"This book is a must-read for all business executives and IT-decision makers with or without previous offshoring experience. Eltschinger's work makes it critical to put China at the top on the list of IT services and outsourcing market destinations. It provides an excellent, practical insight into China and how the market is becoming the key to gaining a competitive advantage in the global services race. Eltschinger's deep expertise in China and outsourcing make the messages credible and powerful."

—*Eric Verniaut, CEO, T-Systems Region America*

"Cyrill Eltschinger's book provides a unique perspective on this amazing country and insight into the next wave of outsourcing. With China asserting itself as a major force in the world economy, the book provides the first hard look at this market."

—*Laurence Barron, President, Airbus China*

"In this book, Cyrill Eltschinger captures the dynamics for an impending global shift in demand for outsourcing services to China. Indeed, as utilization peaks in India and surfeit talent hits the Chinese market, the tide swells for China's IT service sector. Fortunately, China has already begun preparing for this shift by enhancing its legal infrastructure, acknowledging the need to cultivate new industries and committing to increase the level of language skills among its graduates.

But widespread demand for China's IT service sector is also predicated on a shift in emphasis from product-oriented software development processes to service-focused software outsourcing and from low level one-off contracting work to larger scale project management business. And this presents the possibility for another kind of sea change we will have to watch as IT service providers in China climb their own experience curve."

—*Toshihiro Soejima, Executive Vice President, Mitsui & Co., Ltd.*

"This book is giving excellent practical insights when it comes to many aspects of doing business in China. As technology outsourcing continues to play an important role in the globalization strategy of leading enterprises, the demand for qualified talents keeps on rising—well discussed in the book! It is a 'must read!'"

—*Peter Lorange, President, International Institute for Management Development (IMD) The Nestlé Professor*

"Sourcing IT in 'low cost, high performance' countries like China is the key success to qualitative, cost effective IT services and application development. For a growing number of industry players, across sectors, sourcing

IT services in China will guarantee a future and will help them to maintain leadership in the global market. Mr. Eltschinger's book gives a very comprehensive overview of the gain in momentum taking place in the field of IT outsourcing in China. This will help CIOs, IT executives, procurement specialists and top management to grasp a strategic vision into the Chinese IT outsourcing market."

—Bjarne Erik Roscher, Chief Information Officer, SIEMENS SLC

"Although one can always quibble about exact timing, a successful engagement in business support and IT services to China is a strategic asset for today's leaders. There can be no doubt that the center of the economic world is rapidly moving toward Asia Pacific in general and China specifically. I personally found, *Source Code China* an excellent resource and I have already referred it to a number of colleagues"

—Dennis McGuire, Founder and Chairman, Technology Partners
International (TPI)

"*Source Code China* is a must read! With enterprises increasingly depending on advance data and information processing systems to ensure business success, sourcing quality services from the right shore and at an effective rate are undeniable critical success factors to 'winning' in an always more global economy. Mr. Eltschinger's book is an excellent, long-awaited 'wake-up call' in sharing knowledge with a professional audience on what China has to offer in terms of high-tech sector framework, talents, key players and why this market is an 'essential shore' when it comes to making a strategic decision, today, on technology outsourcing and related business support services."

—Dave Weber, Director, MIT Sloan School of Management

"Having spent over 13 years in China, and given his extensive IT experience and Western origin, Cyrill Eltschinger presents a unique perspective of the enormous potential of China as an outsourcing destination. Through direct experience and research, he understands the global sourcing arena as it compares with China; more importantly, as an entrepreneur, he has lived firsthand the pros and cons of doing business in China. I've enjoyed reading *Source Code China* and considerer it an essential primer for those of us who 'want to be in the game.'"

—Benigno López, CEO, Softtek US, Near Shore Services

"As would be expected from a leading China and globally experienced IT thought leader, Cyrill Eltschinger has provided an insightful, useful, and well-documented book on the technology outsourcing landscape in China. The on-the-ground insights and lessons of experience, from both strategic and tactical perspectives, make this a must-read for senior executives with outsourcing decision responsibility, indeed all executives, considering China as an expanded base."

—William H. Mobley, Ph.D., Professor of Management, China Europe International Business School (CEIBS); CEO, Mobley Group Pacific Ltd., Shanghai

"With China already a leading outsourcing destination and rapidly climbing, finally someone is taking a look at this booming industry. This book is the first professional assessment that analyzes how outsourcing works in China and what decision makers need to use this market effectively and to compete globally."

—David Ho, Chairman, Greater China Region, Nokia Siemens Networks

"Thought provoking and very informative about China; a trigger for some serious soul-searching among India offshoring advocates."

—Gopal Kuchibhotla, Associate Director & Leader, Offshore Advisory Services, PricewaterhouseCoopers, India.

"Few aspects of the 'flat world' economy are more important than the subject of this book, and few people, if any, know more about the subject than its author, Cyrill Eltschinger. Cyrill has been engaged in information technology pursuits since his graduation (from Texas A&M, I'm pleased to say), and has watched in the heart of China how the technology outsourcing industry has emerged as a propelling force in the emergence of China as a global economic power. I recommend this book to anyone who wants not only to grasp 'why China' for technology outsourcing, but also to better understand the current and future leading role of China in that industry."

—Dr. Kerry Cooper, Cullen Trust Professor of Business Administration and Executive Director of International Business Programs in the Mays Business School at Texas A&M University.

"This book provides superb insights into the evolution of China for the recent past, providing compelling discussion as to the landscape and lessons for outsourcing to China. Its great coverage on not only 'why' and 'what' but also 'how' makes this book a 'must-read' for key business executives."

—*Dennis Ku, Managing Partner, Egon Zehnder International China*

"The strength of Mr. Eltschinger's experience in China over the last decade flows through his vision in this book. He demonstrates the power of IT outsourcing in China, and that it will outpace its rivals. For understanding China's upcoming role in global IT, it is required reading and a necessary reference."

—*Ferras Zalt, Chief Executive Officer, AtosOrigin Middle East (AOME)*

"People in the IT industry have been waiting for someone to comprehensively address the issue of the world's fastest growing technology market—China. With well over a decade of experience in China's software and outsourcing markets, Eltschinger's book demands the thorough attention of anyone with a serious intention to effectively deal with transactions there."

—*John K. Halvey, Partner, Milbank Tweed, Hadley & McCloy*

"Mr. Eltschinger writes convincingly on China's growing capabilities for providing information technology enabled services (ITES). Like its great neighbor to the west, India, he shows that China has a promising future in ITES. Like India, China offers its own unique advantages and challenges, in a very rapidly evolving economy."

—*Rafiq Dossani, Senior Research Scholar, Stanford University*

"Cyrill Eltschinger has been a pioneer in China's IT services industry for over a decade and knows the dynamics of China's emerging outsourcing/BPO business from the ground up. Business leaders that will evaluate or re-evaluate China in their global IT outsourcing strategies will find this work to be a very helpful professional reference."

—*Gregory T. Shea, President and Managing Director, United States Information Technology Office (USITO)*

"Organizations not sourcing IT services from China are literally missing the boat. Mr. Eltschinger's book takes readers on an intellectual journey explaining how and why China is becoming the premier offshore destination for businesses all over the world. This is a must-read for any business executive and I highly recommend you knock this one off your reading list immediately."

—*David Etzler, Chief Executive Officer, OutsourceWorld*

"This book demonstrates China's credentials as the new hub of offshore IT services. China has proven to be the place to offer advantages in quality, service, and cost. As businesses move east and grow into Asia, China is where it's happening, and that is where we will be."

—*Steve Little, Senior Vice President and Chief Information Officer D.S.I., Schneider Electric*

"Companies, large or small, are striving to become globally integrated enterprises with the agility to utilize talents from anywhere in the world to deliver products and services to customers anywhere in the world. But many are concerned about handing over critical missions to people in countries that are multiple time zones away and may speak a different language. In his book *Source Code China*, Mr. Eltschinger provides compelling reasons why any company can benefit from IT outsourcing to China, a country that is rapidly becoming the destination of choice for most enterprises."

—*Charles Pau, Director, Globalization Architecture and Technology, IBM*

"This book tells the complete story of how the sleeping giant–China–is awakening to play a major role in the IT outsourcing field. Mr. Eltschinger has made an accurate assessment of the global outsourcing business and an in-depth analysis of why China is becoming 'the new global hub of IT Outsourcing.' This is a must-read to understand IT outsourcing in China and its impact on the rest of the world."

—*Dr. Andrew Lai, VP/GM, Global Delivery China Center, Hewlett-Packard Company; Board of Directors, Shanghai Hewlett-Packard Co. Ltd.; Dean, HP Software Engineering School in China; International Economic Advisor to City Mayor of Chongqing, China; IT Strategy Advisor, City Mayor of Chengdu, China*

"Asia Pacific plays a significant role in outsourcing activities and is now making a major transition to high value services such as IT services. Particularly China and India, with their large domestic markets, world-class infrastructure, low cost base, largest numbers of annual IT talents and capability to shape standards, is becoming a global outsourcing powerhouse. *Source Code China* provides an insightful touch with reality of how China is reshaping the global market for offshore IT services."

—*Prof. Dr. Dr. Klaus Wucherer, Executive Vice President, SIEMENS*

"China was the world's largest economy until the beginning of the 19th century. After some eclipse, China is now re-emerging back to the front. In his book, Cyrill Eltschinger addresses an important perspective: China is not only 'the factory of the world,' it is also becoming a major technology services hub. For all of us, it is a fascinating experience to participate in this impressive evolution."

—*Josef M. Mueller, Chairman & CEO, Nestle (CHINA) Ltd*

"As history has shown so many times, China has an ability to know when to take the next step towards economic advancement. Today, it sees opportunity in the highly competitive arena of information technology outsourcing. Cyrill Eltschinger's *Source Code China* examines the depths of a remarkable shift towards a value added economy. After reading this book, you'll see once again how China is positioning itself for leadership in this growing area."

—*William G. Parrett, Chief Executive Officer, Deloitte, May 2007*

"The next five years will be a critical period of time for the continuous expansion of the world market for software and information services outsourcing, and a period of opportunity for China to speed up the growth of software and information services outsourcing. China will continue to generate strong market demand for the global software industry."

—*H.E. Bo Xi Lai Minister, China Central Ministry of Commerce (MOFCOM)*

Source Code China

The New Global Hub of IT Outsourcing

CYRILL ELTSCHINGER

BICENTENNIAL
BICENTENNIAL
BICENTENNIAL
1807
WILEY
2007
BICENTENNIAL
BICENTENNIAL

John Wiley & Sons, Inc.

This book is printed on acid-free paper.⊗

Copyright © 2007 by John Wiley & Sons, Inc. All rights reserved.

Published by John Wiley & Sons, Inc., Hoboken, New Jersey.
Published simultaneously in Canada.

Wiley Bicentennial logo: Richard J. Pacifico.

For general information on our other products and services, or technical support, please contact our Customer Care Department within the United States at (800) 762-2974, outside the United States at (317) 572-3993, or fax (317) 572-4002.

Wiley also publishes its books in a variety of electronic formats. Some content that appears in print may not be available in electronic books.

For more information about Wiley products, visit our Web site at http://www.wiley.com.

Library of Congress Cataloging-in-Publication Data:

Eltschinger, Cyrill, 1965–
    Source code China : the new global hub of IT outsourcing / Cyrill Eltschinger.
        p. cm.
    "Published simultaneously in Canada."
    Includes index.
    ISBN 978-0-470-10696-9 (cloth)
    1. Contracting out—China. 2. Information technology—Management. 3. Electronic data processing departments—Contracting out. I. Title.
    HD2365.E43 2007
    004.068′4—dc22
                                                                2007014933

Printed in the United States of America.

10 9 8 7 6 5 4 3 2 1

"To Jacky & Big Sam"

Contents

Preface   **xv**

Acknowledgments   **xix**

CHAPTER 1

**Outsourcing: The Most Important Management Trend
of the Past 75 Years**   **1**

Outsourcing as a Business Force   2
Made in China   4
Setting the Stage   6

CHAPTER 2

Battle of the Titans: The Global Outsourcing Landscape   **8**

North America   9
Europe   10
South America   15
Africa and the Middle East   15
Asia-Pacific   17
BRIC Nations   21

CHAPTER 3

China: Your Essential Shore   **33**

Big Numbers from a Big Country   34
Government and Politics   36
Planes, Trains, and Automobiles   38
Educating the Masses   39
Your Essential Shore   41
The Early Years   44
Made in China   44
From Pagers to Market Supremacy   45
The Internet Arrives   47
Not Yet a Green Light   49

India Outsources to China 51
Risks and Concerns 55

CHAPTER 4
Strategies that Work **60**

What Works? What Is the Right Shore? What
Is the Right Model? 63
Captive Versus Partner 65
Build-Operate-Transfer 67
Dual-Shore Delivery 71
Going Captive and Avoiding the Expat Trap 71

CHAPTER 5
Ten Lessons Learned **75**

1. What Works Elsewhere Does Not Necessarily Work in
China 75
2. Develop a Vision of the Future Beyond the Next
Shareholder Meeting 77
3. Establish the Right Partnerships from the Beginning 79
4. Do Your Homework 81
5. Commit for the Long Haul 83
6. Prepare Yourself for an Unprecedented Speed of Change 84
7. Choose an Outsourcing City Based on... 85
8. People, People, People 86
9. Never Give Up 88
10. It Is All About Face 89

CHAPTER 6
Winning the Talent War **91**

English Makes the World Go Round 94
Recruiting Staff 96
Salaries on the Rise 99
Chinese Work Ethics 100
Retaining Staff: Employee Retention and Loyalty Programs 101

CHAPTER 7
China's Outsourcing Cities **112**

Beijing 112
Shanghai 114

Dalian 117
Chengdu 119
Xi'an 120
Jinan 122
Hangzhou 124
Guangzhou 125
Nanjing 127
Shenzhen 129

CHAPTER 8
IT Outsourcing, Business Process Outsourcing, and Knowledge
Process Outsourcing in China **135**

Scope of Outsourcing 138
Global Outsourcing Options for Customers 147
Advantages of Outsourcing to China 148
Disadvantages to Outsourcing to China 149
Selection of Vendor Partners 149
Due Diligence of the Capabilities of Vendors 150
Importance of Business Process Standards 150
Importance of Standards in BPO 151
Application Standards to Different Process Types 152
Process Selection for Outsourcing 152

CHAPTER 9
China's Legal Framework **156**

Market Entry and Establishing a Business in China 157
Intellectual Property Rights Protection 159
Employment Issues 164
Government Policy 166
Currency and Taxation 167
Dispute Resolution and Litigation 171

CHAPTER 10
China 2020 **176**

Pillar of the Economy: Focus on the High-Tech Sector 176
Growth of the Services Sector 177
Satisfying a Fast-Growing Global IT and Business Processes
  Services Demand 178
Overseas Promotions Leap Forward 179
Stable China Market Economic Prospects 180

Rise of Globalization: In the Front Row   181
China 2020: Wild Cards   183

Appendix A: Exclusive Survey of Selected Cities in Cooperation With MOFCOM   **186**

Appendix B: Case Studies   **192**

Appendix C: Contact Information for Major Government Offices, Outsourcing Centers, and Online Resources   **238**

Index   **283**

Preface

It is 4:42pm on a Thursday afternoon, early February 2007. I just landed in Beijing returning from a business trip to Dubai, on an Emirates Airlines flight. I exit the plane, switch on my mobile phone, and start checking my text messages. I make it through Customs and walk to the waiting car, all in 15 minutes. I will be home in 20 minutes, just in time to shower, change, and get back in the saddle toward closing a new deal with an important client this evening along with two of my colleagues. It's great to be back. More than ever I am convinced that China is the place to be outsourcing to.

On the airport expressway, my driver has handed me documents for signature as I slap my CDMA wireless card into my laptop. I start sending our team action items prepared in-flight that our new partners in Dubai are expecting. Also, I am expecting an important last-minute updated presentation file to download.

On the expressway, listening to my cell phone and office voice mails, I cannot help but notice the enormous progress that the construction of the new airport express train has made since I left, less than a week ago. The 2008 Beijing Olympics are just around the corner and everything looks on track.

During the flight back, I was thinking about the successful meetings and related partnership negotiations we had with a major Middle East-based IT services company. I could not help but reflect also on the 180-degree turnaround that has taken place in how businesses from around the world are now coming to China to source IT services and build partnerships.

Just how surprising is this?

As a sneak preview of the massive changes that are currently redefining how the global IT outsourcing roadmap looks, take a peek at a map: if you are established in Dubai, flying to India seems a lot closer than flying to China, and engaging an Indian firm for technology services would seem to be the appropriate thing to do. That is especially true in Dubai, considering the large number of Indian nationals currently working and active in all service sectors there. Against all odds, early in our relationship, my potential client, a major IT group, came to China with a mission to seek out a partnership with a leading China-based IT player and expand in the China market. How surprising is that? Clearly, there are reasons!

In Dubai, the client asked about the quality of our tech talent, their English-speaking ability, the availability of various skill-sets resources, and our staff attrition rate. They were also eager to understand how we protect our partners' as well as our own data on intellectual property rights issues. They were keen to review our CMMI level-3 compliant development processes and related data and information security measures. They were highly interested in infrastructure and telecommunications as well.

It is questions such as these, asked not only by our client in Dubai but also customers and potential customers in other places, including the United States, Europe, and Japan, that led me to write this book. The opportunity for outsourcing and offshoring to China is enormous, both for those providing the services and for those looking to maintain or increase quality at a lower cost. However, after hearing nothing but India, India, India for more than a decade, it is time to give voice to the world's new technology superpower—China.

This book is intended for companies and executives already engaged in outsourcing somewhere in the world, for those just getting ready to dip their toe into the outsourcing pool, and also for those who may already have had their first experience outsourcing to China. For those outsourcing but not to China, this book will serve as an introduction to the China outsourcing and technology landscape, and hopefully demonstrate why China is THE outsourcing destination for the future. For those preparing to take the plunge, it will act as a guide to the outsourcing process in general, and more specifically, why China is the best choice for those who have not engaged in offshoring before. Finally, for those who have already discovered the reservoir of talent that China provides, this book will hopefully show how that experience can be improved even further.

In our initial two chapters, "Outsourcing: The Most Important Management Trend of the Last 75 Years" and "Battle of the Titans: The Global Outsourcing Landscape," we will first look at the growing outsourcing phenomenon, how it grew from an initial experiment into an integral part of mainstream global business. Then we will take a broad view of today's global outsourcing destinations, especially the BRIC nations—Brazil, Russia, India, and China—comparing and contrasting these for their outsourcing potential.

In Chapter 3, "China: Your Essential Shore," we look at China today, its economy, political structure, and education system, and how it is poised to become the next global IT hub.

Chapters 4 and 5, "Strategies That Work" and "Ten Lessons Learned," draw on 14 years' experience in China's IT and outsourcing markets to give you valuable insights into working in China, dealing with other companies, government relations, and human resources, and help you to create a sound

China strategy designed for success, where many companies have simply flown blind—and crashed as a result.

Chapter 6, "Winning the Talent War," delves into the kind of talent available for outsourcing projects in China, and how to manage it effectively. "China's Outsourcing Cities," our seventh chapter, profiles 10 cities that have emerged as outsourcing centers in China, and demonstrates the diversity of outsourcing talent and cost structures available in this growing IT hub.

Chapter 8, "IT Outsourcing, Business Process Outsourcing, and Knowledge Process Outsourcing in China," deals very specifically with the three main types of outsourcing, what is available in China in regards to those services, and effective management techniques for each. Chapter 9, "China's Legal Framework," sets the scene for structuring deals, contracts, setting benchmarks, and protecting intellectual property.

Finally, "China 2020," our tenth chapter, looks ahead at China's economic and political future, and examines the trends that will continue to push China toward leadership as the global IT superpower and technology hub.

Acknowledgments

R udy A. Schlais, Jr. has been a true inspiration, more than just a coach and a mentor. He is a genuine example of leadership with a great heart, and a real judge of character when it comes to dealing with people. It has been an honor to serve under his command while he was president during the startup of GM China. Having had the blessing of his support as a partner and non-executive chairman with I.T. UNITED after his retirement as president and CEO, General Motors Asia-Pacific. It has been an unforgettable experience rich in learning.

I am grateful to the Ministry of Commerce; the Ministry of Science and Technology; the Ministry of Information Industry; and the National Development Reform Committee. Their undivided leadership in supporting the high-tech industry while growing a stable economy, and their long-term vision of positive reforms and planning have brought us to this remarkable milestone of China's becoming the new center for high-end engineering and IT outsourcing services.

I would like to thank Yao Yi, Rick Wang, and their team of expert attorneys at Concord Partners for sharing their specialized legal knowledge in the China Legal Framework chapter. Working with Concord was a thoroughly pleasant experience. With almost 100 lawyers, and offices in Beijing, Shanghai, and Shenzhen, Concord's exceptional foundation in Beijing's foreign economic law, investment law, corporate law, banking and finance, and foreign direct investment, along with their strong intellectual property practice group, made them ideal contributors.

I would like to thank Fei Ning and his team of expert attorneys at Haiwen & Partners. Their specialized legal contribution is reflected in the China Legal Framework chapter. Fei Ning's range spans domestic and foreign commercial dispute resolution—arbitration, litigation, and mediation, and also acting as an arbitrator for CIETAC (China International Economic and Trade Arbitration Commission). Established in China in 1992, Haiwen & Partners has won many awards, and has become one of the leading legal practices in China, with unique expertise in a broad range of practice areas including securities, dispute resolution, corporate and commercial, mergers and acquisitions, banking and finance, and real estate.

Special thanks go to Bruce Hofman, founder and principal of Continuous Improvement Methods for his contribution with an in-depth assessment of the framework of improving the maturity of IT outsourcing enterprises in China. Bruce provided much support for the process-related chapter. He has performed numerous CMMI-related appraisals in China and has a thorough understanding of conducting business in China. He has hands-on experience with China-based IT companies' maturity and operations from a process standpoint. Bruce is focused on helping China-based IT companies engaged in outsourcing activities succeed, as well as helping further develop the China IT outsourcing industry.

Thank you to Anastasia Dzenowagis and Insight Solutions Group, Inc. for your contribution to the business and knowledge process outsourcing aspects of the book. Anastasia works with global businesses ranging from chocolate to steel, from Latin America to Eastern Europe to Asia. Anastasia has practical experience assisting global enterprises expand their business-process models in China through either outsourcing or organic growth for significant business results.

At IDC, I appreciate the assistance of Conrad Chang for sharing his views and in-depth knowledge of the Asian market, specifically the situation in the boom in high-tech and IT outsourcing industries in China. It has been a pleasure to share the stage with Conrad at many conferences and interacting with him during his ongoing research trips to China.

Forrester Research's John McCarthy deserves thanks for his continued support in exchanging notes and information on market conditions here. John has been surveying the China market's IT framework for several years, and is doing a remarkable job keeping current with market changes and how the high-tech sector and engineering services are developing. John's frequent visits to China also give us more opportunities to exchange ideas in person.

Thanks to Jamie Popkin at Gartner for his frequent sharing of resources and notes on how the IT market in China is changing. His regular travels to China give him ongoing insight into developments here, and we have been able to visit both here and at events overseas, certainly to my benefit and I hope to his.

I'd also like to acknowledge Hong Gang at AMA Consulting for his ongoing support, helping hand in sharing knowledge, and providing information on industry activities and outsourcing strategies. His work relating to government officials in China has been of great help. Hong Gang is a driven professional who positively impacts and helps the IT outsourcing industry to take great steps forward, especially by winning key leaders' support for overseas promotion activities.

Thank you, Ben Trowbridge and Curt Riley from Alsbridge, for helping multinationals and business executives understand that China market IT outsourcing framework is part of one of the world's best outsourcing destinations. Your understanding and support of China's IT outsourcing capabilities has been of great value. Your research and street-level experience in China demonstrates your commitment to developing and implementing the most knowledgeable offshore outsourcing strategies for your clients.

Mike Anobile at LISA.org's (Localization Industry Standards Association) industry expertise and frank exchange of comments about international enterprises' views on moving their standards and localization work to the China market and related experiences have been exceptionally valuable both to this book and to I.T. UNITED.

Roy McCall convinced me to do this book, and helped me establish my relationship with our fantastic publisher, John Wiley & Sons. He has been a staunch supporter of the I.T. UNITED team and business model, sharing in the vision from the start that China would develop high-end engineering services and high-tech outsourcing. He has been a friend and sounding board, a volunteer in offering his professional views and expert opinion all along. He is an outspoken business figure, befitting a man of his impressive academic background.

I would like to acknowledge and thank my longtime friends and core team members and associates: Reiko Yuan; Laura Ning; Sandy Huang; Sean Zhao; Ray Yang; Charles Zhang; Mike Ouyang; Felix Yu. We've gone quite a ways together almost night and day since my arrival in China. We've learned from one another, above all that nothing can replace trust. This book in many ways is a reflection of our success. Thank you, guys.

Appreciation to John Tai, who has been contributed to our global efforts to share knowledge with so many. John is a great friend and close supporter, with patience. Thanks again, John.

Thanks to Monika Siegenthaler, for her assistance with many aspects of this book during its writing. Monika is a self-motivated achiever with a very astute professional approach; her presence at I.T. UNITED is missed.

Chahriar Assad offered ongoing support and constructive criticism. He has been following the activities and development of the China IT industry through the development of my work here for over a decade. His pragmatic advice and unbiased views reflecting the opinions of executives in the North American and European marketplace have offered great perspective on the market's development.

I'd like to thank Dave Scherer and his wife Patricia, for their support and constructive input. Not many friends go as far back as Dave and I do, having shared sweat while loading large bales of hay onto 18-wheelers in Washington State what seems like so many years ago. Thanks, 'big brother'.

Armando Vacondio has been a friend and mentor, and has always shared his own insights as an industry consultant and expert with and following the development of my activities in the China market. He was always there to offer thoughts and counseling and has always been available when times got tough.

Thank you, David Beevers, for your support ever since we met in Beijing, many years ago. Your friendship has always meant a lot and your professional personality been an example and a source of strength. Thanks, David.

Frank-Juergen Richter, head of Horasis is one of the consulting minds that I have to acknowledge for his ongoing input and shrewd vision. Frank is an old China Hand and holds the edge on advising firms from Asia, Europe and the Americas. His network is an impressive one, and goes back to long before his days at the World Economic Forum. Thanks Frank for your help and your friendship.

I'd like to thank Pat Horner, chairman of the board and chief executive officer of E5 Systems, for his continued exchanges and relentless efforts in sharing knowledge about the state of and the readiness of the IT outsourcing market in China. Pat has accomplished a lot and has had a very impressive career. He is one of the contributors that supported my own efforts, with a clear vision of how the China market is shaping up as a leader; he has hands-on experience in doing business in China.

Mark Redfelsen at the Outsourcing Institute has been of great assistance through continued exchanges, and sharing notes about industry changes, activities in the North American market, and how China is helping changing outsourcing strategies.

I wish to offer sincere thanks to my father, Ernest, for being such an inspiration. He is living example of success and achievement, having started from simple means. As an artist he is unrivaled in his truly unbelievable ability to transcribe on paper and canvas the shapes, colors, figures, and life that surrounds all of us.

I want to thank my loving fiancée Maureen for her endless smile, positive and constructive spirit, for being by my side without argument, and for being so understanding of my busy schedule: running a company at China's breakneck market pace not withstanding all my other business and community activities, in which I have leadership roles and board responsibilities, she unselfishly allowed me to take yet more time during the ten months needed to complete this book. Love you, Baby.

Special thanks go to my great aunt, Renée de Gottrau, for her unflagging love and her interest in the progress of my entrepreneurial career in

China. Renée has always been a very positive and warm-hearted person, in everything that she has done and said. Her visiting me in Beijing two times, while she was over 80, meant a lot. Merci, Renée, we are praying for you.

Thanks also, Michel de Gottrau, my great uncle, who has also been following my career and supporting my progress, sharing his own experiences and knowledge, and visiting me here in China. Michou always has given me pragmatic, honest, and direct feedback on questions and suggestions throughout the years. Merci, Michou.

I extend my gratitude to Romano Anfossi, for his lifelong support, and sharing ideas, love, and thoughts. He is truly a wonderful human being with such warmth in his heart, expressed through his great poetry, as a successful and shrewd fashion industry entrepreneur, and having successfully materialized his passion for great things in life with his wonderful winery.

Thank you to all those companies and individuals that shared their vision, via the advance praise they offered for this book, sharing a common vision.

I am deeply grateful to Sheck Cho, my exceptionally patient editor, who shepherded me through the process of being a first-time author. His guidance was absolutely indispensable and support invaluable, even as deadlines, and I'm sure his doubts, passed. Thank you, Sheck, the pleasure has been all mine.

And finally I would like to thank my friend Steven Schwankert, who sometimes seemed like a third hand on my keyboard as I wrote this book. He (im)patiently answered all my phone calls, text messages, and e-mails about writing, and generously shared his time to make sure I was on the right track.

CHAPTER 1

Outsourcing: The Most Important Management Trend of the Past 75 Years

The global outsourcing race is on. If you are not outsourcing, your company may not survive. Your competition is earning points ahead of your market share and everything that goes with it. *Harvard Business Review* identified outsourcing as "one of the most important management ideas and practices of the past 75 years."[1] The ability for companies to achieve high-quality results at a lower cost while also reducing head count would most likely have been considered a business revolution some time ago.

At the macro level, the process is triggered by competing forces engaging in outsourcing. Simply by not engaging in it, you are losing out because others are getting into it.

The concept of outsourcing is not rocket science. It is simply about sourcing the most qualified talent at the most effective rates. It allows you to focus on what you do best—your core business. Do what you do best—let some tech nerds do their thing.

Cost is part of the equation, but more so than that is the amount of tech talent. Technology is moving fast; it is hard for people to stay current unless they are constantly learning. Western-educated people have a tendency to get bored easily with perceived low-end programming jobs. This allows both outsourcing firms and their clients to tap into markets where it is easier to structure teams of various sizes in day or night shifts.

Outsourcing is more than just a business process—it is also a matter of face (a very Asian concept). Potential outsourcing customers ask questions like "What are your capabilities in India?" China is clearly a better choice, but it is still a very novel concept that started to appear in 2003. We will spend a bit more time on that later.

Companies that already have extensive Asian market antennas and history are clear on China's position and outsourcing potential and moving into the China market. The majority of companies that have experienced this shift away from India and toward China are making aggressive plans to grow further. Others are afraid simply because they do not know what to expect if they enter the China market. They hear a lot, they are curious, they take a discovery trip, but they are still unclear and worried. For many companies, choosing India is less risky because it is already widely accepted as an outsourcing center.

Managers choosing India may now find this is no longer the safe choice, based on past data, and are making poor recommendations to their firms, in the face of rising costs, high turnover, and a diminishing tech talent pool. Over the course of this book, we explain why China is the clear choice for the future as the leading source of offshore outsourced technology talent.

OUTSOURCING AS A BUSINESS FORCE

Outsourcing as a force of business transformation continues to dominate headlines and boardroom discussions. Utilizing modern infrastructure and sources of talent worldwide, more and more corporations look to focus their resources on their core strengths and businesses, and let outside, professional firms handle other business processes, while reaping cost benefits at the same time.

This trend can only continue. The twenty-first century is a time of globalization, and ongoing technological advances improve every day. The progress made in the past 100 years is staggering: modern air connections ferry passengers from Beijing to New York in just over 13 hours; documents zip back and forth across the world in seconds; whole libraries of information can be searched in moments.

Despite the current trend of presenting outsourcing as a relatively recent phenomenon, it is actually one of the most common business practices. Does your neighbor's son mow your lawn? That is outsourcing. The teenager from around the corner who babysits your children on Saturday nights? That is also outsourcing. Do you hire an accountant to prepare your tax return? That is outsourcing too.

Outsourcing is not like the mercantilism practiced by European countries in the eighteenth century; in fact, it is the opposite of that. Mercantilism used large, government-supervised companies to gather resources from around the world, like cotton, sugar, and gold, and then return them to the home nation or a third country to manufacture finished products. At the time, developed nations needed resources, not labor or manufacturing facilities. The height of technology at the time was industrial manufacturing, not information technology, and those facilities only generally existed in Europe.

Today, the business landscape is entirely different; however, corporations in developed countries are still looking to other parts of the world for resources. While some of that demand is still for physical commodities, there is an increasing need for human resources. Nations that are in the process of modernizing, and some smaller countries that have developed superb educational systems, are in position to play a significant role in globalization, and draw foreign investment, both financial and otherwise, to themselves.

Since the end of World War II, global businesses, especially those engaged in textiles and consumer electronics, have used the cost advantages of manufacturing and assembling particularly in Asian countries, to produce high-quality products at increasingly affordable prices. Early electronics efforts from Japan were dismissed for their poor quality; now, not a single brand of television is made in the United States, and even Japan's TV makers do much of their building in Korea and China, or have allowed manufacturers in those countries to move into the space. "Made in Taiwan" became a household phrase in the United States, first for shoddy products, but later for reliable goods at reasonable prices.

Globalization itself is nothing new, with trade between the continents dating back centuries. However, in the later years of the twentieth century, the process of globalization increased as agreements between countries dropped a large number of traditional protectionist tariffs, and allowed companies from one area to more easily and inexpensively do business in another.

For example, the formation of the European Union (EU), in 1958, along with the 2002 adoption of a single currency—the euro—by many of its member states, paved the way for increased trade and movement of labor. The EU now includes 27 countries, 13 of which use the euro, which recently has strongly outpaced the U.S. dollar.

The 1990s also saw the signing of the North American Free Trade Agreement (NAFTA) between Canada, Mexico, and the United States, similarly reducing or removing trade barriers between these neighbor nations. However, NAFTA does not provide for the freedom of movement or employment that the European agreements do.

NAFTA, did, however, begin to permit a greater degree of outsourcing, especially by U.S. companies that moved manufacturing operations over the border into Mexico, to take advantage of the lower cost of labor there. It was NAFTA more than other agreements that began to cause anti-globalization sentiment, leading in some cases to violent protests by a small, fringe minority. However, most businesses and individuals realize and embrace the concept that trade can only become more global, as communications and transportation make markets worldwide more accessible.

As these global trends began to take hold, a backlash began to grow, culminating in the 1999 antiglobalization protests, and ultimately riots, at the World Trade Organization meeting in Seattle. Antiglobalization forces believe that the increased interlocking of trade between nations is driven by corporate greed, keeping workers in developing countries impoverished by forcing wages down, causing workers in developed nations to lose their jobs, and wreaking environmental havoc by moving industry to countries with lower pollution controls and standards. While there are grains of truth in some of these statements, the movement has largely diminished in the face of the increasing benefits of growing international trade for all involved.

MADE IN CHINA

"Made in China" supplanted the "Made in Taiwan" label during the 1980s. Walk into any major North American or European department store, and it is filled with clothing, shoes, and all kinds of consumer electronics. Since the early 1980s, with China's new policy of openness and reform still in its formative stages, foreign firms began using the existing infrastructure of large, state-owned manufacturers, especially in southern China in established special economic zones. China, of course, had another major advantage: a massive labor pool and tremendous cost advantages.

From the early 1980s of producing clothes, toys, and basic electronics, China is now moving on to value-added services. Where previously one could only expect hardware from the China market, both government and private industry are actively supporting world-class software development facilities.

Because "outsourcing" now encompasses a wide variety of services, for the purposes of this book we will define and expand our terms. At my company, I.T. UNITED, our daily course of business requires us to communicate not only in English and Chinese, but also in French, German, and occasionally Japanese and other languages. As such, we found it critically important to define clearly the various terms that we and our customers use so that we can communicate effectively, either internally or externally, no matter what language is being used. We certainly don't want our meaning—and our business—to get lost in translation!

Business Process Outsourcing (BPO). The transfer of internal business processes, such as customer relationship management, finance and accounting, human resources, and procurement, to an external service provider that improves these processes and administers these functions to an agreed service standard and, typically, at a reduced cost.

A major part of outsourced work today, call centers, falls under this heading. Some top outsourcing destinations provide little or no IT or software-related outsourcing services, and yet rank high in global outsource rankings. For example, the Philippines ranks among the top five in some surveys, and yet does very little IT work. However, it is a major destination for call center agents.

Outsourced call centers simply create benefits for the client company by utilizing lower-cost labor to handle customer service inquiries. Although many companies now utilize complex automated telephone menus to reduce the number of operators employed, some calls (and some customers) are simply unable or unwilling to conduct transactions or resolve questions electronically. Because of the high cost of maintaining such call centers in North American and Western European markets, these services, especially for English-language customers, are increasingly being outsourced to English-speaking talent pools overseas, namely India and the Philippines. Similarly, Cantonese-speaking areas in southern China perform this function for many businesses based in Hong Kong.

Information technology outsourcing (ITO). The contractual vehicle through which enterprises use external sources to provide life cycle service and support operations for their IT infrastructure.

Insourcing. A decision by an organization to retain functions internally rather than outsource. The term is also used in cases where services are being brought back in-house after a period of outsourcing them.

Multisourcing. A strategy that treats a given function, such as IT, as a portfolio of activities, some of which should be outsourced and others of which should be performed by internal staff.

Nearshore Outsourcing. The transfer of business or IT processes to companies in a nearby country, often sharing a border with your own country. Nearshoring is a popular model for companies that do not want to deal with the cultural, language, or time zone differences involved in offshoring.

Offshore. An outsourcing term describing the provision of services from a country that is geographically remote from the client enterprises. For example, China is located far from the United States and is therefore an offshore destination for U.S. enterprises.

Offshore Outsourcing. The transfer of business or IT processes to organizations in other countries.

Onshore Outsourcing. The process of engaging another company within your own country for business process outsourcing (BPO) or IT outsourcing (ITO) services.

Outsourcing. The concept of taking internal company functions and paying an outside firm to handle them. The process of transferring the operation of business processes to an external service provider, which then becomes accountable for those services.

Value-Added Outsourcing. An aspect of strategic sourcing or outsourcing, in which some functional area is turned over to a service provider. The presumption is that the service provider can add value to the activity that would not be cost-effective if provided by internal staff.

SETTING THE STAGE

Twenty years ago, much of what we discuss in this book was in its nascent stages. Ownership of personal computers in the United States had only begun a few years earlier. The only computer likely to be found in the average home was a game console made by Atari or perhaps Intellivision.

Enterprise IT was limited to big companies buying big computers, and a small group of technicians or engineers trained to use and maintain them. Command-line interfaces, not graphic user interfaces such as Windows, were the rule of the day. In fact, it was not even called IT. No one had ever used the Internet and we had never met anyone who worked for something called a dot-com.

Although offshoring existed well before the IT wave began to swell, it was used for the manufacturing of goods, as noted previously. The idea that high-level, value-added services such as software development could be completed outside of known talent centers such as Silicon Valley was never considered. Even if there were potential cost savings, established pockets of talent were few and far between, and project management across multiple time zones, not to mention the cumbersome process of sending data back and forth by essentially analog means, limited the appeal of this option.

It is a different world now. IT is so much a part of even small companies now that we do not know how we would live or perform our jobs without personal computers, Internet access, and Google searches. Basic IT tools have transformed the workplace; in fact, consumer hardware and software are so powerful that we now conduct business in many cases without offices or physical premises of any kind. Could we have imagined telecommuting or eBay stores two decades ago? At that time "working from home" was almost synonymous with "unemployed."

As such, worldwide end-user (both consumer and corporate) spending on IT has reached a level that was unimaginable 20 years ago. Computers, Internet access, and access equipment such as routers or wireless setups, servers—these appear on new business buyer lists even before desks, chairs, and paper clips.

In 2005, worldwide IT end-user spending hit US$625 billion,[2] and is increasing at a 28.4 percent compound annual growth rate (CAGR). Who would not want a piece of that market?

With IT adoption and the demand for IT services growing in a similar fashion, the outsourcing of some technology functions has also increased, and continues to climb at an even higher rate than general IT spending. In 2006, BPO expanded at an 8 percent CAGR, to $182 billion by 2009.[3]

Clearly, outsourcing in its various forms is more than a trend. It is now a permanent paradigm shift in the global business landscape. Ten years ago we began referring to "e-commerce," to indicate purchasing or transactions that had taken place online. Now, this type of buying by consumers and businesses is so common that we rarely specify how it was conducted.

The same will be true of outsourcing. Although we now state that a particular function is being sent outside the company, country, or continent for completion, a decade from now utilizing service companies to handle non-core processes, regardless of their location, will be absolutely essential and fully integrated into corporate management.

We believe that China, as it continues to increase in importance to global business and trade, will similarly become an integral part of this move toward integrated outsourcing. With India's ability to supply sufficient tech talent to meet global needs faltering, China will emerge as the number-one source of outsourcing IT talent. Therefore, any discussion of the future of global IT, and especially IT outsourcing, must not only include China, but must focus on it.

We will now examine the global outsourcing landscape, including the factors that determine a country's success and potential as an outsourcing destination. Inevitably, the factors that point to that success lead to the one country that will ultimately dominate the industry: China.

ENDNOTES

1. Sibbet, David. "75 years of management ideas and practice: 1922-1997," *Harvard Business Review*, A special supplement, September–October, 1997.
2. www.eba.com.hk/english/viewnews.asp?newsid=1006
3. www.zdnetasia.com/toolkits/0,39047352,39393141-39094243p,00.htm

CHAPTER 2

Battle of the Titans: The Global Outsourcing Landscape

With the global business process outsourcing (BPO) and IT outsourcing (ITO) markets now multi-billion dollar industries, countless companies and numerous countries are increasingly looking for a slice of the outsourcing pie. Prior to the wide use of the Internet, value-added outsourcing opportunities in more remote locations were limited. Transmission of project material required lengthy faxes, odd-hour conference calls, or daily overnight or express packages carrying floppy disks.

Smaller, more developed countries and territories with well-educated populations see outsourcing as a way to offset their lack of natural resources, and stem the brain drain to more lucrative and cosmopolitan locations.

For large, developing nations, the benefits of building domestic outsourcing industries are manifold. Chief among them is giving local software engineers and other skilled technology workers the opportunity to interact with and learn from their peers internationally.

As we will see, some countries shy away from providing infrastructure for outsourcing because they believe it will interfere with the development of a domestic software industry. However, the capital and experience that support outsourcing often provide a strong boost to countries wanting their own software industry.

An increasing number of countries and territories are attempting to get in on the outsourcing act. The ingredients seem simple enough: tech talent; basic Internet bandwidth and international communications; strong foreign language capabilities; and the ability to complete business process and IT projects for a lower cost than they would in their home market, usually that of major North American and European markets.

However, theory and practice always differ. Some smaller countries have highly educated populations, solid international communications, and foreign language skills, but their small populations prevent them from offering outsourcers any kind of scale. Malta and Singapore come to mind as examples.

There are also large nations, such as Indonesia, which could potentially offer a reasonable amount of computer science talent each year, and a very favorable wage structure, but the nation's education system is not producing the college graduates necessary to become a significant player in outsourcing. The magic formula for outsourcing success is at very least a triangle, if not a pentagon, and the sides must support each other if an industry that will attract sufficient investment and international interest is to be created.

We will examine each major region where outsourcing is taking place, assessing candidate nations, territories, and markets for their strengths and weaknesses, and looking finally at why the countries that are currently dominating global BPO and ITO markets are doing so.

The following discussion is by no means exhaustive, but it does highlight the major areas where outsourcing is taking place. Many countries are able to send work to less-developed neighbors to generate some type of cost savings, regardless of whether or not that place is officially attempting to attract outsourcing clients. However, these are the most noteworthy and the ones that are most likely to come up on a short list of potential outsourcing destinations for executives based in North America and Europe.

NORTH AMERICA

Canada

The United States' northern neighbor seems an obvious choice for outsourcing: shared social and business culture and language; close geographic proximity and time zones; a high-quality education system; friendly relations between the two nations and peoples; and a currency worth approximately 15 percent less than the U.S. dollar. Its location just over the border earns it "nearshore" status.

While some of those similarities make outsourcing to Canada attractive, they also represent reasons to choose other destinations. The Canadian dollar is appreciating against the U.S. dollar, reaching as high as US$0.91 to the Canadian dollar, a 28-year-high, in May 2006[1] before returning to a lower but still strong position. Five years ago, the difference in currency values gave U.S. buyers as much as a 30 percent cost savings by outsourcing to Canada.[2]

However, Canadian companies themselves are outsourcing to centers in Asia, with the possibility of 75,000 Canadian IT jobs moving offshore by 2010.[3] If Canada's domestic IT industry shrinks, it is unlikely that outsourcing can thrive as engineers move into higher-paying and higher-skilled positions.

Canada may be a good choice for small and medium-sized enterprises that want to get their feet wet in outsourcing, but are not ready for offshoring. Currency differences will offer a slight cost advantage over U.S. pricing, although that will vary, especially if the Canadian dollar begins to rise again against its U.S. counterpart.

Mexico

Mexico is clearly associated in the minds of U.S. businesses and consumers with outsourcing, although that association is likely negative, for the migration of U.S.-based jobs that were moved there in the 1980s and 1990s. However, those jobs are viewed as lower-cost, low-skilled jobs that are mostly in manufacturing.

With the growth of BPO and ITO, Mexico has continued to benefit from its proximity to the United States and lower cost structure. The country has a little-known benefit: it graduates more IT professionals annually than any other Latin American country.[4]

Mexican professionals enjoy opportunities for education and training that would be unavailable to most non-nearshore markets, such as traveling to U.S. client headquarters to gain firsthand experience. Because of the growing size and influence of the United States' Hispanic community, both the language and cultural gap have been reduced in recent years, increasing Mexico's appeal.

Although cost savings of 50 to 60 percent over U.S.-based projects are possible,[5] IT projects carried out in Mexico require more staff and more management than those in the United States.[6] Like Canada, Mexico seems a good choice for companies first testing the concept of outsourcing, and for whom cost savings are a greater concern, although they may need to play off the benefits of lower costs against greater management requirements.

EUROPE

Europe's most important outsourcing destination, Russia, is discussed later in this chapter. However, the growth of outsourcing in Eastern Europe has been sufficient enough to merit attention from industry giants, with even Indian firms opening offices in selected locations. The biggest challenges for these locations are their ability to scale and produce sufficient talent to build a local industry, and offer enough in the way of compensation and benefits to retain top talent. Otherwise, they face a brain drain to more developed European economies like the United Kingdom and Germany, or escalating wages that would make them less attractive as outsourcing destinations.

Bulgaria

Bulgarian IT resources initially advertised themselves and the talent available in their country in a rather unpleasant manner: the former East Bloc nation was, in the late 1980s and most of the 1990s, famous for writing some of the most harmful computer viruses users have ever faced.[7]

Since then, the nation's IT talent has focused instead on providing services to mostly Western European customers, and has become an Eastern European hotspot for outsourcing. In 2006, Hewlett-Packard opened a delivery center in the Bulgarian capital of Sofia to serve EMEA (Europe, Middle East, and Africa) clients.[8] German software maker SAP also maintains a facility in Bulgaria.[9] Boeing, General Motors, Ford Motor, and Lockheed Martin are among the companies that have sent work to Bulgaria.[10] Foreign investment in Bulgarian IT is predicted to rise to US$559 million by 2009.[11]

For Europeans, Bulgaria serves as a nearshore destination, just a couple or a few time zones ahead. It is cited for having a highly educated, multilingual workforce, political stability, and low cost.[12]

Bulgaria seems better suited to larger projects from major corporations and may be a tough sell to North American companies, especially those just beginning to outsource. Although it is considered nearshore for Europe, Bulgarian business hours would lie outside of all but the U.S. east coast's business day. It will therefore need to offer significant cost savings in order to prove attractive to that market. Bulgaria's entrance into the European Union (EU) and the mobility that entrance offers its citizens may see top talent heading west in search of higher wages.

Czech Republic

A favorite destination for some German outsourcers, the Czech Republic lies along Germany's southeastern border. Also a former communist state and previously united with neighboring Slovakia, the Czech Republic offers similar benefits to its neighbors Hungary and Poland: relatively low wages for skilled work, and a highly educated workforce.

The Czech Republic's biggest drawback is its relatively small population size. Computer science graduates enter the market annually only in the thousands,[13] not the tens of thousands or ideally hundreds of thousands required to sustain a full-scale outsourcing industry.

With a small industry and lower local wages, better-qualified staff will head to Germany and other Western European countries in search of improved pay and advancement opportunities.

Despite its reputation for the quality of its IT personnel, the Czech Republic's relatively small homegrown industry seems as it if will struggle to find enough people to grow. It also lacks the buzz of Bulgaria and

Poland as a preferred destination for IT outsourcing. Although it may be able to attract nearshore European work, it is unlikely to become a major destination for North American contracts and will be hard-pressed to offer any level of scale. That said, India's Infosys Technologies felt the country had enough potential to open offices in both Prague and Brno, as have Accenture and IBM Global Services.[14]

Hungary

Another increasingly popular Eastern European destination for nearshore European work and more, Budapest must have known it had arrived on the global outsourcing map when India's largest outsourcing services company, Tata Consultancy Services, opened an office there.[15]

Tata's attraction to Hungary seems to be skill-based. Although Hungarian workers are more expensive, they are likely to be multilingual, operating in German and likely English in addition to their native tongue.[16] As such Hungary is experiencing growth in ITO, but also in BPO areas including call centers.

Hungary shares a proximity to Western Europe with its European neighbors and outsourcing service competitors. It was one of the first former Warsaw Pact nations to join the EU, and therefore faces similar risks in losing its top talent to higher-paying markets, especially Germany.

Both IBM and GE operate their own captive centers in Hungary. An editorial in an Indian newspaper identified a key factor in Hungary's—and Eastern Europe's—appeal as an outsourcing center: sending work to European countries, be they west or east, does not have the same psychological impact as jobs that go to India or other non-Western destinations.[17]

Despite its early success, Hungary faces a similar problem to the Czech Republic: being able to produce enough tech talent annually to keep up with rising demand, both locally and globally. Ultimately the size of the available talent pool will determine how much work can be sent to locations such as this.

Ireland

Ireland is a rare Western European outsourcing destination, fueled by a young population that embraced the Internet revolution early and completely. Accenture estimates that in 2007, the value of the country's outsourcing market will reach €319 million (US$357 million).[18]

The country's appeal as an outsourcing destination is clear: English-speaking, working the same business hours as the United Kingdom and most of Western and Central Europe, and a well-educated, young, tech-savvy workforce, and relatively lower costs. Its proximity to the U.S. east coast, and traditionally strong ties between Ireland and Irish-Americans and Irish-Canadians, give it an appeal the Eastern European countries do not share.

New Jersey–based Prudential Financial is one company with IT operations in Ireland, both for testing and for call center support.[19]

The biggest danger for outsourcing in Ireland is that it is becoming a victim of its own success. Although it had lagged behind much of the rest of Western Europe, the island nation's rapid economic growth during the 1990s—both within and outside the outsourcing industry—led to increases in wages, and as such it is less competitive on price than it was previously.[20] Also, work it would have won in previous years is now sometimes sent to Northern Ireland, which remains part of the United Kingdom but can offer cost benefits its southern, independent neighbor can no longer.

Malta

This Mediterranean island nation with a population of just 400,000 has thrown its hat into the outsourcing ring, promoting itself at outsourcing trade shows as a low-cost, European nearshore destination.

As an English-speaking former British colony, Malta is targeting the U.K. market as an alternative to high IT costs there.[21] It also touts its location as being only three air hours from London. However, as a small and relatively new entrant to the outsourcing market, and because it is not exactly a large market where major corporations are otherwise doing significant business, Malta will be challenged to do more than just provide boutique services or handle small to medium-sized European clients.

Poland

Poland may well be the best positioned of the Eastern European countries for significant outsourcing growth. With a larger population than its nearby competitors (38.5 million[22] compared to Bulgaria's 7.4 million[23] and Hungary's 10 million[24]), the country's risk of losing the best of its talent is somewhat mitigated. However, as an EU country, it still faces the departure of skilled workers, especially to Germany and the United Kingdom.

That larger population will be more attractive to foreign companies wanting to establish a more permanent presence in Eastern Europe, especially those who may be concerned about potential instability in Russia. Indeed in 2005, Hewlett-Packard announced a US$50 million investment in Poland over five years, to establish a BPO center for 1,000 employees in Wroclow.[25] Hewitt Associates, one of the world's largest BPO firms, opened a human resources (HR) outsourcing center in Krakow in March 2006.[26] Both of those cities are emerging as Poland's top outsourcing hubs.

Poland boasts similar offerings to its neighbors, with a well-educated, multilingual workforce. Because of its population size, the country stands to benefit by servicing two historical rivals, Germany and Russia. Indeed, as Russia's own outsourcing industry grows, Poland's earlier ties with that country, including linguistic ties, could see it receiving subcontracting work.

Romania

Perhaps more so than its regional rivals, Romania has been active in promoting its outsourcing industry to foreign buyers. It made one of its first appearances at London's OutsourceWorld expo in 2004 and has been a regular participant in trade shows since then.

Although its self-imposed moniker of "Europe's favorite outsourcing destination" may be a tad optimistic, the country offers similar advantages to other Eastern European countries, with a solid educational system, multiple language capabilities, labor costs of approximately one-third to one-half that of the United Kingdom, and working hours that cover most of Western Europe's business day.

Two drawbacks are a political system that is seen as less stable than Eastern Europe's more mature economies, such as Poland and the Czech Republic, and a reasonably small population—Romania offers only about half the potential workforce of Poland.[27] An EU country, Romania faces significant risk of talent flight as one of Eastern Europe's less-developed nations.

Ukraine

This former Soviet state may be eager to shake off its status as Russia's smaller sibling, but its relationship with its neighbor could help to bring it more attention from outsourcers.

An expanding Russian outsourcing industry could make use of talent in the Ukraine as its own nearshore destination. This would serve as a seal of approval for the country's fledgling industry. With low costs and a good education system, the Ukraine could offer nearshore services to the rest of Europe, but suffers from a relatively small talent pool, is considered reasonably difficult to access in terms of travel and visas, and lacks long-term experience in outsourcing on major projects. It has also failed to generate the buzz that countries such as Poland and even Bulgaria have as outsourcing countries of the future.

SOUTH AMERICA

Argentina

Except for Brazil—which we address later in this chapter—and Argentina, South American countries have so far not jumped on the outsourcing bandwagon. A currency crisis several years ago helped to lower salaries and costs. This, coupled with large-scale investment in telecommunications and other infrastructure during the 1990s, has provided some of the ingredients necessary for development of an outsourcing industry.

Sharing overlapping time zones also helps a market that walks the line between nearshore and offshore for North American markets. Cost savings are roughly equivalent to those in Eastern Europe.

The currency crisis and subsequent economic downturn changed the IT landscape by forcing programmers and IT businesses to focus more on open-source and general license solutions, giving the country's software industry a newfound proficiency in that area.[28]

Aside from its appeal to North America, cultural ties may attract European customers. As many as 70 percent of the country's citizens of European descent carry European passports.[29] While this may lead to greater cultural understanding between Argentina and potential European clients, it may also lead to the equivalent of Argentina's soccer talent drain, where top stars are lured abroad by European wages and lifestyle.

AFRICA AND THE MIDDLE EAST

These two regions have not yet seen significant development of outsourcing nations, although two countries on the African continent are attempting to foster domestic industries.

Egypt

Egypt made a big promotional splash at Outsource World 2004 in London, but doubters will remain for some time. The industry there will be plagued by political difficulties in the Middle East, and a likely unwillingness by U.S. corporations to become heavily involved there. Also because of a general dearth of outsourcing activity in the rest of the region, even Egypt's best efforts to present itself as a worthy center will be a hard sell.

The country appeared on AT Kearney's 2005 ranking of global services destinations at number 12, the highest appearance by a nation from the Middle East or Africa.[30] The survey cited the advantages of emerging

Middle Eastern locations as "very low compensation costs, a segment of highly educated technical workers, and historical exposure to English and other European languages."[31]

Egypt is making a greater push for BPO and call-center work than ITO,[32] and sees itself more as a nearshore destination for Europe than as a potential market for North American clients. One of its biggest challenges, especially in developing ITO, is its small college output: at 250,000 total graduates per year, the country has less talent entering the market each year than China has new computer science graduates.[33]

Israel

Israel has become one of the Middle East's few successful technology centers, developing both a domestic software industry and an increasing outsourcing presence despite a limited population and regular bouts of political instability and violence.

Comprehensive connections with international markets, especially in the United States and Europe, along with capabilities in English and European languages, and shared business hours with Central and Eastern Europe, have set the scene for the rise of outsourcing in this country. Electronic Data Systems (EDS), one of the world's largest IT services companies, has operated in Israel since 1995 and employs approximately 900 people there.[34]

The Israeli government has incentivized companies to bring their business to Israel by offering a US$200-per-month subsidy for each worker employed by a foreign entity.[35] Wages and costs in Israel remain higher than other outsourcing destinations, such as China and India, but still realize savings compared to the United States or major European markets.

Along with limitations on the amount of IT talent that can be produced annually by a nation with a geographic area and population as small as Israel's, the country's relations with its neighbors will have a major impact on the future of any outsourcing there. From terrorist attacks to military conflicts such as the summer of 2006's clash with Hezbollah militants in Lebanon, new investment in Israel's outsourcing services industry will hinge on maintaining some semblance of peace, because there are too many other choices available that can deliver similar quality and cost advantages without the threat of violence.

South Africa

One thing about South Africa is certain: it is not a nearshore market for any country, although it does share time zones and working hours with large parts of Europe. That said, its historical involvement with Europe, although at times detrimental to its domestic political situation, means a multilingual workforce that could bring foreign IT investment as the country continues to develop after decades of isolation.

South Africa is at present focused more on BPO and call-center outsourcing than ITO, with Dutch-speaking markets a primary target,[36] although the country can also offer significant proficiency in English and German. Just under 1,000 call centers are expected in the country by 2008, according to one prediction, with 70 percent of existing centers serving U.K. clients.[37]

ASIA-PACIFIC

Having made their name in outsourcing first as low-cost manufacturing centers, some Asian countries are now making the transition to higher-value, IT and knowledge process outsourcing. Indeed, the world's top two outsourcing nations are also the region's population centers: China and India.

Although significant outsourcing services are available in North Asian countries like Japan and Korea, we have excluded them here because they offer little if any cost benefits, and are more likely to receive contracts for specialized work. Also, they are major offshorers themselves, with some of the world's best nearshore talent at their doorstep. For the purposes of this discussion we are also including Australia and New Zealand.

Australia

Australia seems an easy choice for outsourcing. Essentially a North American or European nation plunked down in the Southern Hemisphere, Australia is a major regional IT center. Although Australia's economy has seen strong growth in recent years, and its currency has appreciated significantly over that same period, the Australian dollar's approximately 25 percent differential with the U.S. dollar can still offer savings and high-quality talent to clients in North America and Europe. Ultimately though, Australia is considered a high-end outsourcing center and will not be chosen on the basis of cost benefits. Tier-one players including Accenture, Capgemini, CSC, and IBM Global Services, to name just a few, all maintain a significant presence in Australia.[38]

Many of these global companies benefit not only from Australian labor for international products, but also attract work from domestic firms outsourcing locally, including the federal government and the governments of various Australian states. Major Indian outsourcers are tapping into this domestic market, including Satyam Computer Services and Wipro, with their revenues growing 50 to 60 percent annually.[39] The total Australian outsourcing services market is now valued at US$100 million per year,[40] demonstrating significant room for further growth.

The greatest threat to Australian outsourcing is ultimately that as other markets mature, it will be subject to price pressure. Australian businesses and even the Australian government have engaged in offshore outsourcing, and as a high-end center, could face increasing competition from lower-cost areas in Asia.

Malaysia

Malaysian government investment in a modern IT infrastructure during the 1990s helped this Southeast Asian nation to a position of prominence in IT outsourcing. In 2005, AT Kearney's Global Services Index ranked Malaysia third overall, trailing only India and China,[41] countries many times its size.

It has vigilantly promoted its IT capabilities and attracted multinational IT companies through coordinated efforts including the construction of the Multimedia Super Corridor, which includes the science park/town of Cyberjaya. This area, which stretches from parts of the capital, Kuala Lumpur, to Kuala Lumpur International Airport, includes tax incentives, transport infrastructure, and communications infrastructure to encourage multinationals to establish a significant presence there.[42] Cyberjaya residents include Hewlett-Packard, DHL, and captive global processing centers owned by Standard Chartered Bank and HSBC.[43]

The country has enjoyed particular success servicing the finance and energy industries.[44] Malaysia currently produces approximately 40,000 new "knowledge workers" per year, with a goal of 60,000 by 2008.[45] Outsourcing Malaysia, the country's promotional body, is an active participant in overseas lobbying and trade shows. As an example for smaller nations wishing to create an outsourcing industry for themselves, Malaysia is a superb example, limited only by population and land area.

New Zealand

New Zealand offers outsourcers the advantages of using Australian staff, but with a cost advantage of about 15 percent over their neighbors. Native English-speaking and sharing a common culture with Canada, the United States, and the United Kingdom, New Zealand is hamstrung by its small population and its remoteness. Still, major outsourcers including EDS and Unisys maintain operations here to take advantage of the country's solid, albeit limited, resources.

The Philippines

The Philippines is an outsourcing up-and-comer, with a largely English-speaking population of 77 million, about 10 percent of whom work overseas.

As an outsourcing destination, the Philippines ranked fourth overall in the AT Kearny Global Services survey 2005.[46] The call-center industry is the nation's fastest-growing and is now valued at US$1.7 billion annually, and is a serious competitor for similar English-language services from India.[47]

Despite its prominence among outsourcing destinations, the Philippines has not been able to move up the value chain in knowledge process outsourcing (KPO) or ITO. Despite its reasonably large population (compared to Malaysia's 24 million people), only 400,000 total college graduates enter the workforce each year, a very small percentage.[48] Management and project experience are lacking,[49] and the country is simply not viewed as an IT hub or major IT market, as one of Asia's poorer nations.

Although a series of terrorist attacks in both Manila and on the southern island of Mindanao have sparked somewhat exaggerated fears of unrest, a failed coup d'etat in 2006[50] did nothing to dispel fears of political instability exacerbating a lagging economy surrounded by other Asian success stories. For basic, English-language–based services, the Philippines can offer significant cost benefits. However, for more value-added services, it will be some time before this archipelago nation can challenge the Asian giants.

Singapore

A first-world city-state at the end of the Malay Peninsula, Singapore's five million people serve as a technological benchmark for the rest of Southeast Asia, and also for other parts of the region. Few other Asian countries or territories can rival its development, and its commitment to high technology is obvious anywhere on the island.

Singapore is a high-end services destination, with an English-speaking (English is an official language, and the language of business and instruction in Singapore), highly educated workforce. Through various development programs and under the guidance of the government's Infocomm Development Authority (IDA), technology is integrated into the lives of Singaporeans from a young age, making them among the most technologically aware in the world.

Aside from speaking English, Singaporeans have Bahasa Malaysia as their other official language. With more than 80 percent of the population of Chinese descent, Mandarin Chinese and a variety of dialects, including Teochiu, Hokkien, and Cantonese, are spoken in homes throughout the country and used to establish connections in various parts of China.

Singapore is also home to a significant Indian population, giving it rare cultural and historical ties to both of Asia's technology powerhouses. Because of its diverse Asian roots, Singaporean firms are often the recipients of localization work for other markets in the region.

Singapore is as much an outsourcer as it is an outsourcing destination. Ranked fifth in the 2005 AT Kearney Global Services list,[51] it sends significant work over the border to neighboring Malaysia, the Philippines, and China, where Singaporean companies have joint-ventured with Chinese entities to build and operate software parks.

Outsourcing in Singapore is limited by two obvious factors: population, which currently stands at about five million, and cost. Singapore is considered one of the most expensive IT services markets in Asia, but is utilized for high-end work, localization, and products aimed at regional customers.

Vietnam

If one medium-sized Asian nation is outsourcing's next star, that country is Vietnam. Some 30 years after the Vietnam War ended with a Communist victory, it seems that capitalism has returned and is making up for lost time. Foreign visitors to Ho Chi Minh City (formerly Saigon) who spent time in China during its early boom years report that Vietnam is now reaching the same pace of development.

Some key outsourcing ingredients are already in place. Vietnam's population of approximately 80 million gives it a sufficient pool from which to draw, especially as more are given access to higher education. Although still in its early stages, the country's infrastructure has improved rapidly over the past five years, from Internet access (although it is monitored and occasionally restricted by the government) to roads and modern airports.

Vietnam has been used as a game development center for game software companies including Microsoft, Electronic Arts, and Atari.[52] On the hardware side, Intel invested US$1 billion in a new chip plant in the country in 2006, complete with a visit from outgoing Intel CEO Dr. Craig Barrett.[53]

It is still early for KPO and ITO in Vietnam, with 2005 software and IT exports totaling only US$70 million.[54] However, Vietnam's historic ties to both the United States and France, fueled in part by ethnic Vietnamese populations in those countries, could help to re-establish commercial links there. Language skills could be an issue, but Vietnam's ethnic Chinese population could potentially drive expansion of nearshoring from China. Cost benefits in China continue to be competitive, but should they begin to veer upward, Vietnam could offer Chinese outsourcers a fresh and available source of talent. Although it would be unable to compete in terms of sheer numbers or experience with China and India, Vietnam could develop along the lines of Malaysia to compete among the world's top ten outsourcing destinations. It is one to watch.

BRIC NATIONS

All of the aforementioned nations offer some combination of qualities desirable, if not absolutely necessary, for the development of a domestic outsourcing industry. Some, such as Poland, Ireland, and the Philippines, seem to have particularly bright futures ahead of them. However, as small to medium-sized nations both in terms of geography and population, their growth and ability to assume outsourcing industry leadership positions will ultimately be limited by these factors.

The countries that make the best cases for outsourcing have three critical traits in common: they are attractive markets because of their population size; and equally essential, they have well-established educational systems, particularly in science and technology, producing thousands of qualified young people—at least 100,000 per year or more—with degrees in computer science or related fields, who also have a command of a foreign language, especially English.

The advantage falls to nations with higher numbers of computer science graduates simply because of scale. Although BPO and KPO can technically take place anywhere, an outsourcing industry cannot be built or thrive without scalability. Ultimately, this kind of outsourcing is a resources-based service business, one that requires both quality and quantity of talent. Without quality, nothing beyond the most basic functions can be accomplished and the industry cannot move into higher-value KPO; without quantity, little more than select, small-scale projects can be supported.

To find the necessary levels of population, education, and cost advantages to support large-scale outsourcing, we must look to four nations that offer all three. We commonly refer to these countries as BRIC for the letters of their first initial: Brazil, Russia, India, and China. Of these four, three are already the world's top outsourcing destinations.

Aside from large populations and geographic areas, the countries share other characteristics: all have swiftly rising Internet populations, yet none has passed 20 percent penetration for Internet use. Similarly, three of the four have mobile phone penetration rates of at least 40 percent—Russia's mobile phone penetration actually exceeds 100 percent!

For each country, we will conduct a basic assessment, along with looking at the issues most relevant to BPO and KPO.

Brazil

Official name: Federative Republic of Brazil
Population: 188 million[55]
Median age: 28.2 years[56]
Literacy: 86.4% (definition: 15 years and older can read and write)[57]
Official language: Portuguese
Total telephone lines: 42.4 million (2004)[58]
Total Internet users: 25.9 million (2005)[59]
Total mobile phone users: 86.2 million (2005)[60]

Brazil is best known not for any particular industry (except perhaps tourism) but for its recreational exploits, namely the success of its soccer players, its beaches, the Amazon River and the rainforests to which it gives life, and annual Carnival that brings a parade into the streets of Rio de Janeiro.

Beyond the fun and games, Brazil is South America's largest nation by area and population, and has a young, growing population, one that lends itself to an aspiring technology industry, including BPO. It currently enjoys a stable, democratic political system and economic growth, although, like most developing countries, disparities remain.

Brazil is also the only BRIC nation in the Western Hemisphere, giving it perhaps the psychological edge of being "closer" to North American markets. Depending on one's point of embarkation, though, both China and Russia may be closer in terms of air hours or distance.

More than distance, the advantage this perceived proximity to North America brings is a similar time zone. Local time in Brazil is only one to three hours different than U.S. East Coast time, depending on the time of year and each country's use of daylight saving time.[61] For companies just beginning to offshore some of their business or knowledge processes, being able to discuss a project with the team for most of the business day, in real-time, may help to alleviate some initial fears.

Since 1997, when the country privatized its telecommunications infrastructure, that area has been an area of significant investment and development.

Another benefit of outsourcing to Brazil is that, because it is a new entrant to the game, it has room to grow, and may have the ability to throw more initial resources toward projects, and less turnover than more developed outsourcing markets.

Even as late as 2003, top outsourcing consultants did not think of the country as an outsourcing destination.[62] Although it has a developing domestic software industry, it is still not seen as an upcoming or established powerhouse the way India or smaller rising upstarts, such as Ireland or Israel are regarded.

One of the biggest factors will be cost. An entry-level IT worker makes approximately US$9,000 per year, seen as yielding a 30 percent cost savings for outsourcing clients, although those margins are easily beaten by other outsourcing destinations including India and China.[63]

Locally, the domestic software industry has moved to create greater international awareness by forming BRASSCOM (Brazil Association of Software and Service Export Companies) in 2004,[64] clearly modeled on its Indian counterpart NASSCOM. The association now has more than 3,000 member companies.[65] The domestic software industry is valued at US$10 billion.[66]

At present, Brazil's two greatest challenges are a lack of experience and a language barrier. Firms in the fledgling industry are often small and inexperienced. The nation's engineering students may be reasonably qualified, but lack fluency in English.[67] Brazil's proximity to North America and traditional ties to some European markets may offer it certain opportunities, but it is unlikely to threaten the largest, most established players in outsourcing in the near future.

Russia

Official name: Russian Federation
Population: 143 million[68]
Median age: 38.4 years[69]
Literacy: 99.6% (definition: 15 years and older can read and write)[70]
Official language: Russian
Total telephone lines: 40.1 million (2005)[71]
Total Internet users: 23.7 million (2005)[72]
Total mobile phone users: 120 million (2005)[73]

North America and Western Europe once lived in fear of Russian technology. Will its continuing technological development now threaten the American and European software industry? For the moment, Russia's greatest threat is to the world's other top outsourcers, India and China. The largest and most important of the former Soviet nations, Russia currently ranks third as the world's top offshore country, in terms of volume.[74] In 2007, overall ITO to Russia is expected to grow 40 to 50 percent, up from approximately 30 percent in recent years.

Russia's legacy as a former communist nation makes it in some ways perfect for outsourcing, with a highly educated population and yet a relatively low wage base. Russian programmers and engineers trained by

Russian universities, and in some cases, the Russian military, makes them well-qualified and in high demand.[75] They are regarded as disciplined, almost to the point of inflexibility.[76]

Salaries in Russia for an entry-level programmer are between US$5,000 and $9,000 per year, resulting in cost-savings of 30 to 50 percent over a comparable U.S.-based project.[77]

Like its counterparts in other countries, the software outsourcing industry has banded together under a trade representative group, RUSSOFT.

One of the bigger drawbacks of the Russian market is its relatively small size—only US$750 million total software exports in 2005,[78] compared to the billions of annual exports generated in India and China.

Although Russia's geographic position puts its business day outside that of the United States, European companies may find that general proximity to be advantageous for real-time monitoring of projects and more regular site visits.

Unlike Brazil, which is hindered by its industry's lack of experience, Russian outsourcing's biggest handicap is instead the infrastructure that surrounds it. Mobile phone penetration in Russia now stands above population (104 percent),[79] but landline and Internet infrastructure has not kept pace.

More important, Russia's social and political stability call the continued growth of any particular industry into question. The country's population is actually declining, as is life expectancy, especially among males.[80] Alcoholism remains a serious problem throughout the country. Although officially a democracy, political rights and the democratic process are under continued threat.

Russia will likely have more success with European outsourcers due to the customers' geographic and time zone proximity. While the outsourcing industry there seems set for healthy growth, it will not threaten the industry's two top destinations: India and China.

India

Official name: Republic of India
Population: 1.095 billion[81]
Median age: 24.9 years[82]
Literacy: 59.5% (definition: 15 years and older can read and write)[83]
Official languages: Hindi, Bengali, Telugu, Marathi, Tamil, Urdu, Gujarati, Malayalam, Kannada, Oriya, Punjabi, Assamese, Kashmiri, Sindhi, and Sanskrit. English is widely spoken by primary speakers of other language groups as a bridge.
Total telephone lines: 49.75 million (2005)[84]

Total Internet users: 60 million (2005)[85]
Total mobile phone users: 149.5 million[86]

I always like to say that no one will get fired for outsourcing to India this year, although maybe that is no longer true, or will not be for too much longer. However, any discussion of offshore outsourcing would not be complete without first addressing the development of India's outsourcing capability, but just as important, the difficulties it now faces.

Outsourcing to India began in the 1980s, with Indian engineers trained in the United States and elsewhere. These engineers, who had found employment at top multinational corporations, moved directly into BPO, then ITO, unlike China or some other Asian countries that had first undertaken significant outsourced manufacturing.

During the 1990s, two phenomena occurred that facilitated swifter growth of outsourcing as a whole with the specific development of the industry in India: the increasing trend toward globalization and the rise of the Internet.

India was not always a target for technology activity. As recently as the mid-1970s, it was seen as an impenetrable market, with IBM deciding to pack up and head home, as import duties of over 100 percent made PCs simply too expensive to reach any significant market.[87]

The tide seemed to turn in 1985, when then-Prime Minister Rajiv Gandhi urged the country to embrace technology in a speech,[88] although it would be almost another decade before telecommunications, and the commensurate lowering of tariffs on international calls and other overseas communications that gave the outsourcing industry a fighting chance.[89]

In 1999, with the Internet overseas but bandwidth and the number of users in India still limited, the country and its fledgling outsourcing industry received a boost from a looming doomsday event: the Y2K bug. Expected to wreak havoc on code written decades earlier when processors were designed to handle year dates only with two dates, and not the four they would need to function properly after January 1, 2000, billions of lines of code were sent to India to be corrected. For many companies, this was their first taste of outsourcing in India.[90]

While the Y2K bug did not bring ruin to IT systems across the United States and elsewhere, the end of dot-com era exuberance in early 2000 left the technology industry reeling and looking for low-cost, high-quality alternatives. Wall Street and Silicon Valley's loss was certainly in this case the Indian outsourcing industry's gain. U.S. tech industry hiring declined and layoffs burgeoned, but in India, the experience was exactly the opposite, with a hiring boom to pick up the slack.[91]

Outsourcing in India continued to build on its own success, seemingly in a technology vacuum to the rest of the country. As China quickly became the second largest Internet market in the world, and venture capital and other investment poured in for another chance at a dot-com gold rush, India's Internet use remained under 20 million total users out of almost one billion people.

Travelers to tech centers like Bangalore and Delhi were impressed with the engineers and programmers they met, but were shocked by having to sometimes travel down dirt roads to reach outsourcing facilities, and complained of being unable to get online or access their e-mail during their entire trip to India. Clearly such centers were islands surrounded by areas very much under development.

Only since 2004 has this situation begun to change significantly, with rules on foreign investment changing to allow overseas corporations the opportunity to participate in the construction of domestic networks.

India simply has not yet had the telecommunications build-out that China undertook in the 1990s. That may be good news for suppliers of networking equipment, but it means that the country's existing mobile and fixed-line networks are still far from being considered modern or world-class.

Due to the overall size of its population, and perhaps aided by a new class of low-cost mobile handsets becoming available, India will easily and quickly surpass the United States as the world's second-largest mobile phone market.

However, those same low-priced handsets will also fuel a new burst of growth in China, which has spent the better part of two decades developing its wireless and fixed-line infrastructure into a state-of-the-art, nationwide network.

India's Internet population can also be expected to surpass the United States, again because of sheer size of total population, but by that point the United States will already have slipped to second place after China. Chinese estimates state that the country will surpass the U.S. for total Internet users as early as 2009, but a five-to-ten-year window is more likely.[92]

As of 2007, India's outsourcing market is valued at US$23.6 billion[93] (2012). To date, India has been able to offer approximately 50 percent average cost savings[94] on projects, which has continued to be the most compelling reason to outsource there.

However, that growth is now coming at a price—rising talent costs, increased turnover, and most critical—inability of the industry to produce enough software engineers and programmers to support its hiring needs.

In 2005–06, we saw US$1 billion investments in India by major multinational companies, including IBM and Cisco Systems.[95] Pouring big bucks into the market, at this stage, may guarantee that those companies and others making large investments can attract top talent to themselves. However, ultimately that drives up the price of labor and begins to reduce the savings that outsourcing to those firms can offer—which is the whole point of BPO and KPO in the first place.

One very daunting study, conducted in India by Indians, estimated that given current levels of talent, research, and development, India remains 163 years behind China in terms of scientific research.[96]

Despite these advances, we are left with significant concerns about India in the future. One cannot ignore that 40 percent of the nation is illiterate. Of the BRIC nations, the next lowest literacy level is Brazil, which still offers 86 percent adult literacy. This does not indicate to us that basic levels of education are reaching enough people or enough parts of the country. As we will discuss shortly, India's outsourcing industry is facing a talent shortage—less than 60 percent literacy does not demonstrate to us that there will be a sufficiently large future talent pool to rectify the situation.

While we absolutely recognize the value of cultural, ethnic, linguistic, and religious diversity, and certainly its contributions to the development of nations in North America, Europe, and Asia, India's lack of a single, official language (or even its ability to narrow the list to two or three), can mean ongoing communications problems, with speakers of Hindi comprising only 30 percent of the population. India is also involved in a continuing rivalry with its neighbor Pakistan, one punctuated by the possession of nuclear weapons on both sides.

More practically and probably more important, India has simply not emerged as a desirable market in its own right. Although telecom service providers and mobile phone handset manufacturers are now flocking to India to cash in on growth there, this is an isolated market. We simply do not see the same sustained rate of economic growth there that we do or have in East Asian markets; basic infrastructure such as roads and transport, cannot match what we have seen in other countries, especially China.

There are other indicators of where India is, or is not, going. China is hosting the 2008 Olympic Games, and will be a serious competitor in the overall medal count there. By contrast, no Indian city has ever made a serious bid for the Olympics, and Indian athletes do not compete in the same number or at the same level as their Chinese rivals.

Since 2002, China has been among the world's top five tourist destinations,[97] welcoming 120.29 million foreign visitors in 2005, and is predicted by some to be on track to become the world's most visited country by 2020.[98] India does not make the top ten. As strong believers in the aforementioned Gartner maxim of "Company before country," India does not meet the criteria.

For us, the turning point came when the world's most famous outsourcing organization—India's National Association of Software and Service Companies—said that in 2008, it was expecting that with present levels of computer science graduates from the country's universities, the industry would fall 500,000 hires short of its needs by 2010, based on its current rate of growth.[99]

That is not a rounding error. That does not fall within margin of error for a reasonable survey. Even if that number were wrong by half, coming up 250,000 people too few for a growing industry is a serious shortfall. This leaves India's outsourcing industry with one choice—to itself outsource to another destination with the necessary technology talent.

Other considerations for outsourcing to India include the time difference between there and North American cities (10.5 hours for the Eastern Time Zone, 11.5 hours for the Pacific Time Zone, both on standard time), and the language barrier.

The study and use of English in India, as part of its legacy as a British Crown Colony, is well known. We do not question the widespread study and use of English throughout the country. However, there has been a backlash against call centers based in India, especially from U.S. consumers, who sometimes have trouble understanding the person on the other end of the phone, or who feel alienated by the fact that the operator answering their call is not only not in the same time zone, but not even on the same continent.

We believe that by its own actions, the Indian outsourcing industry has indicated where it—and by proxy, the rest of the world's industry—is going. India's number one destination for its own outsourcing is the world's number two: China.

India's choice of China as its own outsourcing destination is not new. Since the late 1990s, Indian outsourcers have been opening offices in China and shipping projects there. In 2005, Tata Consultancy Services, India's largest outsourcer, opened a joint venture (JV) in Beijing.[100] In early 2007, Tata inaugurated that JV and scooped up a Chinese government currency system contract at the same time.[101] Also in 2007, Satyam Information Services, part of Sify, opened a new development center in Nanjing. It already operated two support centers in Dalian and Guangzhou, and an office in Beijing.[102]

The success to date of the Indian BPO and KPO industry cannot be disputed, and until recently, the maxim that "no one will get fired this year for outsourcing to India" was true. However, with China now the number two destination for global BPO and KPO, and having become the number one choice for Indian companies that cannot satisfy demand with their own talent, we believe that China's time as an offshore outsourcing power has come. In our next chapter, we explain why we have chosen to throw our lot in with China, and why companies currently outsourcing elsewhere or preparing to do so need to consider IT's next powerhouse.

ENDNOTES

1. www.globalinsight.com/Perspective/PerspectiveDetail5869.htm
2. www.computerworld.com/managementtopics/outsourcing/story/0,10801,84817,00.html
3. www.pwc.com/extweb/ncpressrelease.nsf/docid/717933D0D5F89E2985256E6D004E89F4
4. www.outsourcing.com/mexico_trends/mexico.html
5. www.computerworld.com/managementtopics/outsourcing/story/0,10801,84829,00.html
6. Ibid.
7. www.wired.com/wired/archive/5.11/heartof.html?topic=hacking_warez&topic_set=newtechnology
8. www.sfgate.com/cgi-bin/article.cgi?f=/c/a/2006/05/16/BUGANIS78M1.DTL
9. www.businessweek.com/magazine/content/04_09/b3872010_mz001.htm
10. www.sfgate.com/cgi-bin/article.cgi?f=/c/a/2006/05/16/BUGANIS78M1.DTL
11. Ibid.
12. Ibid.
13. www.cio.com/offshoremap/czech.html
14. www.forbes.com/free_forbes/2006/0417/074.html
15. Ibid.
16. Ibid.
17. www.indiadaily.com/editorial/1791.asp
18. www.accenture.com/Countries/Ireland/Research_and_Insights/GuideIreland.htm
19. http://computerworld.co.nz/news.nsf/news/38954EAD25185304CC256D9F00687838
20. www.iht.com/articles/2004/06/05/mireland_ed3_.php
21. http://outsourcingmonitor.eu/articles/malta-nearshore-solution.html
22. www.cia.gov/cia/publications/factbook/geos/pl.html
23. www.cia.gov/cia/publications/factbook/geos/bu.html
24. www.cia.gov/cia/publications/factbook/geos/hu.html
25. www.hp.com/hpinfo/newsroom/press/2005/050415b.html
26. www.oswmag.com/news/viewArticle/ARTICLEID=945

27. www.cio.com/offshoremap/romania.html
28. http://news.zdnet.co.uk/itmanagement/0,1000000308,39161721-2,00.htm
29. Ibid.
30. www.atkearney.sk/main.taf?p=1,5,1,168
31. Ibid.
32. http://services.silicon.com/offshoring/0,3800004877,39156347,00.htm
33. Ibid.
34. www.eds.com/about/locations/israel/
35. www.blogsource.org/2006/11/israels_native_.html
36. http://in.news.yahoo.com/041121/43/2i0e4.html
37. Ibid.
38. www.idc.com/getdoc.jsp?containerId=IDC_P540
39. http://australianit.news.com.au/articles/0,7204,21251353%5E15341%5E%5Enbv%5E15306-15317,00.html
40. Ibid.
41. www.atkearney.sk/main.taf?p=1,5,1,168
42. http://en.wikipedia.org/wiki/Multimedia_Super_Corridor
43. www.sourcingmag.com/content/c060510a.asp
44. Ibid.
45. Ibid.
46. www.atkearney.sk/main.taf?p=1,5,1,168
47. http://online.wsj.com/article/SB117210101864315430.html
48. Ibid.
49. Ibid.
50. www.time.com/time/world/article/0,8599,1167191,00.html
51. www.atkearney.sk/main.taf?p=1,5,1,168
52. www.businessweek.com/technology/content/dec2006/tc20061211_099877.htm
53. Ibid.
54. Ibid.
55. https://www.cia.gov/cia/publications/factbook/geos/br.html
56. Ibid.
57. Ibid.
58. Ibid.
59. Ibid.
60. Ibid.
61. www.computerworld.com/managementtopics/outsourcing/story/0,10801,84869,00.html
62. Ibid.
63. www.sourcingmag.com/content/c060201a.asp

64. Ibid.
65. Ibid.
66. Ibid.
67. www.iht.com/articles/2005/05/17/business/outsource.php
68. https://www.cia.gov/cia/publications/factbook/geos/rs.html
69. Ibid.
70. Ibid.
71. Ibid.
72. Ibid.
73. Ibid.
74. www.neoit.com/gen/newsevents/press_release.html
75. www.computerworld.com/managementtopics/management/outsourcing/story/0,10801,82761,00.html
76. Ibid.
77. www.computerworld.com/action/article.do?command=viewArticleTOC&specialReportId=360&articleId=84874
78. www.russoft.org/docs/?doc = 927
79. www.reksoft.com/blogs/russian-ict/
80. https://www.cia.gov/cia/publications/factbook/geos/rs.html
81. https://www.cia.gov/cia/publications/factbook/geos/in.html
82. Ibid.
83. Ibid.
84. Ibid.
85. Ibid.
86. www.infoworld.com/article/07/01/16/HNindiamobilephoneusers_1.html
87. http://news.com.com/Indias+renaissance+Move+over,+China/2009-1041_3-5751994.html
88. Ibid.
89. Ibid.
90. Ibid.
91. Ibid.
92. http://technology.guardian.co.uk/news/story/0,1998039,00.html
93. www.infoworld.com/article/06/06/01/78823_HNindiaoffshorerevenue_1.html
94. Top by 2020 reference
95. http://newsroom.cisco.com/dlls/global/asiapac/news/2005/pr_10-19b.html
96. www.businessweek.com/globalbiz/blog/asiatech/archives/2007/02/india_163_years.html
97. http://geography.about.com/b/a/005864.htm

98. www.time.com/time/magazine/article/0,9171,503060807-120
    7866,00.html

99. www.infoworld.com/article/06/06/01/78823_HNindiaoffshore
    revenue_1.html

100. www.infoworld.com/article/05/06/30/HNtatamsoutsourcing_1.html

101. www.itnewsonline.com/showstory.php?storyid=8767&scatid=
     8&contid=2

102. www.iht.com/articles/2007/02/08/bloomberg/sxsatyam.php

CHAPTER 3

China: Your Essential Shore

China has arrived as a sourcing destination in the global IT services and outsourcing market. Buyers, especially those with operations in China, are beginning to see the value in diversifying their sourcing through Chinese suppliers. A small yet increasingly sophisticated set of Chinese vendors are prepared for global sourcing relationships. And the Chinese export IT services and outsourcing industry is receiving a strong unified boost from the Chinese Ministry of Commerce. While competition will remain tough from Indian and "near-shore" providers in multiple geographies, savvy Chinese providers are rapidly finding their paths to market.

Jamie Popkin, Group Vice President, Gartner Inc.

As the examples on the preceding pages demonstrate, China did not decide to have an outsourcing industry overnight, nor did it. It was neither the aim of government nor of private industry to begin attracting this type of foreign business or investment to the country. Initially, China was more focused on developing its own hardware and software businesses internally. In its earliest stages, it did not see the value of establishing the country's name in the outsourcing field, and then devoting educational or industrial resources to competing in that field in a way that was not entirely focused on the domestic industry, especially when success was far from assured.

However, since former leader Deng Xiaoping began the process of reform and openness in 1978, and especially in earnest since 1992, China started to lay a foundation that would fuel a host of industries and ultimately allow it to begin competing against the rest of the world.

BIG NUMBERS FROM A BIG COUNTRY

We should first look at the big picture. It is important that a general understanding of China be conveyed before beginning a more specific discussion of outsourcing and the software outsourcing industry here. Doing business in China is not like doing business in the United States or Europe. Although your counterparts may wear suits and ties, eat McDonald's, and even listen to iPods, it does not mean that they or their nation are like you or yours. Success in China requires understanding.

China is a nation of superlatives. It has the largest population in the world, with 1.3 to 1.4 billion people. By land mass, it is the third largest country in the world, just edging out the United States. It covers three time zones but maintains a single national time standard, Beijing Time. The nation prides itself on having 5,000 years of history, a figure that is often quoted, although the lines of archaeology and mythology blur on how far back that really goes. Suffice it to say that China has one of the world's oldest cultures, and its people treasure that heritage deeply.

The country is comprised of 23 provinces and 5 autonomous regions. The latter includes the Xizang Autonomous Region, known better in the West as Tibet; the Xinjiang Uygur Autonomous Region in the country's northwest; and the Inner Mongolia Autonomous Region, which stretches along its northern border with Mongolia (the nation) and Russia. Beijing serves as the nation's capital, and has since the establishment of the People's Republic of China (the country's official name) on October 1, 1949. Along with the majority Han people, which make up about 95 percent of China's population, there are 56 recognized minorities, including Manchus, Tibetans, and Caucasian-looking Uygurs from Xinjiang.

China is home to some of the world's most significant geographic features. Mt. Everest—known in China as Qomolongma—the world's tallest mountain, lies toward its southwestern edge, with its treacherous north face on the China side; its summit ridge forming part of the border between China and Nepal; and its south and west faces in Nepal. The Yangzi River, known in China as "Chang Jiang," or simply "The Long River," is Asia's longest and the world's third longest, with its headwaters forming in Tibet and flowing past Chongqing, Wuhan, and Shanghai into the East China Sea.

China shares land borders with North Korea, Russia, Mongolia, Afghanistan, Pakistan, India, Nepal, Bhutan, Myanmar (Burma), and Vietnam. It now has peaceful relations with all of these countries, including visa-free relationships with some either for Chinese citizens or for travelers from those nations or both. Its last military confrontation with a neighbor was a brief clash with Vietnam in 1979, although ties between the two are now strong and friendly. Chinese passport holders may now travel to Vietnam visa-free.

EXPERT OPINION

China: The New Global Tech Hub

Traditionally, the growth of Chinese IT services industry has been interlinked with the dominant domestic manufacturing industry, particularly in areas like package implementation, embedded systems and system integration. Consequently, these enablers ensured that China possesses a large and vibrant domestic IT services market.

Catalyzed by global sourcing, changing external perception about China, investment flow, inherent advantages of a low-cost and skilled labor pool, and strong government support, the country's IT services export market is in a high growth phase (see Exhibit 3.1).

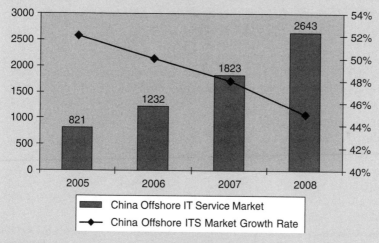

EXHIBIT 3.1 China Offshore Market Size and Forecast (million USD)
Source: neoIT (www.neoit.com)

China's competitiveness as a preferred offshoring location is witnessing a remarkable shift. Japan will remain the most lucrative market and its potential will be instrumental in the rapid growth of Japan-focused Chinese companies. Simultaneously, affinity toward China among the Western countries is growing. While domestic market demand was traditionally the driving force behind investments in

China, the focus is shifting toward leveraging China as a global services sourcing destination. Organizations are looking at China to service both Asia-Pacific and global locations.

Strong skill sets coupled with extensive domain experience make China a suitable outsourcing destination for IT and telecom clients. Application development and projects in the embedded software space are strong market drivers. Software implementation and support, and application management services are also areas that will witness high growth. Broad based growth covering high-end application development, integration, and management along with low-end Web-based development will happen.

While there is opportunity to be realized, there are some challenges to overcome as well. Proficiency with English, though rapidly improving, remains a concern. Moreover, Chinese service providers need to enhance their marketing activities that are targeted toward Western organizations. In addition, project management and delivery skills need to be further improved.

These challenges will be overcome by progressive Chinese IT outsourcing (ITO) service providers who are able to respond to the more demanding needs of U.S. and European organizations, provided there is industry and government support for English language skill improvements. The key to tapping the Western market is to create vertical industry skills, improve the client acquisition process, enhance quality adherence processes, and build up project management skills. Service providers also need to adapt to working on strict contract terms and watertight project specifications. If carried out successfully, these initiatives will transform China into a global tech hub. Early signs are already showing evidence of this transformation process.

neoIT

GOVERNMENT AND POLITICS

Since 1949, China has been led by the Communist Party of China (CCP), and as such, remains officially a one-party state. However, China has always referred to its political philosophy as "socialism with Chinese characteristics," and over the past 25 years those characteristics increasingly resemble a market economy. There is no longer any danger of being denounced as a "capitalist roader" today, once a serious accusation. Citizens are not required to join the Communist Party, and now even qualified entrepreneurs are welcomed into its ranks. As of 2005, there were just over 70 million CCP members.[1] Although CCP membership is not required to serve in government, the vast majority of upper-level government officials and bureaucrats do belong to it. In parts of China's vast countryside, local officials have been democratically elected with success.

China's current head of state is President Hu Jintao, who became the country's leader in 2004. Hu also heads the CCP's leadership council, the Central Committee of the Politburo, of which he is general secretary. The National People's Congress (NPC), China's parliament, meets annually in March and selects the Central Committee.

When President Hu took over for his predecessor, Jiang Zemin, in 2004, international media inaccurately referred to it as "the first orderly transfer of power in Communist Party history."[2] In fact, since the establishment of the People's Republic in 1949, China has overall enjoyed great political stability and continuity. Political events may have led to a reshuffling of potential successors for the highest government posts, but there have been no coup d'etats or coup attempts, as we have seen in other Asian nations such as the Philippines and Thailand. Without that stability, China's current economic growth would simply have been impossible, and social stability receives the government's highest priority.

Among its numerous tasks, China's central government directly administers four cities: Beijing, Shanghai, Tianjin, and Chongqing, the newest and largest such city, with 30 million residents. Residents of the latter three do not think of themselves as being residents of any of the nearby provinces, and as such have their own distinctive character. Because Chongqing was part of Sichuan until 1997, and is still surrounded by that southwestern province, its residents still identify themselves as being from there. The central government's move stripped Sichuan of the title of China's most populous province. The province of Henan now reigns as the nation's most populous, with about 100 million residents.

The central government also oversees two Special Administrative Regions (SARs): the Hong Kong SAR, a former British Crown Colony returned to Chinese sovereignty on July 1, 1997; and the Macau SAR, a former Portuguese colony returned on December 20, 1999.

China regards Taiwan as a breakaway province. Since the end of the Chinese civil war in 1949, Taiwan has maintained its own government and still holds sway over some islands directly off the coast of Fujian province, namely Jinmen (Quemoy) and Mazu (Matsu). It has never declared independence, a move that China said will mean war. While the two sides enjoy significant commercial and investment relations, they are still separated by political differences and have no direct air connections. Political tensions sometimes make headlines, but most believe that despite occasional saber-rattling from both sides, the two are too deeply linked culturally and economically for any kind of military confrontation to occur.

PLANES, TRAINS, AND AUTOMOBILES

In terms of other business infrastructure needs, China leads the region and the world in many cases. The number of air connections to and from China is overwhelming. By 2010, almost 250 flights per week will link U.S. destinations and China, with more than half of those routes dedicated to cargo operators. In January 2007, the two nations' capitals were finally connected by nonstop air service, with United Airlines winning approval to fly between Washington Dulles and Beijing's Capital International Airport beginning late March 2007.[3] About 200 flights per week cross back and forth from Europe. These routes are also increasingly appealing to Chinese carriers, and two of the largest, China Southern and China Eastern, are publicly listed in the United States.

Recent research has shown that China's aviation market, both cargo and passenger, continues to grow at an incredible rate and still has significant room for more growth:

> *Along with the rapid growth of China's economy, airport construction has achieved great development during the tenth Five-Year Plan period (2001–05). By the end of 2005, China has had 135 civil scheduled-flight airports in 133 cities. In 2005, the total passenger throughput of China reached 284.35 million person times, increased by 17.5 percent over the previous year; cargo and mail throughput was 6.331 million tons with a year-on-year growth of 14.6 percent.*
>
> *Among all civil airports in China, there are 42 airports whose annual passenger throughput exceeds 1 million person times, accounting for 94.7 percent of total passenger throughput; there are 7 airports whose annual passenger throughput exceeds 10 million person times, accounting for 52.1 percent of the total; and the passenger throughput of airports in Beijing, Shanghai, and Guangzhou shares 37.3 percent of the total. Besides, China has 39 airports whose annual cargo and mail throughput are over 10,000 tons, accounting for 98.5 percent of total cargo and mail throughout. And cargo and mail throughput of airports in Beijing, Shanghai, and Guangzhou accounts for 56.9 percent of the total.*
>
> *At present, the turnover of Chinese civil aviation occupies only 0.55 percent of the total turnover of the whole transport system,*

and the passenger traffic of civil aviation accounts for only about 10 percent of the railway passenger traffic. However, the turnover of U.S. civil aviation occupies 9.5 percent of the total turnover of its comprehensive transport system. With regard to the airport density, China has 1.4 airports per 100,000 square km while Japan has 23.3 airports per 100,000 square km. And even in eastern China where airports are most concentrated, there are only 4.8 airports per 100,000 square km, while Xinjiang and northwest China only have 0.6 and 0.8 airports per 100,000 square km, respectively.[4]

Despite this massive growth in civil aviation, China's largest transportation network remains its railroads. China operates the world's third largest railroad network,[5] trailing only the United States and Russia. This network now includes trains to Lhasa in Tibet, a new line that opened in 2006 and is considered by the Chinese to be a major engineering feat. Travel by rail in China is inexpensive, fast, and comfortable, especially in sleeper compartments. Shorter journeys like Beijing to Tianjin and Shanghai to Hangzhou or Nanjing, and Guangzhou to Shenzhen and Hong Kong have now reached the speed and efficiency of commuter trains in other parts of the world.

China's highway network has been under construction and expansion until the 1990s, and started coming into its own earlier this decade. In late 2005, China's large-scale road system had a total of 1.87 million km, containing 34,300 km of highway, and the number of the automobiles was more than 29 million.[6]

In 2004, 6.2 billion passengers were transported by road for a total of about 874.8 billion person/kilometers. Cargo sent by road reached 12.5 billion tons, covering 73 percent of the nation's total freight.[7] China's highway network is already second only to the United States',[8] and plans for construction continue until 2020.[9]

EDUCATING THE MASSES

One of China's most formidable challenges, and top triumphs, is in educating its people. Chinese students and scholars are renowned throughout the world for their diligence, their hunger for knowledge, and their ultimate success. Education is at the core of the society and the family. Adult literacy now stands at 91 percent.[10] Of the world's five most populous nations, only the United States can claim higher literacy.[11] Primary school attendance in China, which is compulsory for all children, stood at 99 percent in 2005.[12]

China's value of education is historical. Prior to the establishment of the People's Republic, China adhered primarily to a Confucian value system, which allowed little opportunity for social mobility. However, the imperial examination system, established during the Han Dynasty (206 BC–220 AD), sought to bring the country's most talented into government service, and offered them the opportunity to do so via a standardized testing system. The U.S. civil service examination is in part designed on the Chinese system, which was abolished in 1898. However, that opportunity for the children of peasants in far-flung reaches of the empire to engage in government service—a highly-prized position that offered stability and chances for wealth—led Chinese society to place a high value on education early in its history.

Education is more important in China today than it has ever been. Gaining admission to a university, especially a top university, can make or break a person's career. Failing to get into college not only is a great loss of face for a student and his or her family, but it can also mean significantly reduced job prospects. Unlike other countries such as the United States or those in Western Europe, a university education is generally a one-shot deal: get in on the first try or start considering other options. It is an unforgiving environment, but at present China has approximately 16 million university places[13] for a population of 1.3 billion people.

Ni Hui Shuo YingYu Ma? (Do You Speak English?)

One of the biggest questions I face when I go overseas is, do young technology graduates speak English? One thing is for sure: these graduates certainly *read* English. As the owner of a start-up IT company once told me, "if you don't read English, you can't work in IT. The amount of material simply unavailable in Chinese would prevent you from keeping up with new developments and making any kind of progress in your field."

Young graduates increasingly come out of the country's main institutions of higher learning speaking excellent levels of English. The government identified English as the language of modernization, and therefore, you find professionals in the industry who speak English very well. That spreads across management layers. What is really significant is young graduates and their interest in absorbing Western culture, and the advent of the Internet and how its proliferation in the country really ushered that in.

We are still working against the perception that most people think China does not speak English. It will be some time before people realize how far developed in its English education China has become. But already the data is on our side. One Gartner analyst already indicated that by 2008, China's IT industry will have the world's largest English-language capability,[14] pushed in part by a language-education drive toward the 2008 Olympic Games.

YOUR ESSENTIAL SHORE

At I.T. UNITED we chose "China: Your Essential Shore" as our slogan. This is based on the Gartner research group's motto of "Country Before Company." When it comes to outsourcing, they—and we—believe that you must first choose the market you are preparing to enter, where you want to compete and grow your business, and then choose an outsourcing partner within it.

In the global economy, when a company is trying to decide where it wants to outsource, it should identify what the markets are for its core business and choose a country that is one of their core markets, to outsource there, and to use it as leverage with their core competencies. If you were already going to a company for business, why not consider it as an outsourcing destination for some of your business processes? Especially in a country like China, where linguistic differences and the need for language localization is so critical for market success, to attempt to handle much of that work elsewhere is either impossible or foolish.

The attention that China is getting is starting to snowball. Corporations are considering China for business functions beyond their core competencies, and as a result, outsourcing is picking up. For more than 20 years, the market was labeled as the manufacturing factory floor of the global economy, and it is now taking that success into high-end engineering services.

As we saw in the previous chapter, while India continues, for the moment, to lead the world's software outsourcing market, it is still not a compelling market for overall business. China has a singular advantage that India does not: it is without question the market that most major international corporations, and many, many smaller ones, are chasing.

China has been the target market of every Fortune 100 company, and so many other Fortune 500 and even tiny start-up firms, since it first began welcoming foreign investment in the late 1970s. The Chinese consumer, and reaching him or her with a product or service, has become an almost mythical quest for CEOs and executives. "If I could just get every Chinese person to buy my product just once..." Of course this type of thinking was long ago discredited, but China remains the market of choice for any corporation seeking significant expansion of its business.

As a business destination, China is number one. A survey of experts found that China ranked number one among attractive global business locations, placing ahead of the United States, and number one among transnational corporation executives, ahead of both the United States and India by a wide margin.[15]

Whereas Tokyo, Hong Kong, and Singapore were once the most common cities for Asian regional headquarters, that trend is now shifting to focus on the area's most important market. Companies that have made Shanghai their Asia-Pacific headquarters include General Motors, Alcatel (now Alcatel-Lucent), National Semiconductor, the BASF Group, Korn/Ferry, and Honeywell. That list will only grow.

China continues to be a major destination for foreign direct investment (FDI). FDI leveled off in 2005 at just over US$60 billion per year, but began to see growth again in early 2006.[16] Hong Kong remains the number one supplier of FDI to China. Use of that FDI is concentrated in coastal provinces, with Jiangsu, Guangdong, Shandong, Fujian, and Shanghai soaking up 65 percent of total investment.[17]

The country has maintained strong Gross Domestic Product (GDP) growth for the past two decades, hitting 10.5 percent in 2006,[18] and with an average of eight percent growth predicted by Chinese economists until 2010.[19]

EXPERT OPINION

China: The New Global Tech Hub

It is an exciting time to be in China—these words may sound clichéd, if not jaded, but hold true today more than ever before. Ever since China opened its doors, the country has established itself as the world's manufacturing factory and now sits at the cusp of becoming the world's next technology hub. Critics may claim that IT services and technology are not China's forte but belong to India; however, the signs of what is seen today in China point to a future whereby it is a question of when China becomes the hub, not if. The following are compelling reasons for China's case:

- **Infrastructure is key.** Unlike India, the Philippines, and other developing countries, the infrastructure in China's key cities earmarked for tech development is superior and impressive. From gleaming tech parks to a reliable power supply, having good and dependable infrastructure is the key foundation toward building a solid tech centered economy.

- **Cost effective labor.** Long known as a place with cost effective blue-collar labor, many multinationals and tech providers have begun to realize the large and deep pool of cost effective white collar labor in China's major cities today. The millions of engineers,

PhD graduates, and IT personnel produced by China per annum are more than the entire population of Singapore!

- **Promise of a potential domestic market.** While China will continue to be a major exporter of technology related services, there are sound indications that several sectors domestically offer good potential as local consumers. As banking, manufacturing, and telecommunications services grow, more companies within these sectors are looking toward technology as a springboard for them to leapfrog to new markets overseas and benchmark to global standards.

Nevertheless, China is not without its challenges in its pursuit of dominating global technology, chief of which are:

- **Language skills.** Currently, most of the technology-related work done in China involves very few voice components due to a lack of spoken English skills suitable for a worldwide customer. Nevertheless, this situation is fast changing as more efforts are being poured into improving spoken English amongst technology and outsourcing workers.
- **Lack of a coherent representative body.** There are too many local state governments competing for the same investment dollars instead of presenting a unified, coherent voice akin to Nasscom in India. Such a body would act as an effective marketing, public relations, and lobbying body to represent a unified China that collectively offers a suite of skills, potential, and capabilities.
- **Judiciary and legal systems.** One of the cornerstones of building a strong technology hub is the presence of strong judiciary and legal systems. This is important to ensure intellectual property protection, trademark protection, stemming of piracy and that the written contract is legally binding and enforceable.

While the challenges are great, there is every indication that China recognizes these obstacles and is putting in place processes and programs toward building up a strong tech centered economy. The determination and openness shown by the entities at stake (i.e., governments, private sector, and public sector) are encouraging. It is still at the nascent stages of development but the signs do point to the fact that China is doing the right things to steer itself in the right direction.

Conrad Chang, Research Manager for BPO, IDC Asia Pacific

THE EARLY YEARS

Admittedly, it was a frustrating start as that door creaked open after years of relative commercial isolation. Both the Chinese side and its foreign partners learned a lot from each other in those early stages, but that investment of patience as much as capital is now paying dividends for those who saw that China required a long-term commitment, far more so than any other market to date.

One of China's greatest national and commercial assets is its infrastructure. State of the art infrastructure supports the country's technology drive, and the market supports that infrastructure. The government moved to support high-tech development some ten years ago, and it makes a big difference if the government of any country or any market makes that commitment to support it. We will discuss this commitment and what it means for the outsourcing business in more detail a bit later in China's Legal Framework section.

In other outsourcing markets, we see companies forced to provide all their own equipment, including in some cases their own power generation. Once you leave their premises, that infrastructure ends. These companies are, essentially, infrastructure islands stuck in a given market they chose out of labor considerations, since that nation seems to offer them little else in the way of support or advantage.

MADE IN CHINA

Outsourcing to China came very early during the process of modernization and reform; in fact, it is safe to say that it was outsourcing that first fueled business interest in modern China, as selling to China's domestic market was either restricted or logistically impossible at that time. The nation's levels of affluence had also not yet begun to rise to the point where consumer goods were readily available to them, so the "China market" was all about the future at that point.

The first Special Economic Zones (SEZs) were established in 1980, giving both Chinese and their foreign partners the opportunity to dip their toes into the waters of this newly emerging market. One SEZ, Shenzhen, just north across the border from Hong Kong, is now China's second-richest city, behind only Shanghai.

To early investors, China had two great assets: a vast supply of inexpensive, unskilled labor; and an underutilized heavy industry infrastructure. For this reason the earliest arrivals into the China market engaged in offshore outsourcing, looking for low-cost ways to manufacture their products, in the same way that had been done in other Asian territories in the 1960s and

1970s, with plastics, textiles, and electronics. Slowly but surely, the once ubiquitous "Made in Hong Kong" and "Made in Taiwan" labels and stickers that were on so many products were replaced with "Made in China." Today those tags dominate whole retail markets. In the United States, department stores seem to have been stocked en masse with Chinese-made goods. The ability to consistently produce high-quality goods for a low price opened the doors not only for further expansion of outsourced manufacturing in China, but also has created a reputation for quality that now extends into other areas, including BPO and knowledge process outsourcing KPO.

A U.S.-based journalist spent a year avoiding Chinese-made goods. "After a year without China I can tell you this: You can still live without it, but it's getting trickier and costlier by the day," she said.[20]

One U.S.-based company has made more of this outsourcing relationship than any other: Wal-Mart. In 2004, the company purchased US$18 billion worth of Chinese goods, either directly or from China-based suppliers, and would rank as China's eighth-largest trading partner, ahead of Russia, Australia, and Canada.[21] Wal-Mart's trade relationship also accounts for about 10 percent of the U.S. trade deficit with China.[22]

FROM PAGERS TO MARKET SUPREMACY

During the 1990s, the technology and telecommunications industries participated in a once-in-a-lifetime event: China's technology build-out. Although people in the automobile industry may have had a similar experience, seeing China come of age technologically, in terms of IT and telecommunications, was an amazing process.

Travelers who visited China in the 1980s and the first half of the 1990s will remember having to go to an office of the Ministry of Post and Telecommunications (now the Ministry of Information Industry) to make an international phone call, sometimes waiting hours for the privilege—and paying a lot of money to do so. Telex numbers on business cards were de rigueur well past the point where companies elsewhere in the world had switched to facsimile machines.

Perhaps one of the biggest changes in the 1990s was a leap past analog. Early that decade, people who had never had a phone in their home before began to have them installed. But by the late 1990s, many urban residents, who could now afford to purchase mobile phones, chose to forego their home phones entirely and use only cell numbers. Neither answering machines nor voicemail have ever been popular in China, so not having that point of contact was never an issue. Pagers were a common sight on city streets until the late 1990s, when rapidly disappearing public phones, often run from mom-and-pop convenience stores, made them inconvenient. They were replaced by increasingly affordable mobile phones.

During this time, China began to create competition within its telecom marketplace, leading to improvements in service, shortened installation times, and a diversification of services. From monolithic China Telecom, we saw the birth of China Unicom, a state-run competitor. Since then other players, including China Mobile and China Netcom have each become major influences on the market, with each listing on stock markets or overseas, pushing themselves to acquire more customers, whether those users are buying their first mobile phone or Internet connection. The companies also compete with each other for rates and service.

Also during this period was the start of the in-house research and development activities among China's top technology firms, although at that time there were very few that classified as top tier. In 2000, foreign technology companies began establishing research and development labs in China for product localization and to make use of the low-cost talent, setting the stage in part for the upcoming outsourcing revolution. Companies that maintain labs in China today include Microsoft, IBM, and Sun Microsystems.

Today, China is the world's largest mobile telephony market, with 400 million users and growing. One company, China Mobile, is the world's largest mobile operator. By 2010, China is predicted to have 580 million mobile users, maintaining its lead over the United States and India,[23] with growth expanding as new, even lower-cost mobile phones begin to hit the market.

At present, China's mobile service companies not only offer basic voice and data services, but China Mobile offers 2.5G connections that permit Internet access, especially for e-mail or file transfer on Global Standard for Mobile communications (GSM) systems. China Unicom, which operates the country's only Code Division Multiple Access (CDMA) network, offers services that allow CDMA cards to be used as mobile modems for laptop and notebook computers, for areas that do not have Wi-Fi coverage.

Business travelers can rely on China Mobile to provide them with roaming service for cell phones from their home countries, including push-mail service to BlackBerry and other personal digital assistants. However, a more inexpensive option is available shortly after you step off your flight—most major Chinese airports have desks selling prepaid SIM cards with local numbers. In Beijing, you can buy one before you even clear customs! Try that during your next trip to the United States.

Free Wi-Fi hotspots abound, especially in major hotels, commercial buildings, and cafes in Beijing, Shanghai, and more tech-savvy cities like Hangzhou. Some airports offer customers of China Mobile paid Wi-Fi access charged to their mobile phone number, with registration completed by a simple text message, and no additional hardware.

Some major cities in China also offer a service available in few if any other countries in the world: dial-up Internet access without registration. Using a dial-up number, the user simply types in the access number as his or her user-name and password, and the service provider bills the user's phone number.

In early 2007 China was in the final stages of testing its 3G network and awarding licenses to operators. In January 2007, the country conducted its first 4G test and is already looking toward that new mobile technology standard.[24]

THE INTERNET ARRIVES

The Chinese public got its first taste of the Internet in 1995. Prior to that, it had been available only to government-approved academics and scientists. In 1994, China had approximately 10,000 Internet users, every one of them registered with and approved by the government.

In fewer than ten years, China became the world's second largest Internet market with 137 million total users,[25] and is on track to become the number one broadband market in the world sometime in 2007,[26] with at least 79 million users, and will become the biggest Internet market on the planet as soon as 2007,[27] depending on which analysis you believe. In just a few years Chinese has become one of the most important languages on the Internet, and will only continue to grow in importance and stature. As of June 2006, China enjoyed total bandwidth of 214.2 Gb per second, with bandwidth rising steadily since 2003.

Even in the short history of the Internet industry as we know it, Chinese Internet companies have made a significant impact. That impact has been felt not just on Wall Street, but in China as a battleground for foreign Internet companies, and sometimes their Chinese rivals.

From its inception, Chinese Internet companies have had the upper hand. Google has struggled behind its local competitor Baidu. In 2005, Yahoo paid US$1 billion and injected its China unit for a 40 percent stake in Alibaba.com Group.[28] In late 2006, eBay announced it would replace its own China site with a joint venture site operated by Hong Kong–based partner Tom Online.[29] We can expect more such titanic struggles and mergers in the years to come, as foreign companies continue to seek a foothold in a market that already has mature and robust competitors.

China's sustained Internet growth, both in terms of users and band-width, has meant great things for the outsourcing industry. Fluency in Internet use coupled with available Internet access from an early stage allowed companies aspiring to do work with overseas clients to move from the cumbersome model of sending floppy disks back and forth via express delivery services, to all such transfers now being conducted online, and in some cases, real time.

Follow the Money—Why the largest names in IT Services and Software are flocking to China

When a company is considering where to send their business, it is often a good idea to "follow the money." The logic being that if a lot of smart people managing large pools of money independently come to the conclusion that a certain area or region seems like a good investment, that it is likely an attractive place to do business.

As the IT services marketplace has evolved, new areas have become more attractive to investors. As mergers and acquisition advisors to IT services companies, we now see more interest around "offshore" (non-U.S. or Western Europe) IT services companies than ever before. The landscape has grown from India to include China. Large names in India have seen fit to move into the Chinese market. Infosys, TCS, and Satyam have all set up Chinese delivery centers. In the summer 2005, Microsoft acquired a 28 percent stake in Langchao International Ltd. BearingPoint and Sun Microsystems are also developing software labs in China.

The Chinese market has matured to the point where Chinese companies are now acquiring "onshore" firms. Our firm now sees serious interest from Chinese buyers looking to acquire our clients. Notable acquirers in the Chinese IT services space include Freeborders (acquired U.S.-based ITK), HiSoft (acquired Ensemble and Teksen), and CDC Corp. (acquired U.S.-based Vis.align). Beyondsoft plans to list on Nasdaq in 2007.

These transactions are all proof that investors and strategic acquirers consider the Chinese IT services market to have reached a significant valuation level and a maturity level. This flow of capital indicates that Chinese IT services companies are a serious contender in any offshore IT services market, and warrant serious consideration for any IT project underway.

Andy Johnston, Vice President, and Joel Harper, Vice President, DecisionPoint International

NOT YET A GREEN LIGHT

"High-end engineering services"—when you think about how manufacturing worked itself into the Chinese economy, it was based on cheap labor and extremely basic skill sets. As of 2003–04, the perception has gained momentum that China is ready for its next step up the value chain, in terms of producing and utilizing consultants, engineers, and technicians, more skilled roles that the economy requires, both to sustain itself and for further development.

China's accession to the World Trade Organization (WTO) in 2001 set the tone for business in China for the decade. For companies waiting for a sign that the process of doing business in China had normalized, that was it. A new wave of foreign corporations renewed their investment, and new players began to enter.

One key issue, one in which China again leads the other BRIC (Brazil, Russia, India, China) nations, that is a major factor for trade in general and outsourcing specifically is convertibility of the currency. While it may seem like a cost benefit to be earning dollars or euros and paying in reals or rubles or rupees, expatriating funds in those currencies is a difficult process. While China's renminbi (RMB) is still not entirely convertible, since 2005 it has made great strides.

Previously, the RMB was pegged to the value of the U.S. dollar at 8.3 to 1. However, China's continuing trade imbalance with the United States, coupled with the overall expansion of China's economy, led the United States to call for China to float its currency[30] and allow it to appreciate, a move which would help U.S. exports to China. China's government resisted the calls, saying it would handle its currency in its own way, but did allow the currency to be valued against a greater collection of currencies, and by early 2007 had appreciated just over six percent, eclipsing the Hong Kong dollar, which remained pegged to the U.S. dollar at 7.8 to 1, with a minimal fluctuation permitted. Chinese tourists to Hong Kong and other destinations in Southeast Asia now spend or convert RMB freely.

Since the late 1980s, China has been engaged in projects to promote technology investment and development, attracting multinational corporations to take up residence at high-tech parks in exchange for tax breaks and other incentives. Perhaps the most prominent among these programs is Torch, which as of 2005 included 53 high-tech parks and 29 national software parks throughout the country. The construction of the parks has also allowed some cities to expand in directions previously unavailable, or to move high-technology businesses closer to universities or other sources of talent.

EXPERT OPINION

China as the Technology Services HUB in the Future

I am often asked why a company should do business with China. I find that this question usually comes from people that do not have much exposure to the market conditions in China today.

China has recognized the lead India has taken in the outsourcing industry and is quickly working to not only make up the gap, but has put their collective sites on aggressively pursuing that prestigious role of leading the pack in Asia. Mr. Zhu Ziqi, director of the Zhongguancun Software Park in Beijing pointed out to me the rapidly expanding infrastructure that is being put into place throughout China. Outsourcing centers such as the Zhongguancun Software Park are rapidly expanding in strategic cities across China. Match that commitment with the tremendous availability of skilled workers at very competitive labor rates coming into the marketplace, and you can quickly see the draw of outsourcing projects to companies in China.

Driving the transition of China as a technology hub is the development of the growing economy in China as documented in *The Wall Street Journal*. The continued expansion and level of growth of the economy in China has not previously been seen or experienced in modern times. This will lead to tremendous opportunities.

Having personally reviewed and evaluated a number of companies and their processes in China, I have seen how they are dramatically focusing on internationalizing their practices and providing services at levels competitive anywhere in the world. The obstacles of the past are being broken down partly because of the incredible need for China to develop in order to address the significant issues with supporting a population far greater than most countries can imagine.

Further demonstrating the road to the future is the increasing number of international companies scurrying to get involved in the expansion and growth in China. China's growing economy and deep resource pool will be a bastion of technology and internationally competitive prices which many companies find far too attractive to ignore any longer.

Bruce Hofman, Founder and CEO, Continuous Improvement Methods

2004: What We Had All Been Waiting For

For the outsourcing business, 2004 was the turning point. Although we certainly believed in China's outsourcing potential, that year it was able to deliver the goods, in the form of more than 100,000 Chinese computer science graduates. Only that level of talent graduating every year could sustain the building of a domestic outsourcing industry in China.

That year, the Chinese government sponsored a pavilion at the Outsource World London 2004 trade show. Presentations made at the show demonstrated that China had 140,000 technology professionals. This was a major wake-up call for the global economy. The increased output is the result of the Ministry of Education's reform and efforts over the past ten years, supported by the central government's focus and commitment to the nation's technology industry. We are now seeing the results of a decade of investment by the government in the technology sector.

In 2005, China graduated more than 640,000 engineering students.[31] This number was disputed in a report[32] issued by Duke University's Pratt School of Engineering, which stated that more than 292,000 of those had received degrees from two or three-year programs, equivalent to U.S. associate's degrees. China's Ministry of Education never disputed this, and subdivided the numbers and categories in its own report. Based only on the number of bachelor's degrees in engineering issued in 2004, China still had more than 350,000 new graduates added to the workforce. That number will only continue to climb.

By contrast, U.S. universities issued 137,437 bachelor's degrees in engineering, and India, 112,000.[33] When we look at the future of the outsourcing industry, especially in terms of the supply of future talent, and with India's NASSCOM already projecting a shortfall of 500,000 talents by 2010, China becomes the clear choice.

Up until 2006, nobody would get fired for outsourcing to India. Now, we can see that this is no longer true.

China's outsourcing market is predicted to be 35.6 percent annually until 2009, and reach a value of just under US$29.5 billion that year.[34] Software exports are expected to hit US$10 billion by 2010.[35] Japan remains the number one market for China software outsourcing services at 59.2 percent, with the United States and Europe placing second with a combined 22.5 percent.[36]

INDIA OUTSOURCES TO CHINA

One of the most convincing pieces of evidence that the global outsourcing market is shifting to China is the expansion of India's top outsourcers into it in order to take advantage of lower costs and a sufficient supply of available talent.

Since 2005, these companies have come to China in force. In February 2007, Tata Consultancy Services, India's number one outsourcer, began operation of a new joint venture (JV) in Beijing's Zhongguancun Software Park (zPark).[37] Although the venture is aimed primarily at support for its multinational clients globally, Tata's China JV also picked up a contract for a Chinese government foreign currency management system.

India's number two, Infosys Technologies, entered China in 2003 in Shanghai's Pudong Software Park.[38] In 2005, the company announced it intended to grow its presence in China to 6,000 employees by 2010, with centers in Shanghai and Hangzhou and a total investment of US$65 million.[39]

Satyam Computer Services, fourth among Indian outsourcers, operates facilities in Shanghai, Dalian, Guangzhou, and in early 2007 added a new center in Nanjing.[40] This demonstrates an advantage of the China market that India has yet to replicate: geographic diversity of available resources. While almost all of India's major outsourcing facilities are in or near Bangalore, India's outsourcers themselves have chosen a number of different locations in China to operate centers. This offers outsourcers, Indian or otherwise, opportunities to locate their projects based on factors including cost and proximity to existing operations they may already have in China.

This returns to our original concept of the Essential Shore. Outsourcing to China offers not only advantages in terms of quality, cost, and available talent, but an IT services strategy here can be incorporated into a complete China strategy, given the existing or developing presence of most major corporations. India's outsourcers, who had little or no presence in China, had to come to China in order to support their multinational clients.[41] By choosing country over company when selecting an outsourcing market, China's continuing attractiveness as a global business destination makes its use as an IT outsourcing services location all the more obvious.

In July 2007, IDC research confirmed what we have known for a long time: that China would surpass India as the world's top destination for outsourcing services. Using IDC's Global Delivery Index (GDI), Chinese cities, namely Dalian, Shanghai, and Beijing, are poised to unseat their Indian rivals by 2011, "because of massive investments made in infrastructure, English language, Internet connections, and technical skills, which are favorable towards offshoring."[42]

The Future: Expanding into the Global Technology Services Industry

For the first time in its recent economic history, China is gaining wide interest from Western markets and executive decision makers for its suitability into the next value-chain segment: the technology outsourcing services industry. This is a huge economic milestone.

This formidable new economic transformation will take place, one way or another. The real question is: how fast and how successful will China, as a market, maneuver to scale up its capability and reputation as the new leading technology outsourcing services global hub?

International stakes are huge and the competition is extremely fierce. Current players are not going to let their leadership in this industry just fade away. Besides the existing competition, there are many additional challenges that China has to face before it can take the lead. The biggest of all is getting perceptions of China to change, perceptions that overseas markets, executive decision makers, and buyers have of China when it comes to services.

Western markets and mature economies consider the China market the manufacturing backyard of the global economy. But the situation is about to change by adding technology outsourcing services to its repertoire. Whether this change will be swift or slow all depends on the road ahead and key government and industry supporters' vision to listen, and shape the future with an innovative and international mindset.

Outsourcers of China, Unite!

The technology outsourcing services industry in China is facing a fundamental challenge: the lack of a solid national industry association, recognized by the government for taking the lead in coordinating and effectively supporting all promotional efforts, domestic and overseas, under a common brand name to carry out a consistent global strategy.

To date, China as a high-tech market has been relatively passive when it came to promoting its industry services and related products at overseas trade shows. There is obviously a large number of trade shows in China, and historically the modus operandi was to invite foreign buyers and investors to China. However, participation in overseas trade shows in the services sector is now critical.

China has started to attract global interest in its engineering technology outsourcing services industry. This interest is mainly due to: an increase in the worldwide demand for outsourcing services; a flat supply of Indian tech talent; and high turnover of Indian outsourcing staff.

China can seize this massive global opportunity to take the global lead in the technology outsourcing services industry. To succeed in this new chapter of its economic development, it is critical that an effective international strategy be drafted, with the support and assistance of an expert panel from the industry. Now more than ever, active participation in overseas trade shows, international conferences, symposiums, and summits has become critical.

Promote China First Overseas

To date, provinces, cities, software parks, and associations are geared toward one goal: promotion to attract foreign direct investment, more enterprises, and more commerce. These efforts are mostly deployed domestically, with an interest to increase overseas promotions. While this situation is very

---

EXPERT OPINION

China: An Essential Part of the Global Outsourcing Marketplace

When I produced my first China Outsourcing Summit in Beijing in September 2003, it was literally one of the first-ever global events on the topic to be held in the country. Our second event, held a year later, was just one of four outsourcing conferences taking place in Beijing that month, proof positive that China had almost overnight become an essential part of the global outsourcing marketplace.

And, every indication is that its rapid rise will continue if not accelerate. Why? Most importantly, because the world is heading rapidly toward a shortage of talent unimagined during the hey-day of the Western baby boomers. Those 75 million baby boomers in the United States, for example, are soon to be replaced by only about 30 million Generation X-ers. Not even the rapid absorption of talented workers from India, China, and other parts of the world are going to be able to offset the shortage of skilled workers the world faces. In fact, Korn/Ferry International predicts that by 2020, only about a dozen years from now, there will be a 14-million-person shortage in skilled workers globally. So like it or not, the new, virtual, outsourced business model with its ability to concentrate and share skills across hundreds of companies, not just one, will prevail.

And China is a growing part of that new model. In fact, for the first time in 2007, China's Neusoft cracked the top 25 on the International Association of Outsourcing Professionals' (IAOPs) list of the world's top outsourcing service providers. Established in 1991 and headquartered in Shenyang, Neusoft now has more than 10,000 employees and 40 locations worldwide.

Michael F. Corbett, Chairman, International Association of Outsourcing Professionals (IAOP) and author of *The Outsourcing Revolution*

competitive in nature, there is a fundamental flaw: most buyers are not yet sold on trusting China for high-quality technology services delivery.

Because China is still seen as the world's manufacturing backyard, to position China as the new global tech hub is the first step toward convincing overseas buyers, especially in the technology outsourcing industry play.

It is pointless to try and promote to overseas buyers the advantages and commercial value of any city in particular unless buyers are first convinced that China is the right market choice.

Action is needed to establish and structure a national organization that is recognized by all government bodies and may potentially receive subsidies from government agencies, but will be independent of those agencies. Many industry experts recognize India's NASSCOM's (National Association of Software and Service Companies) strategic importance as a key driver of what India's technology outsourcing services industry success has been to date, and rightfully so.

Government agencies and commercial enterprises must not only unite for the domestic market, but also and especially for overseas promotion. Professional and strategic guidelines must be established for this international marketing effort. Without these guidelines, the image of China may quickly become distorted or fail to take root, which could negatively influence the outsourcing services industry's reputation for all the key players.

Long-Term Government Subsidies Commitment

Long-term government subsidies for China-based companies effectively promoting overseas technology outsourcing services to China are critical for the industry's growth. Why? Because most of the other key outsourcing countries already provide competitive subsidies to their own industry's players.

It takes time to develop a brand name overseas. A China-sourcing brand name is emerging overseas, but expect at least a ten-year committed approach to subsidizing efforts to generate sizable results.

The global outsourcing industry stakes are huge. When considering the size of the outsourcing industry worldwide, BPO has a larger outsourcing industry output value compared to ITO. But when comparing the offshore components, ITO is far larger than BPO.

RISKS AND CONCERNS

Based on the evidence presented here and our own experience in China's IT industry of over a decade, we are clearly convinced of China's future as an IT and ITO superpower. That said, we know that there are, like doing business in any other market, risks and concerns, especially for new entrants to the market, and created by misperceptions and in some cases, disinformation designed to reduce confidence in the China market.

As such, we will address these concerns, as we have done not only for our clients, but as we have had to address them ourselves in this rapidly developing market.

English Language Capability

We have discussed this earlier in this chapter, but given the emphasis that it receives from potential clients and naysayers, it is worth revisiting.

China is neither a former British colony (except for Hong Kong), nor does it need English as a bridge language to cover a multitude of different ethnicities. Therefore, it cannot claim to have the innate English experience that India, or other countries such as the Philippines or Singapore have, where English is the language of instruction.

That said, English is the foreign language of choice in China. It is taught and studied more than any other foreign language, and becomes part of the curriculum in the sixth grade. Families with the means to do so start their children learning English as early as kindergarten. Students and professionals alike view English ability as a key to advancement in business and society. Opportunities in the offices of any multinational corporation or internationally focused business are simply not available to individuals who are not just competent, but fully functional in English, from the receptionist's desk to the corner office.

English capability is now required for entrance into university in China, as it is part of the stringent college examination process. And with the approach of the 2008 Olympic Games, English communication is being emphasized like never before.

Five years ago, people said that there was no ITO in China, and now it is already the world's number-two outsourcing destination and rising. Given how important English is not only to China's business landscape but also to personal success among China's white-collar workers, and especially those in BPO/ITO fields, we believe that in a similar time frame—approximately five years or fewer—this complaint will also fall by the wayside.

Intellectual Property Rights and Information Security

Chapter 9 discusses intellectual property rights (IPR) issues in depth. However, China has made great strides in the protection of IPR, and Chinese courts now regularly rule against and punish copyright violations. Certainly none of the other BRIC countries can claim superiority in terms of

IPR protection, and China's recent progress indicates its commitment to international IPR treaties and its obligations as a member of the WTO.

Protection against this kind of theft is as much a part of the due-diligence process when selecting a partner in China as any legal system. China's legal system continues to evolve, and as such, while great progress has been made, for the near-term the legal system may not provide the kind of legal protection to which Western businesspeople may be accustomed. Traditionally, resolution of disputes via the legal system is a course of last resort in China; therefore, it is absolutely crucial that outsourcing partners are chosen on the basis of their track record and proven, independently verified reliability. Writing a detailed contract is not nearly as important to establishing a business relationship as a comprehensive survey and investigation of the partner's own procedures and reputation.

As for information security, this is also discussed in Chapter 5, "Ten Lessons Learned," but again, we emphasize the need for thorough review of the partner's practices. If security—either information or physical—is seen to be lax prior to signing a contract, one cannot realistically expect that the situation will improve after a project has been confirmed. Make sure that you take your common sense with you when doing a site assessment or other due diligence; standards unacceptable in your home country or your own operation should not be overlooked in your outsourcing partner.

China is reaching international levels in terms of best practices for information security; however, companies engaging China-based firms should be prepared to apply greater management control on these projects to ensure that their own standards are upheld. The same would be true in any other emerging market.

Staff Loyalty and Turnover

In the mid-1990s, as most multinational corporations in China were moving toward localizing their middle management, it was not uncommon for top candidates to have three different employers in the same year, such was the dearth of qualified people. That image seems to have lingered in the minds of would-be foreign investors and potential outsourcing clients, although if job-hopping has taken hold of a particular market, that market would be India, not China.

It is turnover in India's ITO industry that has turned many potential outsourcing customers to what China can offer. With large foreign enterprises making significant investments in their own captive centers in India and wanting to attract top talent by offering superior wages and packages, costs have gone up and turnover in India has increased. These are key factors that are fueling that country's upcoming talent shortage. In contrast, because China is producing a larger number of available software engineers each year, as discussed earlier in this chapter, that greater supply means that the market itself is more stable, and with cost increases and turnover occurring at lower rates.

Project Management Skills

It would be almost impossible to find a Chinese manager with 20 years of IT outsourcing project management experience. There, we said it. We certainly acknowledge the early point from which a few Indian firms began developing their IT outsourcing management skills. While these skills are important, we believe that the continuing availability of talent to fuel the outsourcing industry's growth in China is even more critical. China's top outsourcing firms have already demonstrated their ability to scale and add new talent to projects. At the same time, India's own outsourcing firms continue to tap Chinese talent for their own growth. Clearly these companies are finding the talent that they need here and not in their own country. If China is India's outsourcing destination of choice, then why not choose China in the first place?

ENDNOTES

1. www.chinatoday.com/org/cpc/
2. http://news.bbc.co.uk/1/hi/world/asia-pacific/3671106.stm
3. http://english.people.com.cn/200701/10/eng20070110_339709.html
4. www.researchinchina.com/report/Aviation/3641.html
5. www.mapsofworld.com/world-top-ten/longest-rail-network.html
6. http://english.peopledaily.com.cn/200509/28/eng20050928_211282.html
7. Ibid.
8. www.usatoday.com/news/world/2006-01-29-china-roads_x.htm
9. http://english.peopledaily.com.cn/200509/28/eng20050928_211282.html
10. www.unicef.org/infobycountry/china_statistics.html
11. https://www.cia.gov/cia/publications/factbook/print/us.html
12. www.unicef.org/infobycountry/china_statistics.html
13. www.edu.cn/20010903/200991.shtml
14. english.peopledaily.com.cn/200512/08/eng20051208_226553.html
15. www.unctads.org/fdiprospects
16. www.uschina.org/info/chops/2006/fdi.html
17. www.adb.org/documents/books/ado/2005/update/prc.asp

18. www.ft.com/cms/s/046e73d0-ab75-11db-a0ed-0000779e2340.html
19. www.chinadaily.com.cn/english/doc/2005-03/21/content_426718.htm
20. www.csmonitor.com/2005/1220/p09s01-coop.html
21. www.chinadaily.com.cn/english/doc/2004-11/29/content_395728.htm
22. www.alternet.org/workplace/27829
23. www.embeddedstar.com/press/content/2005/4/embedded18249.html
24. http://news.com.com/Report+Chinas+4G+wireless+launch+leapfrogs+3G/2100-1039_3-6154100.html
25. www.cnnic.net/html/Dir/2007/01/22/4395.htm
26. www.ovum.com/go/content/c,377,66667
27. www.vnunet.com/vnunet/news/2163552/china-lead-broadband-world
28. www.iht.com/articles/2005/08/11/business/web.0811yahoo.php
29. www.cw.com.hk/computerworldhk/article/articleDetail.jsp?id=393870
30. www.ft.com/cms/s/e7da9b74-9cc3-11da-8762-0000779e2340.html
31. www.moe.gov.cn/edoas/website18/info14477.htm
32. http://memp.pratt.duke.edu/downloads/duke_outsourcing_2005.pdf
33. Ibid.
34. www.przoom.com/news/3685/
35. http://english.analysys.com.cn/3class/detail.php?id=234&name=news&&daohang=News&title=China%20Software%20Industry%20to%20Grow%2030%25%20Over%20Next%205%20Years
36. www.sourcingmag.com/content/n060519a.asp
37. www.networkworld.com/news/2007/ 021307-**tata**-begins-outsourcing-joint-venture.html?fsrc=rss-outsourcing
38. www.rediff.com/money/2003/aug/27infy.htm
39. www.infoworld.com/article/05/08/04/HNinfosyschina_1.html
40. www.infoworld.com/article/07/02/08/HNsatyamchina_1.html
41. www.itworld.com/Man/2701/061002indiachina/
42. www.infoworld.com/article/07/07/05/China-top-offshore-destination_1.html

CHAPTER 4

Strategies that Work

There are four main options when it comes to offshore outsourcing:

1. Offshore partner (third party)
   a. Fixed-price short-term engagement, often a one-off project. Advantage: fulfill a specific a need, paying only for what you get. Disadvantage: staff members may be unavailable for future projects or for follow-up.
   b. Staff augmentation, long-term focus (retainer-based, dedicated team). Advantage: build knowledge in the team, have resources at hand any time. Disadvantage: fluctuation of work load, fixed cost even if time not used.
2. Captive (establishing your own subsidiary)
3. Acquisition
4. Build-operate-transfer (BOT)

The opportunities and risks of each model are outlined in Exhibit 4.1. This exhibit is intended as a suggested primary decision matrix, but by no means pretends to be comprehensive as the grounds for decision-making will vary from one enterprise to another.

One reality to grasp is that there is no secret formula or single path to ultimate outsourcing happiness. The right outsourcing strategy may be different from one company to another, depending on the company's size, key market expansion focus, and type and volume of services required. Many multinationals demonstrate with success that a mitigation strategy mixed with different engagement and delivery models, as well as a spread over different locations, may be the right approach for them. The old adage of "not putting all one's eggs in one basket" certainly holds true in this case.

At the same time it has become obvious that China has become a bigger, sturdier basket for one's eggs. According to the Gartner motto "Country before company," wherever your strategic market is, it will benefit you and your firm to build a strong presence and partner network in that given market.

EXHIBIT 4.1 Preliminary Decision Matrix Based on Suggested Advantages and Disadvantages (i.e., Opportunities vs. Risks of Offshoring Outsourcing Strategies)

Strategy Option	Suitable for	Advantages / Opportunities	Disadvantage / Risks
Captive	▪ Organizations with market strength and available capital ▪ Strategic outsourcing market	▪ Customized model, 100% based on actual business needs ▪ Intellectual property (IP) control ▪ Knowledge management ▪ Retain training investment ▪ Cultural fit ▪ Build strong market presence	▪ High initial investment ▪ Ongoing capital expenses ▪ Requires local knowledge
Acquisition	▪ Organizations with market strength and available capital ▪ Strategic outsourcing market	▪ Faster than captive, but slower than outsourcing ▪ Tap into smoothly running operations and a fully functional team ▪ IP control ▪ Knowledge management ▪ Retain training investment ▪ Build strong market presence fast	▪ Highest initial investment ▪ Due diligence/ transparency (smoke-and-mirror techniques) ▪ Selected company may not fit business needs 100% ▪ Ongoing capital expenses ▪ Cultural fit ▪ Change management
Outsourcing Retainer-based/staff augmentation	▪ Several projects, similar scope (knowledge retention)	▪ Fastest approach ▪ Flexible staffing ▪ Pay on a monthly basis	▪ Risk of workload fluctuation— possible idle time ▪ Limited control of staff

(*continued overleaf*)

EXHIBIT 4.1 *(Continued)*

Strategy Option	Suitable for	Advantages / Opportunities	Disadvantage / Risks
	▪ Rapid implementation schedule ▪ Limited budget/cost driven ▪ Option for small and medium-sized enterprises (SMEs)	▪ Knowledge retention	▪ Limited process transparency
Outsourcing firm-fixed price (FFP)	▪ Short term ▪ Clear work scope ▪ Tight implementation schedule ▪ Limited budget/cost driven	▪ Flexible staffing ▪ Rapid establishment ▪ Clear start date, number of resources, clear total cost	▪ Higher hourly cost than retainer ▪ Limited control over staffing ▪ Limited process transparency ▪ No or little knowledge retention
Build-operate-transfer (BOT)	▪ Not enough cash on hand, but enough capital ▪ Strategic expansion market	▪ Lower initial investment than captive and acquisition (staggered investment) ▪ Benefit from partner's local market and process knowledge ▪ Process based on BOT client corporate culture ▪ Monthly or based on milestones ▪ Build market presence	▪ Implementation quality ▪ Change management during/after transfer ▪ Changes in business needs

Despite a forecasted growth rate of eight percent gross domestic product (GDP) for 2007, slightly lower than 2006's 10.5 percent, China's continued rapid economic growth over the past decade, its market size, and its potential, make China undeniably the key global strategic expansion market of choice for all major multinationals and successful small and medium-sized enterprises (SMEs). It is not really a question of if, but rather a question of when any one enterprise will be able to get into the game.

WHAT WORKS? WHAT IS THE RIGHT SHORE? WHAT IS THE RIGHT MODEL?

Although this may come across as an unexpected wake-up call, it is actually the best advice that can be given to enterprises looking at outsourcing today: "Think China" and check out things for yourself on site! A proper procurement process or some form of due diligence is indeed crucial to confirming that a partner is right for your organization. Gut feelings do not always work. Find out whether your strategy is compatible with that of a prospective vendor. Does the supplier prospect have a clear path to growth determined? Have you asked for and validated references?

China is unique in relation to other markets. Regardless, some basic principles remain the same wherever you go. While everyone is ranting and raving about attractive rates and drawing up price comparisons with other popular offshore destinations, the truth is that if you pay rock-bottom rates, you are going to get rock-bottom quality. In other words: quality comes at a price, in China as well as in other markets. But at the same time China is still less expensive than other markets!

Given the fact that experienced engineers with a high level of English proficiency are in high demand, globally, it is indeed no surprise that in the view of more multinationals moving in to set up captive centers, salaries for certain skill sets have started to soar in some major outsourcing cities. While rates may experience a natural increase, the output or supply in the China market keeps climbing. As the supply keeps climbing, the amount of available talent that enters the workforce has a positive impact on the demand coming to China. It is important to note that until now, primarily only university graduates have been making up the numbers of tech graduates. It is to be expected that the blue-collar programmers graduating will start adding to the supply of qualified tech talents in the near term.

As the government has selected technology as one of the key pillars and engines of the economy, it is a safe industry to work with and count on. China does not do things halfway.

EXHIBIT 4.2 Barriers and Success Factors for Outsourcing Transactions

Top Ten Barriers	Top Ten Success Factors
▪ Competing resources (48%)	▪ Ensuring top sponsorship (82%)
▪ Functional boundaries (44%)	▪ Treating people fairly (82%)
▪ Change skills (43%)	▪ Involving employees (75%)
▪ Middle management (38%)	▪ Giving quality communications (70%)
▪ Long IT lead times (35%)	▪ Providing sufficient training (68%)
▪ Communication (35%)	▪ Using clear performance measures
▪ Employee opposition (33%)	(65%)
▪ Human resources	▪ Building teams after change (62%)
(people/training)issues (33%)	▪ Focusing on culture/skill changes
▪ Initiative fatigue (32%)	(62%)
▪ Unrealistic timetables (31%)	▪ Rewarding success (60%)
	▪ Using internal champions (60%)

Source: IBM Survey of Global 500 (a survey of 500 top global executives, published by IBM Corporation)

Studies all point clearly to the fact that any successful outsourcing transaction relies heavily on the people aspect of what needs to get done and how. IBM's survey (see Exhibit 4.2) suggests that nine out of the top ten success factors and barriers in a successful outsourcing transaction are people-related.

From a management point of view, the following factors are extremely important for any offshoring project:

▪ Be clear about your objectives and the system requirement specifications. Up to 50 percent of your success depends on a clear description. Carefully thinking everything through before even beginning to talk to potential service providers will pay off in the long run.

▪ Use internal project champions to carry the initiative forward and secure support for the offshore team and/or smooth the path to high user acceptance for any remote developed system or software.

▪ Clear project ownership and responsibility for the overall success of the project. As for any project, unclear responsibilities poison even the best project setup.

▪ Ongoing monitoring and meaningful reporting, with necessary adjustments being made within an agreed time frame.

▪ Depending on the chosen engagement and delivery model, it will also be extremely important to provide some kind of team building for the offshore team and let the team members feel they are part of a bigger picture.

■ Actively managing onsite staff relations. Often, outsourcing triggers a lot of fears and current employees may resist the shift to offshore work in view of their fear of losing their own job. It makes sense to openly communicate about the project scope and the organization's strategy when it comes to outsourcing.

CAPTIVE VERSUS PARTNER

Going captive or finding a partner that you can trust: which is better? Security and controls are usually at the heart of this debate.

For some corporations, this is not up for discussion: captive is the only way to go. A captive center is a development center that is a proprietary operation of a corporation. Captive centers human resources typically are the direct employees of the corporation running the center. Captive centers are popular with corporate players, as many decision makers are uncomfortable with the idea of opening up their own backyard to a third party.

Corporate entities operate in a captive format back home, so why would they do anything different offshore, goes the thinking. True, but operating a development center offshore does not come without a few major hiccups and drawbacks. The complexity involved in running a center in a different market is not necessarily well adapted for a set of common corporate rules.

Then there is the expat-related added cost, during the initial stages; that is, for corporations that intend to localize their management, transitioning high-cost expats to local nationals at some stage. Besides, such management localization plans are not as straightforward or as easy as one wants to believe. Also, there may be a number of added costs involved in running a captive center offshore when one operates it like a foreign enterprise to emulate the environment back home. Even if no one likes to face that reality, it is part of the equation.

The coup de grace of it all is talent wage inflation! Captive centers established in offshore markets adversely affect the market rates, often quickly, depending on the speed and number of corporations entering a given market or region. Captive centers hire talent at a premium. As rates for talent increases in a market, captive centers keep up the premium to retain it. Inflation starts kicking in and market rates begin their unstoppable ascent. Offshore captive centers are and always will be strong-armed into providing higher rates than the market bears, given their mode of operation principles. That is also true in China.

For those that have decided to go captive, no matter what, and willingly accept the drawbacks of doing so, then build it yourself from the start and have your own key management do all the hiring. So-called build and transfer captive centers will not provide the expected results upon transfer. We cover this later in the "Build-Operate-Transfer" section.

Finding a third-party outsourcing or offshoring partner to work with, alternatively, is another choice. That path requires trust between the two companies involved or it should not be explored. Without trust there can be no outsourcing partnership. Offshoring to a third-party partner takes proper evaluation and selection. It is no more cumbersome than going captive; it is simply different.

When looking at the top ten success factors and top ten barriers in a successful outsourcing transaction (according to an IBM survey of Global 500 companies), nine out of ten factors on either side of the equation are people-related. Offshoring work is people-intensive. Under such circumstances it is obvious that executive decision makers and corporate procurement buyers all plan carefully the selection, appointment, and ongoing performance measurement process behind the value that their outsourcing partner brings to the table.

The focus then turns to what represents a successful methodology for partner selection. Among the favorites are long Microsoft Excel sheets filled with questions and sent to prospective partners being evaluated. The exact content of such requests for information (RFI) varies from one company to another, but in principle covers similar areas of interest. These areas usually cover a mix of company history, talent capabilities, client/project references, some sort of internationally recognized process maturity label (CMMI, ISO, ITIL), and financial data.

Excel questionnaires or surveys can often be misleading, but it is the most obvious approach to some sort of initial ranking of prospective vendors, yet that is the way most selection processes begin. There is nothing wrong with conducting a survey to assess a prospective list of potential partners, as long as it is not the only method used to proceed.

What is more meaningful than an Excel questionnaire is to focus on what the likelihood is that both company cultures will mix well. Do both parties understand each other and communicate on the basis of similar values and company culture? What is the management team experience with partnership and commitment track record? How rapidly can the prospective partner ramp up with the required skill sets? What is the history of the partner in putting together successful team(s) in various application types and service lines? That usually will be best accomplished via onsite visit(s) to the partner's premises. It is important to meet the key members of the management team and assess the business culture at the top level, and its similarity or divergences with the buyer's own.

If top management does not find ways to feel comfortable with the other company's executives, who says that the other levels below will?

Outsourcing or offshoring to a partner is about building an overseas extension of your own team. If you define your working relationship with your team and teammates as one of trust, then it really should be no different with your offshore partner.

Eventually, the upsides of working with a partner that you trust and that delivers expected results are very positive. You get to access a vast source of qualified talent with little to no burden to your hiring quota, no added imposition to your company pension plan, nor any other company-related liability. You also get to tap into the market's most talented resources at the most competitive rates. Rates are usually linked to agreed work volume and time commitment.

Finally, a partner has the advantage of a well-established presence in the market with extended business network benefits, to pool resources on short notice. A partner may also have a large client base in the market, which is a unique advantage to get into the China market itself.

BUILD-OPERATE-TRANSFER

Many organizations need to focus on other strategic businesses areas but are at the same time faced with the challenge of building new service offerings and/or entering a new market within a short time frame. It is hard to jump-start operations in an unknown land—especially a market as complex as China.

While a BOT scenario is not recommended for starting to do business in China, many executives look at a BOT showcase as an ideal with which to go to market. The BOT strategy is a flexible combination of application development and outsourced system launched to prepare operations. As an engagement strategy, BOT is the ideal model for companies that look for a partner with in-depth knowledge of the local conditions to hand-hold the company in the early days.

From a legal point of view, a BOT project is a concession contract in which a principal grants a concession to a concessionaire who is responsible for the construction and operation of a facility, over the period of the concession before finally transferring the fully operational facility to the principal, at no cost. Put more simply, BOT means that the client has a right to own the facility, while the third-party vendor builds the facility, hires the employees, and gets the operation running for a certain period of time, and hands over the operations to the client after an agreed period.

The BOT model has proved very successful in the infrastructure and construction industry, but when it comes to offshoring it is another story. Typically, a company builds a highway or bridge only to operate it for a period of time and later hand it over to a government agency. It is important to note that this model is based on specialists bringing in the best knowledge and skill sets for establishing a project. The model places the early stages of a project in the hands of specialists who then hand it over to someone else, like the government, once the project is running smoothly.

Increasingly, clients in the United States and Europe are demanding that the BOT model be adopted, as it is being seen as a preferred model in the BPO space. With many companies adopting this model, BOT is recently being hailed as the next big wave in outsourcing.

So what is BOT all about?

In theory, BOT projects build the foundation of long-term association between the outsourcing vendor (service providers) and client with the advantage of traditional models like the Offshore Development Center (ODC).

The BOT model gives customers the opportunity to get an ODC up and running to suit their business needs. The staged process helps the client evaluate the risks involved and helps them check feasibility before investing in a full-fledged manner. This model also gives the client the option of acquiring the operations at the end of the contract period.

BOT usually follows a three-step approach:

> **Step 1: Build.** Set up the facility and infrastructure, staff the development center, and establish knowledge transfer.
>
> **Step 2: Operate.** Manage the offshore organization: program management, development, quality assurance, maintenance, enhancements, and product support.
>
> **Step 3: Transfer.** Register a new offshore subsidiary for the customer, transfer assets, and hand over operations.

According to Gartner research, CIOs, IT leaders, and business leaders in aggressive industries should incorporate engagement models that make offshore vendors an integral part of their value chain. They must begin building relationships with offshore IT services companies that deliver value-added business process services which supplement their development, production, and delivery of final products and services.

The BOT model offers a number of variants:

- Operate (which really just boils down to traditional outsourcing models)
- Build and transfer
- Build and operate
- Build, operate, and transfer

Apart from the option of transferring or gaining ownership of the operations for the project after a period of time, the principal difference between build and operate (BO) and BOT is that the building of an operation is based on client specifications. The infrastructure is set up, the processes are followed, corporate philosophy incorporated, and resources trained and customized as per the client's needs. At the time of transfer the integration of the BOT unit into the "new" parent company is therefore usually smooth. This is also the reason why BOT is considered suitable for BPO/KPO outsourcing.

However, there are some concerns associated with the BTO delivery model. How can the buyers ensure they have the freedom and flexibility to inculcate their own culture and values into the BOT team? The recruiting is also potentially harder with this model than directly into a subsidiary. There are risks associated with future events too. In particular, will the transfer occur smoothly and on time? Will all the BOT team members transfer or will some want to stay with the vendor?

The bottom line is that the BOT model is not suited for the complex, relationship-based environment that prevails in China. An exception is always possible. But to think that you are going to be that exception is to play Russian roulette.

As with other outsourcing engagements, there are some common concerns that need to be taken into consideration:

- Quality
- Security
- Intellectual property rights (IPR) as well as legal structure issues
- Time zone difference
- Connectivity
- Transparency

Who should be looking at BOT, and what are the key advantages?
BOT may be the right model for:

- Organizations that wish to start business operations in a country where they have no existing base. Getting a partner (service provider) with an extensive local network to set up operations will reduce the risk of venturing into the new country, but it is not advisable in a relationship-heavy market like China.
- Organizations that have no prior expertise in a given process, and want to pool specialized and dedicated resources to execute that process. Partnering with a service provider who has mature processes in place allows the organization to benefit from expertise and knowledge. It is also not advisable in a relationship-heavy market like China.

Major advantages of the BOT model include:

- Rapidly build market share (i.e., address an urgent need in a short period of time and/or launch a complete end-to-end solution in a short period).
- Keep the strategic focus and concentrate on the organization's core competency while setting up a new venture.
- Access the best-in-class skill sets.
- Reduce capital expenditure.
- Cost-effective outsourcing during the initial period of build-out and operation.
- Reduce operating risk.
- Retain knowledge of related sensitive processes.

Setting up a BOT partnership? Here are some key points to consider:

- Who has the controlling stake when the project starts?
- How will the board be composed?
- Which of the partners has what kind of say on board appointments?
- What are the milestones that need to be tracked to ensure that the project progresses in line with expectations?

Before making any decisions, the buyer organization will have to conduct a feasibility of approach to set up the project on its own or work out a BOT model. If it opts for the BOT model, then it pays to short-list service providers and initiate the dialogue with them early on. Sharing the BOT parameters with the short-listed service providers enables them, and their intent is ascertained as to whether or not they would be keen to proceed with such an arrangement. It is very important to find an experienced service provider because it should have the right domain knowledge and expertise to help get the optimal return on investment.

The BOT agreement spells out the nature of the contribution that each of the participants will bring to the table, mentions the time duration for the transfer of the project, and the rights of each party. These rights are referred to as the "put" and "call" options, as in whether one of the participants in the venture will put up its shares to be taken up by another, or whether they will call for the shares of the other partner.

Typical components of a BOT delivery arrangement include:

- Application development project management, network testing, and operation functions

- IT management monitoring and surveillance, fault management, configuration management/provisioning, performance management, operations support system management, on-site support, and preventive and corrective maintenance
- Billing operations, on-the-job training, formal implementation of world-class network operations methods and procedures
- Transfer

DUAL-SHORE DELIVERY

While its name may sound impressive, the dual-shore delivery model is straightforward and is rooted in common sense: it synchronizes the objectives of the onsite and offshore teams with regular and formal knowledge transfer sessions. The main objective of this model is to leverage technology, practices, and accountability of the "parent" organization with the scalability of the Offshore Development Center (ODC) to deliver a sizable value proposition to clients. The dual-shore model mitigates the risks and uncertainties of pure offshore remote development by offering business analysis and project management control directly onsite at the client's premises. For that very reason the dual-shore delivery works best in combination with either the BOT or staff augmentation/workforce extension model.

The key advantage of the dual-shore model are the reduced IT costs due to the fact that the majority of the work is being shifted to low-cost yet highly competitive regions.

GOING CAPTIVE AND AVOIDING THE EXPAT TRAP

We like expatriates. We *are* expatriates. Heck, most of my working life has been spent abroad, first in the United States, and for more than 12 years now, China. But we also understand well that there is a temptation among people coming to do business in China to err on the side of hiring people who look like them, talk like them, and eat like them.

At least, settling expats in China is no longer an issue these days. The infrastructure is world-class, sometimes even better than North America or Europe; you find any possible product you are used to overseas, as China has everything you can imagine from the Americas, Europe, and Asia; housing is luxurious and in abundance; finding a Western school is not a problem for families; and the living environment is one of the best you can expect. China is no longer a "hardship" location.

Put simply, an expatriate is usually an executive from a company doing business in a foreign country, the man or woman "from home office," in many cases. The term often carries with it a certain amount of status, as that person enjoys benefits from the company such as a housing allowance, paid leave, more vacation, amenities like a car or driver, and often international school tuition for her or his children. They are distinguished from both local hires—foreigners who join the local office of a company without the accompanying package—and local staff, who are nationals of that particular country and are hired based on wages commensurate with local conditions.

Western businesspeople have done great things for China over the past 25 years. Without foreign investment, management, experience, and technology, it could not be where it is today. Although business agreements in China are frequently couched in the language of "friendship" and "cooperation," the fact is 99 percent of these firms and people would not be here unless they thought they would eventually make a significant profit, and frankly, neither would their Chinese joint venture partners. Whether or not companies make a buck is another question, and many do not necessarily come out ahead in the end.

For companies taking their first steps in China, or even taking their first steps in new directions such as outsourcing software development, they tend to want to put their guy in place, and there is nothing wrong with that. Having someone that you know and trust overseeing a project 13 hours by air from headquarters is probably a good idea in the early stages.

Outsourcing businesses walk a fine line in China when it comes to expats. Their primary customers are companies primarily in North America and Europe, and also Asia-Pacific nations like Japan, Korea, and Australia. Therefore, being able to communicate with these customers is mission critical. In this case, communication requires far more than just translation of words from one language to another; it is the translation of business concepts, corporate culture, customer expectations, and standards, along with language, that is required. Here, "lost in translation" often results in losing something far more important: the customer.

The expatriate, especially one who may have linguistic experience in a given market, may also have the advantage of understanding a country's corporate culture, the way projects and deals are done, the way information and people are managed, and how those affect the expectations and outcome of any project. He or she is sometimes the person speaking to head office, providing updates, relaying messages in each direction.

Despite their obvious advantages, expats have two major faults. The first and most obvious one is the cost. In the 1990s, corporations dispatched armies of expats into the China market, to open offices and build teams and markets. However, as that decade progressed, CEOs and boards of directors began to wonder where the return was on all their investment in China, and why they were spending so much money to send their employees' kids to international schools if they were not bringing home the bacon. The latter half of the 1990s saw most major corporations transition to local, middle management, and, in many cases, senior management.

Since 2001, with China's accession to World Trade Organization (WTO), we have seen a new influx of expats as companies previously too scared or barred from entering the market are lining up for a slice of the China pie. Because of its resident population of diplomats and students, Beijing always seemed to have a large number of foreign residents; however, in the past three to four years, a huge number of expats have made Shanghai their home.

The second disadvantage of expats is cultural understanding. The ability of a foreign manager to win the respect of his or her Chinese team is a challenge not to be underestimated, and not simply solved by speaking the language, although that is an enormous help. In many ways, Chinese staff members feel that their foreign managers do not understand them, and therefore are indifferent to their situation, their concerns, and factors that may affect their performance.

For example (and these are very generalized examples), the average expatriate's lunch may cost more for one week than his staff members may spend on transportation all month. He or she takes taxis to and from work; they take the bus, the subway, ride their bicycle, or walk. The expat may eat at a Western restaurant near the office; local staff probably eat in the building's cafeteria, get lunch at a cart outside, or brown-bag something that can be heated up or prepared with boiling water. If the expat is single, he or she may not understand the family concerns that face staff members, especially female staff members, who are often charged with picking up children from school or after-school activities (we realize this is certainly not limited to China). None of this includes the fact that staff members know their foreign superiors make many times what they do and resent it.

The expats themselves are also not perfect employees. Their status, both within the company and the local office, can make them difficult to work with. They, their spouses, or children get homesick or physically ill. Their vacations or home leave most likely correspond to Western, not Chinese, holidays, thereby interrupting workflow.

Most expats, or foreign professionals who consider themselves as such, have a short shelf-life in the workforce. Most of the expats float in the market on corporate assignments that range from six months to five years. On average, three to four years make the cut on such assignment duration. At the end of their assignment, some may be asked to extend their stay, but that is not necessarily a popular corporate practice these days.

As expats get to spend time in the market, there is a usual tendency for them to get stressed and overworked. For one thing, the adjustment to the new environment does not always come easily. Then the work style of the market is quite heavy and fast, giving the sweats even to workaholics. Finally, the added reporting or ongoing requests that come with the job to the regional management, the Asia-Pacific management, and the groups' global headquarters management can truly be exhausting and overwhelming.

Not withstanding that some headquarters never seem to understand what time zones mean or how they work, expats may experience a total hectic working environment with incoming calls from multiple time zones and under the flood of constant masses of e-mail pressures.

It is therefore not surprising that many married expat couples or families break under such a work-oriented lifestyle, leaving almost no time for themselves, especially after they factor in business trips, domestic and international.

In any case, what has been known to happen to expats on the ground is that they learn over time what works and what does not work with relation to making things happen in the market. The knowledge absorption does not come easily to everyone and, in fact, many must first fail in their own entrenched corporate-sponsored ideas and plans in order to realize it. Some will need to fail several times in identical occurrences in order to "get the point."

There is little use giving advice to newcomers: they do not listen, they do not believe a word of what wisdom out here seems to be simply because they have a totally different thought process at the time. Look at it as a certain mental state of corporate-induced colonialism merged with home-front education and experience divide. They arrive on the ground for two days and, one business trip later, they call themselves China experts.

All right, so it is not a surprise that many foreign professionals will tend to make plenty of mistakes until they learn. The irony of the cycle is that those expats who eventually learn the ways of doing business in the market may not always be those who are most successful in their corporate environment, depending on the conservative nature of their market of origin and of their headquarter's corporate model dominance.

These are basic strategies that can apply to any outsourcing market, but are of particular value in China. In the next chapter, we discuss how these strategies have been applied, and how we learned valuable lessons from these and other experiences.

CHAPTER 5

Ten Lessons Learned

O ne of the first questions I am invariably asked when I meet people, both Chinese and non-Chinese, is how long I have been in China. As noted earlier, I have been here since 1994. Regardless of who the person is, that answer is almost always met with some expression of surprise (although Chinese people then ask why my Mandarin isn't better).

It has been fascinating and rewarding so far; the speed of change here is so rapid that sometimes I need a neck brace—I think I have got cultural whiplash!

Although I would be the last person to be considered a China expert, more than a decade of experience does provide some insights into doing business in this country.

Here are some of the most important insights and lessons that I have learned from running my business here; they can both help you with your own pursuits in China and in selecting a partner in the China market.

1. WHAT WORKS ELSEWHERE DOES NOT NECESSARILY WORK IN CHINA

Just because a particular plan or strategy works somewhere else does not necessarily mean it is going to work in China. Most business people based outside China invariably draft their plans to expand in the China market based upon commonly accepted international assumptions, operating standards, and Western performance metrics, especially revenue-wise. These plans are made using the experience that created the overarching framework upon which a given company has based its success elsewhere.

When the first team—the "sacrificial lambs"—is sent over for market expansion, they are charged with a clear vision of what the company must be in China: It is a large market, they need to expand there, they cannot afford not to be in China, and so forth.

Those people are usually well-indoctrinated with company goals and culture, values, protocols, talent training, and high-potential local succession planning. Many of the people being sent to China, historically and even now, have little understanding of Asian culture, especially Chinese culture and the environment in which they will be operating. They have little training about cultural differences, how to respect them, and how to utilize them effectively. For some, China will be their first-ever overseas assignment, although we see less of this now than a few years ago. And there is a tendency to send people to China who look Asian, regardless of their actual ethnic heritage and cultural background. They "look" Asian, so they will fare better, right?

Upon arrival with their mandate from headquarters, they attempt to re-create a little America, or a little Europe, or a little Japan or Korea in building teams, usually adopting a quasi-colonial approach. They try to behave like they would back at headquarters, and when they encounter difficulties, blame the environment for not being up to snuff rather than their own unwillingness or inability to adapt. It is never their fault—it is the local hires, the government, excessive regulation, or whatever the perceived problem is. They are trying to meet their overseas-established goals with overseas strategies, attitude, behavior, and communication methods, and nine out of ten times those plans do not go anywhere.

Most of the expatriates being sent are usually assigned for two to four years. Only when they arrive do they begin learning about the environment, and are generally hostile to that environment, beyond perhaps a mild curiosity about the culture, language, and food. As time goes by, those who are open to different cultures will start learning about the environment and the market and its ways. Others will simply stick to their expatriate life, commuting from within a walled compound to work, then to a foreign bar or restaurant, and then back home to the compound. For them, their stay turns out to be little more than a very long business trip in China.

Those who start learning about the environment will begin communicating with headquarters in a manner that the company's executives are not expecting: that certain parts of the plan are not possible, at least not in the way imagined, or that some goals are unreasonable.

Members of the team choosing to live a more expatriate lifestyle tend to remain within the company's vision, even if that vision is unrealistic or unattainable. There is also a tendency for any person who has spent a reasonable amount of time in China to be seen, or see themselves, as a "China expert." This is a mistake I have strenuously avoided, even after more than a decade in China.

In either case, headquarters will feel that these people are burned out because they are not producing the anticipated returns, or that they have gone astray because they talk about "nonsense" to which no one can relate back in the home country. At this point, a new wave of fresh corporate tourists is dispatched, and the process repeats.

To remedy this situation, it is necessary to empower local management from the get-go, and nurture that local management by employing foreign experts merely as consultants in a training role.

It is essential that hiring decisions are not made by temporary expatriate resources only, and overseas executive management should be involved if necessary.

Those being sent to China require preparation before their departure. Their expectations must be reasonably set. By making market specialists available to those managers and executives who will go to China, and sending them to a "China boot camp," a company can to earmark its staff for success, as opposed to failure.

This "boot camp" is a crash course in how to avoid major problems and difficulties, and prepare the staff for the environment in which they will be working. It may include language training, depending on the amount of time available before departure. However, at minimum, it needs to teach basic cultural survival skills, such as the use of chopsticks and Chinese table manners. It may also include Chinese history, especially modern history, and how the past 30 years have influenced and affected the present-day business environment.

Upon emerging from the program, the executives should be far more prepared. It should dispel long-outdated notions of China that may have been gleaned from old movies or television shows. Chinese women do not wear pigtails anymore? There will be available running water? Will we have electricity? These may seem like ridiculous stereotypes that should have dissipated long ago, but we are consistently amazed at the ideas with which people arrive in China.

Strategies must be inspired by and formulated according to how business is done in China, not in the home country.

2. DEVELOP A VISION OF THE FUTURE BEYOND THE NEXT SHAREHOLDER MEETING

There is no way that anyone is going to make an investment in China if they are looking for a quick, bottom-line return within six to eight months.

Most companies coming to do business in China are completely stressed by Western business standards. That means that the pressure of shareholder expectations for growth and revenue is huge, dictated by the bottom line and performance metrics that only consider Western results as the norm, especially for publicly listed companies. Only the largest companies can afford to invest for anything beyond the short term. Results must be delivered on a quarterly basis or within a year.

It simply takes time to get things structured properly and going with the right momentum. One quarter, and in most cases, one year, is just not enough time to accomplish even the most basic goals for a new operation in China, beyond hiring a team commencing operations.

How can you follow the rules of the market, engage in relationship-building, create partnerships, and maintain a long-term focus, while constantly looking over your shoulder at the board and their three-to-six-month expectations?

Very few companies are able to have a long-term commitment to China of a 10- or even 20-year vision as part of the company's future. That is why it is extra hard for small and medium-sized enterprises (SMEs) to enter the China market. This is not as a result of executive strategy, but simply because of cash flow. It is hard to make a living in a market where nine-digit annual revenue is considered small.

Those companies that do not understand that it takes a long-term vision to be successful in China are constantly caught making short-term mistakes, such as investments, simply because those investments cannot be linked to short-term returns; not investing in relationship building because it takes time, and, similarly, that there are few or no short-term returns; and approaching business deals with a one-track mind, instead of considering longer-term benefits and not just near-term rewards.

It is necessary to cut some slack to the China operation, in Western board of director terms, to allow those teams building the business in China to have a chance to be successful, or revise their goals in a "way of doing business in China" mode rather than Western performance standards.

Most business people come to China with a single-minded approach: It is a big market; we should go there and make money. However, there is no true vision of the future with those people making decisions. Wanting to make money in China is not a vision; they do not necessarily ask themselves where the China market is going to be in five or ten years, and simply think in terms of where they want their own business to be.

Market conditions have changed from foreign companies coming over to China and putting in foreign investment, to the maturation of the domestic market and its own growth, and Chinese groups and organizations are now expanding outside the domestic market to international ones. They expand outside of China with a long-term vision of how to succeed abroad, often hiring experienced foreign executives to help them do that.

Board members with a short-term vision of how to expand in China may very well find themselves acquired by China-based competitors who trump them with their own long-term outlook for international expansion!

3. ESTABLISH THE RIGHT PARTNERSHIPS FROM THE BEGINNING

Asia, and particularly business in Asia, revolves around partnerships and relationships. China is definitely no different; in fact, in China, this maxim is true in the extreme. To conduct business in China, whether it is in the IT sector or other industry, one needs to be able to demonstrate the ability to build long-term partnerships with their team, as in building a partnership with colleagues, staff, and hiring the right people to create internal partnerships. One needs also to forge partnerships with external sources, people coming from within the supply chain, such as vendors, contractors, and customers. Perhaps even more critical is building alliances at the government level. If the building of partnerships is a weak link in the leadership within an organization, the organization will not succeed, or will be forced to overcome a high number of hurdles and dead-end business deals. Those who do not understand this essential fact of life and how business is conducted in this particular marketplace are simply left with making excuses as to why they fail to perform.

The challenge of this situation comes to a climax for those people who are naturally averse to developing partnerships and relationships. The value of the relationship only grows over time, so it does not matter how good you are, it will take time to nurture, establish, build, and grow partnerships to evolve as relationships. Most people who claim they have relationships usually do not have many. Those who have them treasure them and do not go around boasting to whomever will listen what a good relationship they have with Deputy Minister X or Deputy Mayor Y.

The challenge of partnerships and relationships is multilayered. Within an organization, relationships are built on a person-to-person basis. Loyalty is a bond that links two people on a very personal level. Loyalty is usually invested in the hiring manager or the hiring leader. This is a very important concept to remember in China. What it means is that when the hiring leader moves on, that is, changes companies or moves up the corporate ladder, then usually the people with whom they are working have a high tendency to follow their boss. In this case, the relationship becomes a bond that is an asset at the local level.

Establishing a partnership is not a cold-call type of activity. It is highly preferable to be introduced, and the closer to the person you want to meet that your intermediary is, the stronger the chances of developing a new, positive relationship—by baby steps.

At the company level, relationships with vendors and customers are very important. Relationship means trust, and is similar to a family bond or allegiance. The challenge at this level is the constant search for the establishment of relationships, and the establishment of key relationships. Most relationships with foreign professionals in the market are short lived, with the average expatriate shelf life of two to four years. It takes five to ten years and longer to grow and nurture relationships, on average. But as the famous Chinese saying goes, "A journey of 1,000 miles begins with a single step." Take that step now. You cannot build a relationship with an important partner by waiting. Take that first step as soon as possible to get your relationship on its way.

It is rough, long-term, time-consuming, painful, and it can be expensive—but not as rough, long-term, time-consuming, painful, and expensive as it would be without those relationships in place! In addition, you have to put your own personality into it. You must face the fact that you cannot possibly build relationships with whomever you want just because you want to. You are therefore more likely to get along with similar personality types, but not everyone will be like you, and not everyone will like you. That does not mean that a relationship is not possible.

Relationships are built in different ways. It involves a large amount of private time and social activity outside of normal working hours. In China, it means genuinely developing a friendship and mutual respect. The word "friend" is not used lightly in China, and if it is, it is a safe bet that the person using that term for you is not your friend.

There are many approaches to start building a relationship. Some of the most popular social activities that are used and that I have put into play include a large variety of daytime and nighttime functions, from the standard luncheon or afternoon tea or after-lunch coffee, to the morning breakfast meeting, and early evening dinner, to half-day, nine-hole golf outings, or full-day golf experiences, full-day or even overnight hikes on the Great Wall, chamber of commerce luncheon invitation, and combined sport activity—tennis, squash, jogging.

Depending on the importance of the relationship, interaction may expand outside of business hours and into social time and even weekends, covering a range of activities including drinking beer, wine, and the much-praised rice alcohol (bai jiu). Longer, formal dinners and banquets are stronger in terms of generating positive results. After-dinner activities include bowling, karaoke, concerts, and visiting a health spa or sauna facility.

Relationships generally begin with people getting to know one another, and starting to have a mutual understanding of each other's personalities and aims. As the relationship grows, the partnership gets stronger and people will start inviting each other to one another's homes, to meet their friends and families, and to share home-cooked meals. To conduct successful sales in China, one must by all means tap into an established network of relationships, or learn how to accelerate the pace of relationships in order to open up new opportunities. Sometimes it is not easy to build relationships as it may involve extracurricular activities that extend into the late hours of the night.

A relationship requires ongoing maintenance. There is a regular time during the year when it is understood that gifts may be exchanged, not of great value, but it is part of the culture to express each other's appreciation or make a gesture through a token of the other's present.

The period approaching Chinese New Year is one such time. It is the most significant holiday of the Chinese calendar. During the Mid-Autumn Festival, which usually falls in September or October, boxes of mooncakes are sent to the offices of business partners and customers.

Without getting too deep into the complexity of meal etiquette in China, there are some very basic and important rules that apply. Do not turn down an invitation to drain your glass, especially if the leader of the other side is proffering the invitation. A large majority of the meals involve plenty of drinking, and turning down invitations to drink together is bad luck and generates negative energy, and weakens the opportunity to develop a bond between two people.

Some gatherings may involve tea only. Never drink alone. Do not serve yourself, at least not first. Be eager to keep your neighbors' cups full. Do not spill from your glass when you clink glasses, or it is understood you will have to drink up for spilling. Do not put your glass down after you have clinked glasses without drinking, its bad luck. Do not just wait for others to invite you to drink. Invite others to share in a communal toast.

4. DO YOUR HOMEWORK

When choosing your partner, look for similar values in company culture, whenever that is possible. Establish a solid understanding and ease of communication with the management team. Assess the capabilities of the company on a one-to-one basis, with no assumptions. Validate all claims made by the potential partner. Look into internal documented company processes, any documented labels of international quality, such as International Organization for Standardization (ISO), Capability Maturity Model Integration (CMMI), and Information Technology Infrastructure Library (ITIL).

Ask for a copy of the company's business license. Yes, ask for a copy of the business license. You have probably never done this before, and probably have never needed to before. But this accomplishes two things: first of all, it communicates to your potential partner that you plan to cross every "t" and dot every "i." You are serious, you mean business, and you may be doing both of you a favor—some companies will not want to have a relationship with an outside partner that is going to scrutinize them so closely. It also has a more practical function. Despite their desire to engage in outsourcing services, they may not be licensed to do so. While their running into legal or regulatory problems is minimal, it should certainly give you pause that they have not taken steps to obtain the proper licenses. What else does this tell you about them? Do they not have the qualifications or relationships to be approved for those licenses? Or are they just too lazy to do it, and if so, how will that approach affect the work they may do for you?

Visit the premises. Start with an overview by looking around to get a general feel for the working environment style. What is the level of cleanliness and nature of organization in which individuals work at their desk? What is the general noise level in the area? Also, observe more closely what people are doing at their desks. Are they surfing the Internet? Playing solitaire? Trying to look busy while a visitor is there?

Dig deeper and try to see how the premises' physical security is maintained. Do they use passkeys? Swipe cards? Photos IDs? Are employees walking around with recognizable IDs around their necks or hooked on their belts? What kind of badge are you carrying as a visitor, if any? What type of access does your visitor security badge give you? Try it! See what doors it opens.

Ask to see the server or systems room. Look at the level of cleanliness on deployed equipment, as opposed to a large number of cables mixed in a distasteful bundle. Are power plugs out in the open, just waiting for someone to step on them? Are servers hooked up to an Uninterrupted Power Supply (UPS) device? Are all server screens protected with screen savers? Are password windows prompted if you touch any idle keyboard? Is the server room used as a storage room? Is it properly air-conditioned and cooled, or more like a sauna? Where are the systems' back-up tapes stored? Onsite? Offsite? Are fireproof safes in use? Onsite? Offsite? Are they locked? Are closed-circuit television security cameras in use? Are they hooked up? Where does the live feed go? Are sensitive documents left lying around? Are papers left on printers? How are documents disposed of?

Ask to speak to people within the company that you select randomly. You may also want to do this with customers whom are offered as references. Try to validate some of what you have heard about the company, if you have heard anything. Ask to see a general employee manual or other company manual.

Request references of various types of clients and projects. Asking for company financials that have been independently audited may also be prudent depending on the type of partnership that is sought.

Discuss what the basic prototype engagement process looks like. Do the people you are talking with seem knowledgeable? Do the answers seem authentic or staged? Do not be so willing to excuse slow answers just because of communication problems or linguistic differences.

Understand the executive biography or profile of the management team and try to understand the caliber of professionals being proposed for cooperation with you. What is their background; do you feel they have the right experience for your proposed project or work?

What is the average length of time that people in the company have, what is the rate of turnover? What is the average level of experience of those proposed to work with you? Obviously more is better. Ask the HR department how headcount is calculated.

What sort of quality assurance procedure is in place? How are reviews done? How is the sign-off completed? What sort of project methodology is adopted?

What is the networking infrastructure? What is the communications infrastructure available to remain in contact with overseas clients? What are the linguistic abilities of staff members? What is the average level of fluency in English (can be another language if relevant, but English is usually a good indicator)?

5. COMMIT FOR THE LONG HAUL

Establishing a brand and positioning a company in a market that is as complex and vast as China, with so many provinces and major cities, that is as culturally diverse, with so many behavioral and customary differences, is not accomplished overnight. The sheer size and scale to reach the market and target customers, companies, and consumers, is mind-blowing. Just positioning one's brand in cities like Beijing and Shanghai, which are home to about 12 to 15 million people each, is resource demanding, time consuming, investment hungry/costly, and represents a major achievement in itself.

So, it takes time to build an organization's business activities, and reach the market toward business goals, just as it takes time to build partnerships and relationships, and the first ten years will usually be more difficult until a certain momentum has been created and partnerships have matured.

There are activities that are investment heavy that are required upfront simply to pave the way for the organization to flourish, following a set of goals through different strategy levels.

Most companies have a short-term approach targeting a break even, to be reached generally within two to three years. This type of break-even approach is generally unsuited to the China market and unrealistic. However, that is the measurement Western companies use for Western-based strategies in Western markets, and therefore these benchmarks mistakenly make their way into this market.

The "long haul" in China means a minimum of ten years or more. Now, I realize, who makes a business plan these days for that length of time? It takes a lot of time to get acquainted with just how fast the marketplace moves, how entrepreneurial the people are, and how much talent really is here. It also takes time to groom a stable and productive team.

Market conditions are continuously evolving. New regulations come into effect, superseding older ones, offering both opportunities and challenges on an ongoing basis. It takes time to train your teams or your partners to the point where you feel each is an extension of the other.

6. PREPARE YOURSELF FOR AN UNPRECEDENTED SPEED OF CHANGE

Via the centralized planning that is utilized in China today, plans that are promulgated from the central government and implemented by provincial and local governments, perhaps no other nation has the ability to initiate and complete the massive projects that we see undertaken here. Since the establishment of the People's Republic in 1949, five-year plans have been, and continue to be, the norm. At minimum, your own plans need to be made along these lines because this is the benchmark upon which your partners will be operating.

Numerous cities have had their entire landscape drastically changed just in the past five years, with new districts and "new towns" being added to expanded and incorporated environs.

During the 1990s, China witnessed an unprecedented construction of IT and telecommunications infrastructure. In just a decade, China went from the average citizen not having their own home telephone, to the largest mobile telecom market in the world and the world's second largest Internet user base. In 1995, the Internet first dribbled into China via slow dial-up connections. Now, broadband is widely available and easily installed in first- and even second-tier cities. A visitor landing at Beijing's Capital International Airport can buy a SIM card for a GSM phone before even going through customs. Without even being admitted to the country, you already have basic connectivity!

Business districts and commercial premises have been well laid out and grouped to foster economic progress and development. Public transportation has increased massively. In brief, what has occurred in China over the past almost 30 years is the subject of a book in itself—and has already been documented by many fine writers, with more to come, I'm sure.

Perhaps most important, there is a commitment from Chinese leadership, at the highest and provincial and local levels to continued economic development, to support the infrastructure and conditions necessary to promote the market as it keeps growing.

7. CHOOSE AN OUTSOURCING CITY BASED ON. . .

Choosing a city in which you want to establish your team or in which you want to assess a partner is of critical importance. Key measurement elements involve the type of infrastructure available in that city or province. What sort of Internet connectivity is available there? What major Internet service providers operate there? What are the general infrastructure readiness, quality, and availability?

What is the cost of office space, net or gross? What is the mobile network access from inside buildings or in different locations throughout the city? What is the traffic situation there? How far is the airport from the city? How often do trains to other major cities run? What about flights to other cities? Are there international flights available? From your company's headquarters, how many plane changes or stops would be necessary to reach this city?

Government-sponsored commercial incentives—tax breaks, special software or technology development areas, tax refunds, available subsidies, access to government tenders, employee-related mandatory benefits (personal insurance, social security insurance, health insurance, housing fund), Labor Bureau-specific rules. Government accessibility—what sort of support are key government officials willing to offer? Is meeting with key government officials simple, impossible, tedious, difficult?

What is the efficiency of the cost of the building site? Is there any advantage to locating in high-tech zone or software park? The primary advantage of a high-tech or software park in China is that they will provide commercial benefits—usually tax breaks. Conceptually, it is part of a planned expansion of the city hosting the park, and therefore is usually well-linked to other parts of the city by public transportation and with ample housing in the vicinity for easy commutes for the workers. Working close to home is an important criterion in job selection for Chinese employees, some of whom still return home each day for lunch.

There is a concern over locating in high-tech parks with the close proximity of numerous technology companies, because employees are more likely to jump from one company to another. This is sometimes countered by the high-tech parks' own worker database, which registers employees and creates an employment record for them to prevent this kind of job-hopping. Ask if the software park you are considering has this type of plan or monitoring in place.

What is the framework for universities and other leading institutions that are graduating tech talent in that city or area? The nation's university graduates, in terms of quality and quantity, typically come mostly from Beijing and Shanghai, having the most universities and therefore the most graduates and having the largest talent pool, followed by Xi'an, with Chengdu fairly close after that. Also, what is the availability of people in the surrounding areas to those cities? For example, Dalian rests at the southern end of Liaoning province, and the rest of China's northeast. The ability for people to converge there is somewhat better than other areas in that part of the country. This is obviously a major part of the selection criteria.

What are local salaries in that city like? What is the average cost for an engineer with two years of experience?

From a language ability perspective, first-tier cities may have a greater percentage of the talent that can converse fluently or effectively in English, as those cities have a longer history of international interaction. Other areas may be preferable due to proximity to target language groups. For example, Shandong province has investment from numerous Korean businesses, and therefore the infrastructure for interacting with that market is generally better than in other parts of the country.

In a second-tier city, salaries will be lower and there may be greater access to high-ranking government officials. But the downside is that language-wise, there is a tendency that the professional workforce will be less fluent in a second language, such as English or Japanese, and that lower salaries prevailing in those areas may draw better talent out of those areas and toward first-tier cities and metropolitan areas in search of better compensation.

8. PEOPLE, PEOPLE, PEOPLE

Pieces of the human factor have been covered among these lessons and throughout this book. However, some important concepts I have learned along the way are important to share with anyone wanting to be involved in software outsourcing in China.

My 13 years in China have taught me that Chinese workers are brilliant and talented. They are quick to learn, open to new ideas and methods, and inclined to embrace new technologies and modern ideas. They are eager for personal development and very conscious of their future and developing career opportunities. Chinese culture harbors the notion of challenging oneself in order to promote growth, and the people with whom I have had a chance to work have demonstrated this almost to a man—or in many cases, a woman.

To perform under the right leadership but in a relationship-based market environment, vision and direction becomes all that more important in order to drive the workforce. Because the workforce comes from such disparate and diverse backgrounds, with different levels and types of experience and education, it is crucial to emphasize training, corporate culture, behavioral expectations, and norms, so as to create a baseline for what is acceptable, what is the proper way of handling situations, and establish some guidelines that people can refer to in creating an overall workforce momentum that leads ultimately to a general set of values by which everyone conducts business.

Training is also a highly regarded, indirect value that employees will be seeking within a company structure. Should employees feel they have exhausted the training and progress options within their company, they will start looking elsewhere for personal and career advancement opportunities.

It is important to provide a strong framework for what is expected of the workforce and coach them in what is an acceptable work style to reach the proper level of efficiency and productivity. Offering too many choices within the workplace may not lead to the desired results. A rigid work environment tends to lead to better results in relation to the structure of the market. At this point, the market has not matured to where practices such as flexible working hours and telecommuting will lead to better results.

A lot of education and guidance is required in the process. It is important to continue coaching employees in best practices, as to why a particular process or code of practice is correct and produces the most desirable results.

Also, in developing international cities, for example, Beijing and Shanghai, over the course of their career some employees will end up working for managers from numerous cultures and nationalities. Therefore, what may be asked of them in one workplace may be completely different from the desired behavior that their current employer wants from them. Consistent and regular guidance will assist these employees in finding their way—and produce for you what you want from them.

It is also important to emphasize to employees that remaining with a single employer and producing good work there is in itself a career benefit, something upon which other employers will look favorably. Stability and loyalty are not necessarily the order of the day in a market that is still developing, a market growing at an exceptional rate, in which there is a continuous and strong demand for quality tech talent. However, as the market matures and the internationalization of business in China provides for the acceptance of international best practices, demonstration of that kind of stability and loyalty will become a significant career asset.

Team building is very important for employees to break the ice and get to know each other better. Because interpersonal relationships in China are more formal than those in other countries, particularly North American and European countries, it is important for the employer to break down the barriers that may exist among employees in order to foster better cooperation. I have seen many workers, sitting at adjacent desks or cubicles, in their early days at jobs, communicate with their neighbors only by e-mail rather than simply turning to that person and asking questions. This is something that can be avoided through regular team-building activities and interaction led by management.

As an example, at my company, I.T. UNITED, we have one annual general team outing, designed as a team-building activity. This is complemented by department-specific team activities throughout the year, based on the desire and need determined by department heads. Before the annual Spring Festival, we have a staff dinner for the entire company. We also hold quarterly employee forums. In addition, our human resources (HR) department recognizes employees through awards and other positive citations. This is an ongoing process; it should not be seen as having one or two activities per year is enough. Although we emphasize one or two particular events that occur each year, more regular events foster better communication, better cooperation, and ultimately, better results.

The downside of the HR equation is that there will always be people who will look for loopholes to take advantage and abuse a situation. This, of course, is not exclusive to China. However, it requires vigilance to ensure that bad practices do not begin, and that if they do, they are addressed quickly and completely.

9. NEVER GIVE UP

No matter how difficult things may seem—at least to the newcomer—China is one amazing market from the standpoint that you can actually get things done more easily and more quickly than anywhere else in the world, if you can just find the right angle. It is about finding the right way of thinking and approach, how to tackle an issue, project, problem, goal, or deadline.

The funny thing about it is, the more Western you think, the less likely you will be able to grasp how to reach your goal. You have to tackle the situational challenges with a different approach. When you hit a wall, do not just fall flat on your back. See if there is a way to go under, around, over, or through it. There is a multitude of ways to go about things here. That variety of ways to handle problems makes the market extremely exciting and highly entrepreneurial. However, if you are not a highly entrepreneurial person, and you are coming from a highly rigid and conservative environment, this type of flexible thinking may be difficult, certainly at first. Making things happen and making the transition to the China way of doing business may therefore present some steep challenges, or at least a very steep learning curve.

Face it: with market reforms and the transition to a market economy, people in China want to make money, and that is an important, if not the primary, motivation for your potential partners. Although this will not apply to government officials, they still have interests, including acquiring new business for their particular area and attracting new investment. Working with foreign companies is now standard practice throughout China, so approaching governments and Chinese corporations is at least as competitive as anywhere else in the world, perhaps more. For that reason, keep your partners' interests in mind when negotiating—it may help you that much more to achieve your own.

10. IT IS ALL ABOUT FACE

The manner of expression in Western society tends to make a point from a factual perspective, stating bluntly the way things are, cause and effect. The mode of expression in China is more indirect, and does not always state the obvious, but looks for a more clever way to use an indirect approach to suggest or imply something. Care is usually taken not to implicate people involved in a particular project or task to make them lose face.

Giving face is one of the essential pillars upon which the culture, society, government, and economy rest. In some cases, it is a hindrance because it is hard to improve things if when you are trying to find lessons learned, someone automatically will feel a loss of face. If whatever it was was not done well in the first place, how do you go about improving a working environment where people are not necessarily willing to consider ongoing improvement as a necessary and daily task?

I have this difficulty with one member of my staff, a manager who has been with me for ten years. If he were not a valuable part of my team, and if we did not have a good working relationship, then certainly he would not have lasted so long nor progressed so far in his position and within the company. However, each time I discuss the idea of "improvement" with him, he takes it personally, and believes that I am accusing him of not doing his job.

It requires one to think ahead and be sensitive not to generate conflict, where you inadvertently cause the parties involved to lose face, or create a situation whereby something that was said or done disappointed someone present directly or indirectly. This may include a violation of cultural or business protocol, or failure to adhere to it in a way that gave sufficient exposure to the parties involved. It is very easy to make an entirely innocent remark at a meeting, meal, or other interaction that has far more serious repercussions than could be imagined.

In the mid-1990s, I met some local colleagues in Singapore. I was fresh off the plane from Europe into my new assignment. It could not have gone worse. When I gave my business card to them, I did not present it in the polite, Chinese form: to offer a card with two hands. Similarly, when they offered me their card, I did not receive it with two hands as a demonstration of respect. This tainted my entire relationship with them during my remaining time in the company. Of course, I had no idea that this was the custom, not having had any training prior to my arrival. Still, in this case, even an innocent mistake had significant consequences, and my relationship with them just never got off the ground.

While negotiating a project implementation with a government agency, the country manager of the company I worked for was invited by the head of a Chinese government bureau to toast with a tiny glass of rice wine during an official banquet. Our country head had some reason why he declined to return the toast. That was it. That was all it took. The deal was over. Insulted, the agency chief refused to deal with our country head any further.

Following protocol in China—in any country, really—demonstrates respect and at least a basic understanding of the culture and its customs. Not drinking a small glass of rice wine does not seem like a capital offense. But what it says is, "I do not care about the way things are done here." It sends a message from the outset that you are going to be a problem. And someone who is willing to offend the head of a company, department, government agency or bureau, or country over a small glass of rice wine—or a two-handed business card presentation or any other seemingly miniscule point of social minutiae—is not someone who's going to make a good business partner.

CHAPTER 6

Winning the Talent War

T he sheer size of China's population makes the country the world's biggest talent pool. In 2005, the working-age population was estimated at 918 million or 70 percent. By 2013 that number is expected to climb to 72.14 percent of the country's total and peak at 997 million.[1]

The phrase "War for Talent," coined in the late 1990s by Ed Michael, then Director of McKinsey, has never been truer than in China. While the rapid growth of China's economy is a blessing for most companies, it is also a headache for management faced with the challenge of attracting, developing, and retaining top talent. Lured by abundant job opportunities in the booming market, talented employees are always ready to consider a better offer and move on. One feature of China's job market is that it has plenty of talented professionals to offer. Another feature is that demand for talent exceeds supply. The rapid growth of the Chinese economy has resulted in a booming demand for people in professional and managerial jobs. McKinsey estimates that China will need to produce about 75,000 globally capable executives over the next five years[2] to satisfy demand for talent required by both China's corporations and multinationals.

In the IT market, the number of graduates has been rapidly increasing over the past years. However, the numbers vary greatly and the reliability of the statistics has been questioned at various occasions as the way data is collected is pretty much left to every district.

In 2006, the total annual output of university graduates in computer sciences and related degrees reached 290,000, with 350,000 predicted for 2007.

In May 2006, Vivek Wadha, Executive in Residence/Adjunct Professor with the Pratt School of Engineering, Duke University, testified before the U.S. House of Representatives Committee on Education and the Workforce. This was widely covered in the U.S. media because of the debate about U.S. engineering competitiveness in comparison to both China and India. Wadha raised a central question: if a certain type of engineering job can be done more cost effectively in India or China, why should the United States invest in graduating more of those types of engineers?

Based on a 2005 study, McKinsey argues that although China boasts hundreds of thousands of university graduates, the country is facing a talent shortage that will hamper China on its way to becoming a giant in offshore IT and business process services.[3] According to McKinsey, there are two issues: (1) few of China's graduates are capable of working successfully in the services export sector, and (2) the fast-growing domestic economy absorbs most of those who could.

Far from predicting a thriving offshore services sector, McKinsey's research points to a looming shortage of homegrown talent, with serious implications for the multinationals now in China and for the growing number of Chinese companies with global ambitions.

China has also been challenged on the quality of its engineers. One of the regular refrains is a "factory approach" to producing resources for the high-tech industry. It needs to be taken into account that in the past five to eight years the capacity of the universities has been expanded dramatically. While in 1993 the total number of graduates was 1.7 million, in 2006 it reached 4 million, as Vice Premier Wu Yi said in a speech at a forum in southwestern Xiamen in September of that year. Wu continued, adding that China's huge pool of talent fit well with high-end industry outsourcing. China announced its plan to restructure its low-end manufacturing economy by investing in services, outsourcing, high-end manufacturing, and research and development services.[4]

In only a generation, since 1978, China has roughly 20 percent of its college-age population in higher education, up from 1.4 percent. In engineering alone, it is producing 442,000 undergraduates per year, along with 48,000 graduates with master's degrees and 8,000 doctorates.[5] The higher education expansion launched in China since 1998 has ushered in mega-universities enrolling 20,000 to 30,000 students. Large public teaching universities have been merged to form American-style comprehensive universities, with the intention of creating world-class institutions focusing both on research and teaching.[6]

And if "an unlimited supply of workers with similar skills is available at the end of a broadband wire for a tenth of the salary," as Nayan Chanda, Director of Publications at the Yale Center for the Study of Globalization[7] so nicely puts it, the textbook economics are very clear on the right thing to do. That's where China's power as the world's biggest talent resource comes fully into play.

The majority of resources for the outsourcing industry come from universities, coming with degrees as different as computer sciences, engineering, telecommunications, English, or any business degrees including marketing and business studies. The 2,273 universities that were operating in 2005, included 481 adult universities catering exclusively to students who already have a first university degree. Seven hundred of the universities were entitled to award bachelor's, master's, or Ph.D. degrees. The total number of students enrolled on campuses was 23 million, including the 5 million new students who entered university that year.[8]

China's educational system has four different kinds of institutions for higher education:

1. Core universities such as Tsinghua University, Peking University, Shanghai Jiao Tong University, Fudan University, Nanjing University, or Zhejiang University. These universities attract the country's top talent[9] and are part of the famous "Project 211," comprised of 106 universities and colleges in the twenty-first century conducted by the Chinese government and aims at cultivating high-level talent for national economic and social development strategies.[10] Core universities receive full government support and the competition at the entry level is extremely tough.
2. All universities other than the core universities, including adult universities.
3. Colleges that offer only associates' degrees, usually three-year programs.
4. Vocational universities, like technical institutes or vocational schools in the United States, with two- and three-year programs.

Reflecting China's development needs, the areas of focus for higher education are science and technology. The government is ready and willing to spend billions of dollars to transform its top universities into the world's best within a decade, wooing big-name scholars to China to build first-class research laboratories. The model employed is simple: recruit top foreign-trained Chinese and overseas-born ethnic Chinese to well-equipped labs, surround them with the brightest students, and give them tremendous leeway. Officials at Peking University estimate that as much as 40 percent of its faculty was trained overseas, most often in the United States. While it will not make a difference in the short term, China will be able to leverage this approach in the longer term. Because of central government control, when China moves, it moves on scale that no one else can match.

Although the vast majority of universities in China are public, for the past 15 years there has been an increase in the number of privately funded universities emerging. In Xi'an, for example, there are about 80 government-funded and 80 privately funded universities. Many of the private universities that were founded in the early 1990s started out with a few dozen students, only expecting to ultimately enroll a few hundred students per year. The influx of students, however, quickly turned these institutions into campuses with several thousand students.[11]

In a short time, private universities have rushed to obtain more land and build more buildings, while doubling and tripling enrollments. Within a few years more than a dozen of them have joined the ranks of mega-universities with 20,000 students or more.

At university, the focus of most engineering courses is on so-called hard training, the technical skills. Students study and learn the fundamentals such as mathematics, database structure, programming theory, and popular technologies such as Java, C/C++, or PowerBuilder. The technical ability of many graduates is excellent. However, while an English level of CET 4—a Chinese basic certificate in English based upon passing a standardized test—is required to qualify for degrees in many courses, soft training such as professional business behavior, communication skills, project management, or intercultural competence are recognized neither by the educational system nor employees, at this point. Merrill Lynch concludes in its 2005 report about the state of China's outsourcing industry that it is only a matter of time until the required improvements regarding project management and English will be remedied through better education. Meanwhile, training provides outsourcing companies with an opportunity to differentiate themselves from their competitors.

So, what is the actual situation? How do Chinese companies view the situation? For Chinese companies—much as for any of their competitors in other markets—the key to success is attracting and retaining talent. The following sections outline the key challenges for China-based outsourcing providers from an HR point of view, starting with recruitment, then managing and retaining talented employees.

ENGLISH MAKES THE WORLD GO ROUND

English is the global language of business. English proficiency makes the business world go round—and that is equally true of the outsourcing world. Hardly surprising, English proficiency in China is exploding. The Chinese school system has been placing increasing emphasis on learning English and the 2008 Olympics to be held in Beijing has further fueled this trend. Since the 1990s, English has been mandatory starting in the third year of primary school, but many children start earlier. A number of Chinese kindergartens have started teaching English, showing that demand is high for English-language training from an early age. In Shanghai, for example, about a fifth of kindergartens provide English-language lessons.[12]

At the same time, the quality of English education is often criticized and some worry that the English focus is detracting from studies in Chinese. Nevertheless, China pursues its objective of making every citizen literate in English by the 2008 Olympics with ambition and single-mindedness, although this effort is likely to fall far short. By contrast, as late as 2005, the government of the Indian state Karnataka still held on to its 15-year-old ban on English in primary schools despite huge popular pressure.[13] It would seem that a state whose capital is Bangalore—the symbol of India's success in the global economy—and which derives its competitive advantage from its mastery of the English language should be more progressive in embracing English as a way of enhancing its competitiveness. Meanwhile, Bengal and Gujarat, realizing their mistake, immediately went back to teaching English after discovering they had created an unemployable generation. Although in both India and China there are voices who fear that English proficiency will lead to the loss of proficiency in their mother tongue, the difference between China's certainty and India's ambivalence is instructive. It seems that China is willing to pay the price to modernize the country and join the world.

The Chinese are enthusiastic about learning English, and publications about English learning and books in English are becoming ever more popular to read. China has established a complete system for English teaching that covers the path from primary school to college and this system has improved a lot over the past two decades.[14]

In addition, in 2001 the Chinese government also started implementing a nine-year voluntary education program, which uses a standard English course to replace the former teaching outline. The new standard adopts the international system according to which English language education is divided into nine levels. This has changed the old style of teaching, which attached primary importance to grammar and vocabulary. Adopting the new standard helps to develop the students' ability to use English in their daily life, arousing their interest and encouraging their participation with the help of their own experience. The new method places a lot less emphasis on reading and writing in favor listening and speaking skills. The pupils start learning English from grade 3 in primary schools. After grade 6, they should reach level 2, and after grade 9, level 5. Students graduating from high school should have reached level 8, while those from foreign-language high schools or schools with foreign-language specialties are expected to have reached level 9.

For young professionals, English has become an integral part of boosting their career prospects and enabling Chinese talent to work for foreign companies.

College entrance exams require testing in Chinese, mathematics, English, plus another subject as relevant to the college.[15] Far from being reluctant to comply, Chinese students are embracing English learning as a ticket to a better future.

RECRUITING STAFF

Finding the Needle in the Haystack

As part of an industry that was born out of the need to cut costs, outsourcing providers face several issues. As a result of being cost driven as much as personnel driven, the outsourcing industry is viewed by top talent as a low-level opportunity. This image is also linked to the fact that at this stage most services provided by China-based outsourcing companies remain focused on small-scale Application Deployment Management (ADM) projects and other work, localization, and testing.[16] As the industry matures (and all the signs are pointing to the rapid ascension of China as the new global IT hub), it will move to providing increasingly value-added services such as consulting or complex systems, and this issue will most likely take a back seat.

When recruiting raw talent, outsourcing providers not only face competition from other subindustries in the high-tech sector such as software producers or dot-com companies, but also from world-class IT companies such as IBM, Microsoft, or many others building a presence in the China market. Because the dream of most IT personnel is to work for such a world-famous company, they usually view working for a China-based outsourcing company as a stepping stone to the clients they serve.

In order to keep a hand in the game, professional HR processes with a clear talent identification system and carefully maintained candidate databases are just the starting point. Successful employers use detailed candidate profiles based on their specific corporate culture and competency model, which helps them identify the kind of people that fit with their work environment.

Like most companies operating in China, outsourcing providers use a mix of strategies to narrow the talent gap:[17]

- Recruiting Chinese candidates who have studied abroad and thus increased not only their language proficiency, but also their intercultural competence. These resources are much sought after for positions that interface directly with the client, and therefore require a high level of English skills. There are a growing number of students from China who go that way. In 2005 alone, more than 62,500 students from China studied in the United States, which makes China the second-largest source country for such students.[18]
- Expanding expatriate programs for experienced professionals (a relatively expensive option that will not be sufficient in the long term).

- Recruiting talent from Chinese elite universities such as Peking University or Tsinghua University (the latter being the first to launch an MBA program in 1991).
- Targeting experienced people from global Fortune 500 companies with Chinese subsidiaries.
- Building advanced online recruiting tools into their corporate Web site.

Popular Recruiting Channels

The most popular recruiting channels for finding talent resources are:

- **Online recruiting Web sites.** The top three online job portals—www. zhaopin.com, www.51job.com, and www.ChinaHR.com—control nearly 70 percent of the online job market with 51job.com leading the pack with a 39 percent market share, followed by ChinaHR.com at 15 percent and Zhaopin.com with roughly 14 percent.[19] Those portals are the starting point for staff on the lookout for a new career opportunity. There are also an increasing number of online platforms for career planning and development.
- **Headhunting agencies.** Increasingly popular in a fast-growing industry, headhunting agencies are sprouting all over the place. Apart from established global players such as Heidrick & Struggles, Hewitt, Mercer, or Korn Ferry, there are a number of local, specialized boutique firms that cater to the tech industry such as Dice, Topjobway, or Chance.
- **Campus recruiting.** Campus recruiting is becoming more and more competitive.[20] When recruiting students, instead of paying for online recruiting ads with the big three, many companies have turned to free job postings on university online bulletin boards (BBS). This is actually where the majority of students will start looking for their jobs.[21] Meanwhile, for IT talent there are more and more training organizations that run technical training programs, which can also be great resources for industry talent.[22]

Despite the challenges China's outsourcing industry is facing, The Outsourcing Institute highlights that overall China is in a reverse brain-drain situation and can rely on its fast-growing IT talent pool.[23] The current workforce of about two million software developers in China has been growing at 22 percent annually. In addition there are currently 5.86 million engineering graduates, a number which is also growing at an impressive 13 percent annually.

Moreover, many China-born, U.S.-educated businesspeople and IT executives are returning to China, bringing back with them Western business approaches. These so-called "sea turtles" or "hai-gui" are tech- and business-savvy entrepreneurs who use the knowledge and experiences gleaned from the best universities and companies in America to reap the rewards in their homeland. One of the best-known sea turtles is Dr. Charles Zhang, founder of Chinese Internet portal Sohu.com (market cap: $540 million). Zhang, a 1994 physics graduate from the Massachusetts Institute of Technology, got in on the ground floor of the Internet market in China. Starting off in 1996 as a copycat of Yahoo, he financed his company with personal savings and a loan of US$225,000. Peggy Yu came back to China in 1998 after 11 years in the United States to start DangDang.com, and now heads up one of the most successful online bookstores in China.

For outsourcing providers the first challenge lies in finding the right resources and determining what skill level is required for the position at hand. Generally speaking, providers with a clear value proposition and a narrow strategic focus on certain services or technologies will have an easier job than providers who choose to grow with their clients, and are flexible in ramping up new skill-sets for a new project. The factors influencing how easy or hard it is to find the right resource are:

- **Technical skill-set.** The following skill-sets are popular in the in the IT outsourcing industry, which makes them a focus of university education and therefore relatively easy to recruit: Java, .Net, PHP, C/C++, or C#.
- **Experience.** As in other outsourcing destinations, engineers with three or more years of experience are scarce. Like their counterparts in India, China-based providers' biggest challenge is finding staff with three to seven years' experience for program manager, senior architect, or team manager roles.[24]
- **English skills.** While most universities require an English level CET 4 for graduates to complete their degree (meaning they can read or write), it is considerably more difficult to find resources who have a good level of conversational English and are able to easily communicate with overseas clients.

Two kinds of resources are harder to find: engineers who combine a high level of English proficiency with solid technical experience, and engineers who have built knowledge of specific technologies such as those that are not widely used in the market.

Top Qualities Employers Look For   What are the characteristics that professional outsourcing companies look for in their employees? The proper level of technical skill-set is crucial in controlling costs and preventing rapid turnover. Overqualified candidates cost more and will leave sooner than their teammates if the project is not challenging enough.

For obvious reasons, language capability is much sought after. Key languages are English, Japanese, and Korean. Given the cultural and geographical closeness, the latter two are hardly surprising. Japan is already China's biggest business process outsourcing (BPO) offshore market and cities such as Dalian and Tianjin are the primary destinations for that work. Language skills are important for quality and efficiency. However, many outsourcing providers are moving to a team setup where only the account manager or project manager requires conversational English, whereas the rest of the team is managed in Chinese and thus only needs average writing and reading skills to understand English training materials.

Candidates with a proven ability to learn fast and good interpersonal skills are certainly more valuable. As turnover increases, so does the interest of employers in candidates with a stable working record whose resumes show or promise a steady career development. Candidates who demonstrate integrity, respect for standards, and an awareness of information security issues are much in demand. Finally, the candidate should be a good cultural match for the company.

For companies it is important to understand the top five reasons that cause low staff retention:

1. Salaries that do not reflect their true contribution
2. Lack of training and more developing opportunities
3. Lack of respect from others
4. Company's long-term goal and strategy is unclear
5. Lack of company culture

SALARIES ON THE RISE

All things said and done: outsourcing is about reducing costs and saving money. While a number of factors affect the cost-saving potential of any given location, the cost of labor is among the most important. A recent neoIT report concluded that the one factor that has the most bearing on IT outsourcing/business process outsourcing (ITO/BPO) salaries is the supply and demand for people who possess the required skill-set.[25]

According to a survey conducted by Mercer Human Resources Consulting, salaries in China surged in 2006 and are expected to increase further this year.[26] While wages rose an average 7.94 percent year-on-year in 2006, Mercer estimated salaries would continue to increase by 7.7 percent in 2007. The IT industry in particular saw a higher than average increase of 8.3 percent in 2006—hardly surprising, given the increasing number of resources absorbed into the rapidly growing outsourcing industry and the fact that an ever-growing number of players are competing for English-speaking engineers with project management experience. For the high-tech industry, salaries increased in Shanghai, Guangzhou, and Beijing 7.3, 6.9, and 6.5 percent, respectively. The survey also showed that salaries of mid-level managerial staff climbed 8.5 percent, much higher than the average of all employees interviewed. Pay for middle management increased 8.7, 8.6, and 8.4 percent in Shanghai, Guangzhou, and Beijing, respectively, last year. The survey concluded that despite higher pay, middle managers prefer to job-hop, indicating that they are the most sought-after employees in the job market. This goes hand in hand with the growing number of headhunting firms who actively seek out talent and lure them away.

China retains several advantages over its neighbors and competitors, including low overall salaries, even distribution of talent over major cities, and far lower annual salary increases than most other countries in the region.

According to the Mercer study, salary and remuneration packages have become a key factor for employees. However, a decent salary and attractive remuneration package were considered as basic measures. "Employers realize they should adopt a new talent introduction and retaining mechanism," said Brenda Wilson, managing director of Mercer China, in a January 2007 interview. She said this would involve recognizing outstanding employees by widening the salary gap, formulating a quick-response pay adjusting system, and providing good conditions such as flexible working hours.[28]

CHINESE WORK ETHICS

Industrious, Smart, and Hard-Working: Yes, It Is True!

The vast majority of Chinese engineers are very smart and hard-working.[29] They are intent on building a successful career for themselves. At the same time they tend to be emotional in the sense that the feel of the company, for example, the company culture, is very important to them. Chinese professionals are also quite sensitive to management skills and will respond to encouragement rather than penalization. This is an area where the outsourcing industry sometimes has to fight against its image of using people just as a means to an end. However, if Chinese staff feel that their work is interesting, valuable, and good for their career development, they are very loyal workers and willing to do whatever it takes. Companies that recognize their staff's achievements, have a good performance evaluation system including regular performance reviews, and offer their employees the career they are looking for can expect their employees to stay loyal for at least two to three years.

Child Emperors Holding Court at Work?

The new Chinese urban generation in major cities is undeniably more dynamic and exhibits much greater interpersonal skills than their parents. At the same time, as a result of the one-child policy, some young Chinese tend to be spoiled, having been doted upon by four grandparents and two parents whose attention is focused on their offspring's every move and giving them everything they may not have had. These so-called "child emperors" remind some of the post-war generation in the United States and Europe. For China, however, this is a relatively new phenomenon and may impact on staff's work ethics in the medium to long term.

I Have a Sore Throat, I Need to Go to the Hospital...

To the Western observer, Chinese staff can appear somewhat hypochondriacal. Indeed, all over China, health is a major topic in everyday life, and exchanges range from small-talk to lengthy discussions about what ails the other party, peppered with health advice from anyone who feels competent in the matter (and that includes virtually everyone). Because the health system is organized somewhat differently, with hospitals being the first point of contact, it is quite normal to hear statements such as "I have a little bit of a sore throat and need to go the hospital"—something that would sound ludicrous in the United States. More hilarious and probably exasperating (if looked at from an employer point of view) anecdotes about the health obsession of some Chinese staff include a doctor's certificate, confirming that the employee in question cannot come to work because the office environment contains too little oxygen, or other excuses. While disruptive employees will need to be disciplined, regular staff concerns may need to be addressed.

RETAINING STAFF: EMPLOYEE RETENTION AND LOYALTY PROGRAMS

With China's economy almost doubling in the past five years and expected to maintain about 10 percent annual growth for 2007 and 2008, talented employees face abundant opportunities and temptation to leave for new employment. While the rapid growth of China's economy is a blessing for many companies, it is also proving a headache for HR departments across industries. As the war for talent heats up, methods such as decent salaries and benefits, promotion, and well-designed training programs are no longer sufficient to retain talent. One feature of China's job market is that it has plenty of talented professionals to offer. But another feature is that demand for talent exceeds supply.[30]

Like increasing labor costs, turnover rates are a growing concern for China's outsourcing industry as the cost for recruiting takes its toll and the loss of skilled resources impacts directly on profitability. To some extent, the two of them go hand in hand. According to Mercer, the overall turnover rate in 2005 was 12.8 percent.[31] For high-tech companies, it was 13.2 percent, and for the pharmaceutical industry where new research and development facilities are opening up every day, it was as high as 17.6 percent.

In the IT outsourcing industry the reasons for the higher turnover rate can mostly be found in the characteristics of the industry itself. The fact that most China-based outsourcing companies still provide project-based work and low-end services such as coding and testing[32] and have no proprietary core technology will often prevent engineering talent from accepting such an offer; they are concerned about devaluing themselves in the market and about the stability of their job once said project is finished. Current employees who have expanded their skill-set to a certain extent will often feel stuck if they have little opportunity to work on technically challenging projects that add to their experience and provide an exciting and motivating work environment. Adding value for the client effectively also adds value for employees and this will be a decisive factor in the impending consolidation of the IT outsourcing market, which is currently still very fragmented.

A Mercer survey of software professionals indicated that they saw turnover as a result of interactions between various emerging and fragmented industry forces, particularly to the stimulating force of skill shortage.[33] Managers of software companies should take all possible measures within their control, and accept the fact that staff turnover is here to stay, just like technological uncertainty.

It is necessary to understand that the job market in China is extremely volatile in the sense that staff may leave on very short notice if they have decided to make a change. The notice period may be as short as a couple of days; on average it will be around two weeks. One of the reasons is that future employers often push employees to join early and even offer to compensate the current employer if necessary, thus shortening their own ramp-up time.

However, employees will feel they are entitled to their personal freedom, regardless of any contract they have signed. In a culture that honors trust and the other party's promise, there is often precious little awareness that a contract is legally binding. Although more and more employers are seeking protection from this kind of irresponsible behavior, it will take time.

The social changes that the past two decades of opening have wrought in China place the young generation under a lot of strain. They face the burden of medical treatment, housing, cars, and education for themselves, their children, and their parents. In big cities housing costs have increased dramatically; in Beijing it has probably doubled over the past three years. Apart from salary pressure, job hopping is fueled by multinationals that often offer considerably higher salary package, while having a negative impact on the market.

The pressure of making more money also plays an important part in the frequency with which jobs are changed.

Accept Turnover as a Fact of Life — and Develop the Right Strategy to Minimize its Effects

Both the government and China-based outsourcing providers understand that, given the competition for talent and rapid growth in the outsourcing industry, turnover is here to stay. It is a question of facing the facts — and then finding the right strategy to control and minimize its effects. The right solution on how to increase staff retention involves several different approaches.

Survey results show that employees with one to two years of experience are the most unstable group, and comprise around 44 percent of the whole turnover population. There is also a clear indication that employees with five or more years of service are likely to be very stable. Employees within the age group of 25 to 35 years have shown the highest turnover rate. They comprise 87 percent of the whole turnover population.[35] Those most likely to change jobs regularly or quickly are in applications development, customer support, and sales. However, except for the former, the results for the latter two are consistent with many other industries.

Person-culture fit and person-job fit are the two important variables that are closely related to employee turnover, the former being the fit between personal beliefs and values of an individual, and the latter being the fit between the job challenges and achievement orientation of a person. Lack of these fits results in lower job satisfaction and consequently in employee turnover. Both these variables are highly relevant to the software industry — a people and skill intensive industry. Attaining high levels of fit starts right from the recruitment stage, and HR managers need to devise the selection process accordingly.[36]

Building Loyalty So how can a Chinese IT staff effectively be bound to the company? In a nutshell, the best way to keep an IT staff is to provide a creative and challenging work environment, to offer attractive, competitive compensation and benefits packages based on a regular, fair performance evaluation system, to give employees the prospect of a proper career path within the company, and to foster a unique corporate culture. All of those factors need to be taken into consideration if the company intends to keep a highly motivated team of young talent.[37]

A lot has been written about how Chinese employees build loyalty more easily toward their managers rather than the organization employing them.[38] While it is true that staff often build loyalty toward their manager or supervisor, one needs to keep things in perspective. If the project is valuable to their career and adds to their technical knowledge and personal growth, most Chinese professionals will stay on even after their manager has left.

The first step in building loyalty toward the organization is a strong company culture. Open communication will also help give employees a sense of ownership. Traditionally, IT outsourcing is very profit driven; there is less emphasis on values, team building, and employee development. Because the Chinese are more emotional than their Western counterparts in their relationship with the company, the company needs to acknowledge how employees feel and care for a good working environment. Organizations that fail to do so create tension because the employees feel like they are not part of the company, and the leaders have nothing to leverage from to command their team members' loyalty. If the company culture is weak, engineers will automatically build loyalty to their manager, not the organization.

Overall, Chinese employees tend to place great trust in their leaders and managers. In a 2005 study, Mercer Consulting found that in China:[39]

- There is tendency to place trust and confidence in senior management.
- Nearly seven out of ten employees surveyed trusted their management to always communicate honestly, while three-quarters said their organization was well managed.

Trust is important, and so is respect for the individual employee. If employees feel recognized and receive management attention, they will build a sense of ownership. In such an extremely labor-competitive market as China, it can be daunting to place your trust in employees who may leave you to join the competition the very next day. Yet, in most cases, that trust pays off. Obviously, outsourcing is a business so there needs to be a safety net and companies must put in place a control mechanism for those few who may trespass. It is better to communicate control mechanisms in advance.

Positioning a Company as an "Employer of Choice"   Companies need to develop their own employer brand to position themselves as an employer of choice. Just as with products, outsourcing providers will have to establish their own distinct brand and take care to build a good image in the job market. This is proving especially difficult for small- and medium-sized firms. Thankfully, it is not capital strength alone because talents often consider multiple factors when they decide which company to work for.

Offering Professional Career Development   Given increasing turnover rates and stiff competition for experienced resources, many organizations in the region look to enhance their employee value proposition. As a consequence, career management has become a strategic HR issue. Smart organizations have begun using career management as a tool for adding value for their staff—at the same time reducing turnover and increasing their employee's engagement. Particularly in China, the development of a career infrastructure can help organizations build internal functional excellence in areas where it is difficult to hire or keep experienced staff such as marketing, sales, engineering, and research and development.

Career development is not just an HR function. It is also part of a company's management style. People-oriented organizations recognize that in the end it is the people who make the difference—and money. Companies wishing to retain their high-potential employees need to create an environment that allows those people to grow. This is especially true for fresh graduates, who make up the biggest part of the resources for the outsourcing industry at this point. High-potential workers, much more than the average employee, need to feel they have a career path with the company and can build their resume in that position.

In the West, the trend throughout the 1990s had been to encourage employees to manage their own careers, a reversal from the cradle-to-grave employment system that was prominent for decades. The introduction of the flexible workforce strategies like downsizing and right-sizing threatened (some would argue eliminated) the concepts of the psychological contact that supported employment stability.

Over the same period, the East has enjoyed higher levels of employee loyalty given the paternalistic role organizations have traditionally played in society. The idea of mass layoffs and smart-sizing in Asia has not traditionally been a widely accepted way to reduce costs. Today, both employment models are undergoing changes. The West has begun to focus more on career management to encourage commitment and some organizations in the East have begun to focus more on individual ownership and accountability for careers.[40]

Building a Comprehensive Knowledge Management System   To mitigate the risks of turnover, it is important for companies to build a comprehensive knowledge management system to document processes and experiences.

Performance Incentive Systems

Incentives based on performance and other benchmarks have shown, both overseas and in China, to be effective methods of retaining staff. These can include stock options for key staff, pension plans, and loans for children's education. Adopting a proper incentive system creates a favorable working environment and is helpful in motivating and retaining staff.

A healthy working environment includes not only sound benefits, but also well-established working procedures that allow employees to work more smoothly and flexibly and obtain a greater sense of achievement.

Negative environmental factors such as bureaucracy and corporate politics should be minimized. Companies should invest more in training managers, because many employees resign due to the incompetence of their superiors. Companies should retain people with corporate values. Most companies do this by optimizing their salary system again and again. However, what keeps people in the long run is corporate values.

Given the fierce competition for talent in China, companies should not place a high expectation on retention. A Watson Wyatt survey shows that it is good enough for an employee to work for a company for three years. People who choose to stay may not be the best in terms of capacity, but they recognize corporate values and will grow with the company. Developing people inside the company is more important than smart recruitment, given the shortage of experienced talent. In fact, large corporations such as Motorola and Hewlett-Packard all have long-term training programs. Training means investment, which might not bring revenue in the short term, but will surely benefit the company in the long run.[41]

Managing Staff

What is important to understand when managing Chinese IT resources? Chinese culture is results driven, not process driven. For many Chinese as long as it works, it is fine—even if the solution is less than perfect. This attitude can be a challenge when working with overseas clients who expect standardized processes to be followed to the letter. China-based staff need to have a clear understanding of the process (senior-level staff should understand why, and junior-level employees should ensure that the standard is being followed). Implementing the process properly will require continuous management attention and education. Part of this process is weekly department meetings to share experiences, give advice, review projects, and thus learn from mistakes and enhancing the project implementation process. Last but not least: implementing standards is also a matter of selecting the right employees.

In order to achieve better results it makes sense to link staff management to client requirements, such as information security and English skill, and build those requirements into job descriptions and performance evaluation.

Indeed, many Chinese are shy and do not communicate well unless or until they know someone. While Americans learn to stand up and speak freely in front of others from an early age, Chinese are more introverted, which means that their leaders need to be proactive in bringing new employees into the team and in their daily communication. Employees need to feel that they have influence—regular surveys can help.

Good employee relationships will build a sense of ownership—team building and joint activities are critical. Activities to build teamwork and let them know the company's culture—an annual outing, regular activities such as badminton, going out for dinner, singing karaoke—also allow them to have a good time together.

Let them know the company's future. Communicate. Be open to the employees, place trust in them—one of top five reasons why employees leave is that they are unclear about the company's strategy and future.

Many Chinese are entrepreneurs at heart—this goes a long way to explain why sales and post-sales staff have one of the highest turnover rates. For companies this attitude is both a chance and a risk. It is necessary to get staff to buy into the organization and leverage from salary-linked incentives such as variable bonus depending on performance and achievement of agreed objectives.

On three occasions, the whole of China pretty much shuts down: Spring Festival, the Chinese New Year based on the lunar calendar; Labor Day on May 1; and the National Day on October 1. Those so-called Golden Weeks were introduced in 1999 and coincide with important traditional holidays expressing the Chinese traditional orientation toward family culture.[42] Employees working during one of those Golden Weeks receive triple pay as reimbursement. For outsourcing providers it is important to plan around those peak times of travel, as employees expect to be released during the holiday to return back to their hometown and stay with their family. Spring Festival is often the only time many Chinese will visit with family.

Styles of leadership are currently different between Asia and the United States. Culture colors the way things are done, but less so what is done. The differences in styles most markedly reflect the stage of development of the economies and companies of Asia. As Asian companies come to rely more on professional employees of all sorts, and as professional services become more important in Asian economies, the less autocratic and more participative and even empowered style of leadership will emerge.[43]

A Culture of Not Challenging Authority

Chinese culture is one in which people do not challenge authority. This custom goes back 5,000 years to the time of agrarianism, when loyalty and obedience to a familial hierarchy bound laboring groups together. These moral values are still strong in China's culture. Enterprises that need free-thinkers must install a new working culture that even allows junior staff members to ask questions and raise issues when they think there are problems. This is new and rare in many Chinese enterprises. For example, an employee normally would not ask enough questions to understand a process properly, or challenge a senior associate regarding statements he or she made about a project. Also, a project manager would not want to be asked questions for fear of losing face if he or she did not have the answer readily available, or if the answer was wrong. This is a key issue in many companies, and costs extra time and money to resolve technical issues that were not raised earlier. Although largely viewed as a major weakness, this could also be turned into a major advantage for low-end, repetitive types of work.[44]

Training and Developing Staff

As a rule of thumb, the more talented the employees, the more eager they are to learn. Because the right training programs bring new knowledge and skills to employees, this is a smart investment in retaining them. In China, more and more companies increase their investment to employee training in many ways, which also boosted the training market in China since the 1990s. Hundreds of technical schools across China are offering specialized training classes for all kinds of graduates and students.

Nevertheless, employees in China report that they do not think they are given sufficient opportunities for training and development:[45]

- One in four reports that his or her organization does not provide good training opportunities to enhance career options.
- Only about one half of all employees in China report that their managers actively encourage them to participate in training opportunities.

In combination with mature HR processes, training proper career path setting gives more motivation to the employees on the personal development within the organization. If employees know clearly about what position is within their reach if they make the required effort in performance and competency improvement, this will boost motivation and performance (provided the desired compensation comes along too). The employee will be more focused on the target performance standard and make the best of him or herself.

The ongoing development of staff will also provide a good example to other employees to motivate them following the successful development path—establishing goals are always the effective way to motivate more staff.

China's efforts in becoming a future ITO powerhouse are also supported by government officials, many of whom are forging partnerships with multinationals to train IT engineers. For example, IBM has signed deals to train 100,000 software specialists over the next three years. Microsoft is spending $750 million to build a technology center that will expose Chinese hardware and software engineers to Microsoft technology. In addition, Microsoft is donating $25 million over the next three years to develop software for schools, and another $10 million over the next five years to put Microsoft products in elementary schools.[46]

The government focus on technology in the past 20 years has resulted in subsidiaries for the outsourcing industry. For example, many software parks are compensating companies for language training. There are also more and more joint efforts between universities and enterprises for targeted recruiting: students will be working on a joint project (sort of a private-public partnership) to acquire new skills; and may be hired straight away after graduation by the enterprise sponsoring that project.

ENDNOTES

1. www.chinadaily.com.cn/china/2006-09/01/content_678901.htm
2. www.clomedia.com/content/templates/clo_article.asp?articleid=1177&zoneid=111
3. The Emerging Global Labor Market, McKinsey Global Institute (MGI), 2005.
4. www.mybroadband.co.za/nephp/?m=show&id=4164
5. The International Herald Tribune, 27 October 2005 (http://yaleglobal.yale.edu/display.article?id=6422&page=2)
6. www.bc.edu/bc_org/avp/soe/cihe/newsletter/News38/text015.htm
7. http://yaleglobal.yale.edu/display.article?id=3422
8. Ministry of Education, 2006, www.moe.edu.cn/edoas/website18/info20438.htm
9. http://rank2006.netbig.com
10. www.edu.cn/20010101/21852.shtml
11. www.bc.edu/bc_org/avp/soe/cihe/newsletter/News38/text015.htm
12. The Straits Times, 2004 (http://yaleglobal.yale.edu/display.article?id=4441)

13. Outlook India, 3 May 2005 (http://yaleglobal.yale.edu/display.article?id=5675)

14. English Education in Present-Day China, Lin Lin, Associate Professor, Foreign Language College, Chinese University of Political Science and Law, 2002.

15. English Education in Present-Day China, Lin Lin, Associate Professor, Foreign Language College, Chinese University of Political Science and Law, 2002.

16. Forrester Research, China's Offshore Role—Preliminary Findings, 2007 (from John McCarthy PPT).

17. www.clomedia.com/content/templates/clo_article.asp?articleid=1177&zoneid=111

18. http://opendoors.iienetwork.org/?p=89251

19. China Market Research Group and iResearch, 12/2006 (http://china.seekingalpha.com/article/23004)

20. www.wetfeet.com/employer/articles/article.asp?aid=360

21. China Market Research Group, 12/2006 (http://china.seekingalpha.com/article/23004)

22. http://article.zhaopin.com/pub/view.jsp?id=27415&DYWE=1171361 723866.451231.1171361724.1171361724.1

23. The Outsourcing Institute: IT Outsourcing in China: How China's Five Emerging Drivers Are Changing the Technology Landscape and IT Industry, 2006.

24. Forrester Research, China's Offshore Role—Preliminary Findings, 2007 (from John McCarthy PPT).

25. neoIT, Offshore and Nearshore ITO and BPO Salary Report, June 2006.

26. www.chinadaily.com.cn/cndy/2007-01/19/content_787155.htm

27. neoIT, Offshore and Nearshore ITO and BPO Salary Report, June 2006

28. www.chinadaily.com.cn/cndy/2007-01/19/content_787155.htm

29. Forrester Research, China's Offshore Role—Preliminary Findings, 2007.

30. www.chinadaily.com.cn/cndy/2007-01/31/content_796912.htm

31. www.chinadaily.com.cn/bizchina/2006-12/25/content_767048_2.htm

32. Forrester Research, China's Offshore Role—Preliminary Findings, 2007 (from John McCarthy PPT).

33. Mercer Consulting, 2004. (www.mercerhr.com/referencecontent.jhtml/dynamic/idContent/1130215)

34. Forrester Research, China's Offshore Role—Preliminary Findings, 2007 (from John McCarthy PPT).

35. China Employer A&R Survey, 2006.

36. www.mercerhr.com/referencecontent.jhtml/dynamic/idContent/1130215

37. www.hroot.com/companypublish/html/1432.htm

38. http://repository.ust.hk/dspace/handle/1783.1/1568

39. www.mercerhr.com/referencecontent.jhtml?idContent=1182520

40. www.mercerhr.com.cn/knowledgecenter/reportsummary.jhtml/dynamic/idContent/1231750;jsessionid=EP0G4HJS532TKCTGOUGCIIQKMZ0QUJLW

41. www.chinadaily.com.cn/cndy/2007-01/31/content_796912.htm

42. www.chinadaily.com.cn/china/2006-12/18/content_761961.htm

43. http://hbswk.hbs.edu/item/4869.html

44. www.chinadaily.com.cn/bw/2006-08/21/content_669243.htm

45. Mercer HR 2005 What's Working, China, www.mercerhr.com.cn/knowledgecenter/reportsummary.jhtml/dynamic/idContent/1231750;jsessionid=EP0G4HJS532TKCTGOUGCIIQKMZ0QUJLW

46. The Outsourcing Institute: IT Outsourcing in China: How China's Five Emerging Drivers Are Changing the Technology Landscape and IT Industry, 2006.

CHAPTER 7

China's Outsourcing Cities

S ince China began moving resolutely toward becoming the world's leading nation for IT outsourcing (ITO) in 2003, a number of designated outsourcing bases have sprung up to use their various advantages to attract international business. Each has its own benefits and downsides. Some are more accessible but also more expensive; those farther from international points of access may offer greater cost benefits, but a smaller talent pool or less available resources and support.

To guide potential outsourcers who may or may not have the opportunity to visit their China outsourcing partner(s) before making a selection or during a given project, the following descriptions are designed to provide basic background on each of 10 cities that are making their mark on the industry. Included are all ten national software bases.

BEIJING

Population   15 million[1]

Software Parks or Technology Zones   Three major software parks have been established in Beijing: Zhongguancun Software Park (zPark), Changping Software Park, and Beijing Industry University Software Park. The biggest and best-known, zPark, is among the country's largest.[2] Resident companies include Oracle, Siemens, Flextronics, and Wipro.[3]

Top University or Universities   Beijing University and Qinghua (Tsinghua) University are considered the nation's top two institutes of higher learning. In all, 18 universities in Beijing offer engineering degrees, and 10 offer programming.[4]

International Air, Rail, and Road Connections   Beijing Capital International Airport (BCIA) is currently battling Shanghai's Pudong International Airport for the title of China's most internationally connected airport.

With the addition of flights to Washington Dulles International Airport announced in January 2007,[5] the capital is now linked to every other major world capital and financial center. Travelers from Beijing also have the opportunity to fly to rarely visited cities in Asia, such as North Korea's Pyongyang and Mongolia's Ulan Bataar—both of which can also be reached by rail service from the Chinese capital.

As the nation's seat of government, Beijing also offers domestic passengers the greatest number of domestic air and rail links, including train travel to Lhasa in the Xizang Autonomous Region (Tibet), which takes two days, and an overnight train to Hong Kong. Ironically, air service to Lhasa is still routed via Chengdu in Sichuan province.

International rail service from Beijing includes the aforementioned north Asian capitals, along with trains to Vietnam's Hanoi via Kunming, and to Moscow on the Trans-Siberian Railroad's two routes, via Mongolia (faster) or Manchuria (easier for citizens of nations that do not have a visa-free travel agreement with Mongolia).

History and Description   Beijing has served as China's political and cultural capital several times over the past 800 years, and has been the nation's seat of government since the establishment of the People's Republic of China in 1949.

The city, the name of which means "northern capital," first became China's capital under Kublai Khan's Yuan Dynasty (1279–1368). Although part of that capital remains north of the Forbidden City in the form of Beihai Park, the city itself was then centered more around what is now the Haidian District in the northwestern part of Beijing.

Although the capital moved briefly to Nanjing in the late 1300s, upon establishment of the Ming Dynasty (1368–1644), power returned to Beijing shortly. When the Qing Dynasty overthrew the Ming in 1644, they continued to rule from the same city.

Leaders of the Republic of China moved back to Nanjing in 1911 after overthrowing the imperial system, but the Communist Party of China (CCP) once again chose Beijing upon their victory in China's civil war and the founding of the People's Republic of China.

In many ways, the best is yet to come for this city. Having undergone more than a decade of urban renewal, Beijing is gearing up for its moment in the international spotlight as the host city for the 2008 Olympic Games. When they begin on August 8, 2008, Beijing will have expanded its transportation capacity by several times, including new subway lines, a third terminal for BCIA, a light-rail express line to and from the airport, and hundreds of kilometers of new roads, not to mention an almost complete reconstruction of the city's designated central business district.

Beijing is China's leading city for technology businesses. The Zhongguancun area in northwestern Beijing is often referred to as China's Silicon Valley, and the surrounding Haidian District is home to numerous technology start-ups, major tech enterprises such as Chinese computer manufacturer Lenovo, and the China operations of multinational technology firms.

Although most analysts and executives would agree that Shanghai and Shenzhen are better cities in which to do business, China's mix of central government planning and market economics, sometimes called "cadre capitalism," make a strong presence in Beijing, if not a China headquarters, a requirement for any large company conducting business here.

Beijing's long history as China's administrative and political center means that for centuries, the nation's best and brightest have come to the city for both education and then employment. This trend continues today, to the benefit of the city and enterprises based or with operations there. Because of this, Beijing is also one of China's most integrated cities in terms of a mix of people from different cities and provinces, along with representation of many of the country's 56 designated minority groups. However, the pride of native Beijingers regarding their city and history is exceptionally strong. The Beijing dialect of Chinese forms the basis of the standardized form of "putonghua" or "common speech," China's official language.

It is also China's most international city, due in part to the continuous diplomatic presence of so many different countries and organizations, not to mention the large international student population and a growing foreign business community, especially since China's accession to the World Trade Organization (WTO) in 2001.

The concentration of universities often gives enterprises in the capital first pick of local university graduates, who perhaps want to take advantage of higher salaries and greater opportunities than their home city or province may be able to offer.

That lure of greater potential compensation also makes Beijing perhaps less attractive as an outsourcing destination, in terms of cost. Salary packages for software engineers in Beijing are the country's highest.[6]

SHANGHAI

Population   20 million[7]

Software Parks or Technology Zones   Shanghai Software Park, Shanghai Pudong Software Park, Waigaoqiao Software Park.

Shanghai Pudong Software Park holds a designation as a National Software Base. Waigaoqiao Software Park is located in the Waigaoqiao Free Trade Zone in Shanghai's Pudong area and counts IBM among its resident companies.

Top University or Universities   Fudan University and Shanghai Jiaotong (Infrastructure) University are the city's best and among the nation's top institutes of higher learning. Shanghai Jiaotong has the distinction of being former leader Jiang Zemin's alma mater.

International Air, Rail, and Road Connections   Shanghai currently has the distinction of being the only city in China to be served by two major airports: Pudong International Airport, a relatively new facility east of the city; and Shanghai Hongqiao International Airport, the city's original air harbor, which lies northwest of the city center. Upon Pudong's opening, Hongqiao was intended to become a domestic-only airport, although limited service to cities in Korea and also Hong Kong is available.

Pudong International is China's busiest airport for international passenger traffic, and one of its busiest for cargo. Flights from and to Pudong include major destinations in North America, Europe, the Middle East, and Africa, along with every major city in Asia. The airport is connected to Shanghai's eastern outskirts by the world's only regularly scheduled magnetic-levitation (maglev) train, which reaches speeds of 431 km/hour and covers the 30 km distance in seven minutes, although the maglev station's remote location may mean the user then spends significant time in traffic, especially if his or her ultimate destination is on the western side of the Huangpu River.

Shanghai's location in the central coast puts it almost equidistant from Beijing and Hong Kong, with flights about two hours to either destination.

Travelers should be aware that while a huge number of international and domestic flights serve Shanghai's two airports, some of its air routes, such as Shanghai-Beijing and Shanghai-Shenzhen, are among the nation's most crowded air patterns and frequently experience delays, especially when summer thunderstorms begin to form in the area. Avoid scheduling meetings too close to arrival times, and when possible, take the earliest departing flight available, before the pattern begins to fill up and delays begin to have a knock-on effect. For midmorning meetings and depending on schedules, sometimes an overnight train is an easier way to guarantee an on-time arrival than a seemingly short flight.

Shanghai is an excellent place from which to begin a rail journey, with regular express service to nearby destinations including Nanjing, Hangzhou,

Suzhou, and Wuxi. Beijing, Guangzhou, Shenzhen, and even Hong Kong are easy overnight train trips. It appears that regular service to Lhasa, the capital of the Xizang Autonomous Region (Tibet), may soon be in the offing, putting Shanghai's rail accessibility almost on a par with that of Beijing.

A network of expressways links Shanghai with other nearby cities, including Nanjing, Suzhou, Hangzhou, Wuxi, and Ningbo on the Zhejiang coast, all of which can be reached by regular bus service or private car within two to three hours.

Shanghai is also a major Yangzi River port for both cargo and passengers, able to access both cities upstream on China's most famous river, and domestic coastal and international destinations via the East China Sea. Although Dalian, Tianjin, and Hong Kong could be reached by ship from Shanghai, these services offer little advantage to the business traveler.

History and Description Shanghai was the original exotic Asian city to most North Americans and Europeans. Before neon images of Tokyo in the 1980s, before shots of Hong Kong in the 1972 James Bond film *The Man with the Golden Gun*, there was 1920s newsreel footage of Shanghai, throngs of humanity passing back and forth in front of the European architecture of the Bund, Shanghai's waterfront.

Before Shanghai became a treaty port following the settlement at the end of the Opium Wars (1839–42) between China and various Western countries, it was little more than a fishing village upriver from the ocean. Today, one look at Shanghai and the visitor cannot help but think that it is vying for the title of Greatest City in the World.

Shanghai's perch on the central coast and at the outflow of the Yangzi River made it the city of choice for foreign traders from the mid-1800s until the 1930s, and as such quickly became China's commercial capital. The city remained one of China's most important ports after the establishment of the People's Republic in 1949. Shortly after the beginning of the move toward reform and a market economy, Shanghai began to recapture its status as a commercial center, and after being rivaled by Shenzhen for over a decade, it is once again China's richest city.

As a center for outsourcing, Shanghai's universities and quality of life make it a rich pool of talent. High-tech zones and software parks are concentrated in the Pudong district, as the lure of tax breaks and other incentives were used to populate the area and encourage both construction and population by multinational corporations.

Shanghai's biggest drawback for the potential outsourcer is cost. Software engineers in Shanghai are the second-highest paid in the country, trailing only Beijing, and office space there is routinely China's most expensive, excluding Hong Kong. However, many outsourcers and corporations find that the city's infrastructure and talent sufficiently offset the higher costs to justify making it their software base in China.

DALIAN

Population   2,980,513[8]

Software Parks or Technology Zones   Dalian Hi-Tech Industrial Park is a national Industrial Park approved by the State Council in 1991.[9] Resident companies include Dell, Hitachi, Neusoft, Nokia, Sanyo, and Toshiba.[10] Dalian Software Park counts 21 global companies as its residents, including GE, IBM, Matsushita, SAP, and Accenture.

Top University or Universities   Dalian University of Technology (DUT),[11] Liaoning Normal University (LNNU) is one of the key institutions of higher learning in Liaoning Province and located in Dalian;[12] Dalian Maritime University (DMU), one of China's largest and best maritime universities.[13]

International Air, Rail, and Road Connections   Dalian serves as an excellent transportation hub for northern Asia, given its proximity to Japan, South Korea, and the Russian Far East. Daily flights connect Dalian's Zhoushuizi International Airport with Tokyo, Hiroshima, Seoul, and Hong Kong. Regular flights also serve Nagasaki, Nagoya, and Osaka in Japan, Irkutsk and Vladivostok in Russia, and Pusan in South Korea. It also connects Dalian with all major Chinese provincial capitals and commercial cities.

Regular rail connections link Dalian with all major Chinese cities, and can take travelers to the Russian border crossing at Mudanjiang, and the Chinese border city of Dandong, across the Yalu River from North Korea. Dalian is also being linked to other major northeastern Chinese destinations by high-speed rail that can travel as fast as 300 km/180 mph.[14]

As a port city, cargo and passenger service from Dalian is available to Nagasaki and Osaka in Japan, Pusan in Korea, and Chinese destinations including Xiamen, Shanghai, Weihai, Yantai, and Tianjin.

History and Description   From an outsourcing point of view, Dalian has traditionally been an important destination for Japanese buyers. Due to geographical proximity to Japan and the fact that the region was under Japanese colonial rule for 40 years (until 1945), there is a lot of Japanese language capability to be found. Major Japanese high-tech companies, such as Hitachi, Sanyo, and Toshiba, have created presences to tap into the local talent pool, and there are a number of call centers for the Japanese market operating from Dalian.

At the turn of the twentieth century, Dalian was first a Russian colony (then called Port Arthur), but changed hands following naval confrontations between the Japanese and first the Chinese navy, later the Russian navy.

The city is often cited as a model for other Chinese urban areas in terms of cleanliness and urban planning. Few other Chinese cities can offer the same kind of scenic beauty combined with robust economic growth. It is a popular summer tourism destination and Dalian's seafood is famous throughout China.

Dalian is the window for northeast China and the gateway to Beijing and Tianjin.[15] One of the top ten outsourcing cities in China, Dalian is also China's second largest seaport after Shanghai, with an area of about 12,600 sq km. The city is a major industrial and shipbuilding center; a popular tourist destination; a robust retail, fashion, and distribution center; and an important gateway to the country's northeast industrial region.

Located on the southern tip of Liaodong Peninsula in Liaoning Province, Dalian was declared an Open Coastal City in 1984. This was quickly followed by the construction of a highly successful Economic-Technological Development Zone (ETDV) in the area. In 1988, the entire Liaodong Peninsula, made up of 8 cities and 16 counties, was named an Open Economic Zone. In 2000 the Dalian Export Processing zone was established, and Dalian today is a magnet for investment from Hong Kong, Japan, Taiwan, South Korea, and the United States.[16]

By the end of 2005, the total number of approved foreign-funded enterprises in Dalian amounted to over 10,000, about 4,000 of them having started operations. More than 1,900 representative offices and agencies set up in Dalian by overseas companies make Dalian one of the five cities in China with the highest concentration of overseas representation.[17]

Dalian currently does the majority of business process outsourcing (BPO) coming to China from Japan, valued at US$1.23 billion in 2004.[18] Japan is still China's largest customer country for outsourcing. The city often likens itself to the Indian outsourcing hub of Bangalore, and even ran a short-lived ad campaign calling itself "The Bangalore of China."

The city now has an additional advantage to benefit its trade and business: its former mayor, Bo Xilai, credited with helping to make Dalian the business hub and model of Chinese urban planning it is today, is now China's Minister of Commerce. Bo, son of Chinese revolutionary and long-time State Council member Bo Yibo, served as Dalian's mayor for seven years, before becoming governor of Liaoning province from 2001 to 2004, when he became Minister of Commerce.

CHENGDU

Population   10,443,000 (2004)[19]

Software Parks or Technology Zones   Chengdu Hi-Tech Zone became a nationally ranked high-tech industrial development zone in 1991 and ranks fifth among China's 53 high-tech zones. Twenty-eight Fortune 500 companies and other 603 foreign invested enterprises have invested in the zone.[20]

Top University or Universities   Sichuan University; Sichuan Normal University; Southwest Jiaotong University; University of Electronic Science and Technology of China; Southwestern University of Finance and Economics; Chengdu University of Technology; Chengdu University of Information Technology; and Chengdu University.[21]

International Air, Rail, and Road Connections   Chengdu is southwest China's most important transportation hub, and is still the single jumping-off point for foreign visitors going to Tibet by air or road. Chengdu Shuangliu International Airport lies 16 km to the southwest of the city.[22] International flights that serve it are almost entirely with other Asian countries, including Singapore, Thailand, Cambodia, and Japan, along with the Special Administrative Regions of Hong Kong and Macau. KLM also operates regular, nonstop service from Amsterdam to Chengdu. Domestic flights serve all major provincial capitals and financial centers.

Chengdu is the southwest's largest rail junction, with connections to Beijing, Shanghai, Guangzhou, and Kunming. International trains are available, but all pass through Kunming.

Several nations maintain consulates in Chengdu, including the United States, France, Germany, Korea, Singapore, and Thailand.

History and Description   Chengdu is the provincial capital of Sichuan, China's second most populous province, and the nation's fifth largest city. It has served as a regional capital since the third century AD, when it was the capital of the Shu kingdom, one of the three warring states mentioned in the Chinese epic novel *Three Kingdoms* by Luo Guanzhong. The name Shu still is used regularly to refer to Sichuan.

Chengdu's present layout reminds the visitor of Beijing—perhaps because the national capital served as its model for urban planning. Its distinctive, spicy cuisine either delights or punishes visitors—although food there is exceptionally good, there will be no rest for eaters of a bland diet. Teahouses that line the city's waterways are popular with both residents and travelers as inexpensive rest stops to while away an afternoon.

The city has served both as a political and cultural center during its history, once home to two of China's most famous poets, Li Bai and Du Fu, both of whom lived there during the second half of the 700s A.D.

Today Chengdu is probably southwest China's most vibrant economic center, including its development as a base for technology development, and is designated as one of the country's ten national software bases. Chengdu's large university population, coupled with lower costs than first-tier cities such as Beijing and Shanghai, make it an attractive site for outsourcing services. Municipal government estimates placed the value of Chengdu's total software industry revenues for 2006 at 18 billion yuan (US$2.32 billion).[23]

Chengdu's Hi-Tech Industrial Development Zone counts Microsoft, Motorola, Lenovo Group, and Intel among its residents. Intel is now producing 65-nanometer semiconductors from a plant in the zone, and is the largest foreign investor in the city.[24] Electronic Data Systems said that Chengdu was one of five locations in China where it would be expanding its operations.[25] Mark Andrew Boyle, vice-president of Accenture Greater China, said in an October 2006 interview that Chengdu was among the cities that should be encouraged to become a BPO center.[26]

The city has its own outsourcing alliance—the Chengdu Software Outsourcing League—with 49 members, to promote software outsourcing services available in the city, with Singapore being a particular target.[27]

Chengdu is now building itself to be the financial hub for western China and has successfully attracted major international financial institutions, including Citigroup, HSBC, Standard Chartered Bank, ABN AMRO, Bank of East Asia, and BNP Paribas.[28]

The city is also becoming the West China base for domestic financial firms. Chengdu serves as the People's Bank of China's (China's central bank) southwest China headquarters there, along with the regional headquarters of many Chinese banking and securities firms.[29]

Chengdu has also found favor with international consulting firms as a regional base. KPMG opened its first west China office in Chengdu in October 2006. Its arrival was predated by several years by Ernst & Young, an early arrival.[30]

XI'AN

Population   6 million[31]

Software Parks or Technology Zones   Xi'an High-Tech Park (XAHTP) is not one single zone, but comprises several software parks and technology zones, including Electronic Industrial Park, Chang'an Technology Park,

Xi'an Software Park, Hi-Tech Export Processing Base, Xi'an Jiaotong University Science Park, Northwest Polytechnic University Science Park, Biopharmaceutical Park, and Advanced Material Science Park.[32] In its various locations, XAHTP hosts IBM, Hewlett-Packard, Philips, NEC, and Fujitsu.[33]

In 2002, Xi'an was designated not only as a National Software Base, one of ten, but was given the go-ahead to become China's largest such hub.[34]

Top University or Universities Xi'an Jiaotong (Infrastructure) University, Sha'anxi Teachers' University, Northwest University, and Northwest Polytechnic University.

International Air, Rail, and Road Connections Xi'an is served by regular non-stop flights from Japan, Thailand, and Macau. As one of China's most important tourist destinations, it is well-connected with all other major Chinese cities and provincial capitals.

Rail service is available to all major cities in China. Connections to Alma-Aty in Kazakhstan and other destinations in Central Asia are available via Urumqi.

History and Description Xi'an was once the eastern terminus of the Silk Road trade route between China and Europe via Central Asia, and at one time may have been the largest city in the world. Xi'an—originally known as Chang'an—was first China's capital under the Qin Dynasty (221–206 BC), and remained so under the Western Han Dynasty (206 BC–24 AD). It served as the capital for the last time in the Tang Dynasty (618–907 AD), regarded as one of China's greatest periods of expansion and culture.

Xi'an is best known overseas as the home of the Qin Dynasty terracotta army, thousands of life-sized, lifelike statues that were made to lead and protect the Qin emperor into the afterlife. It is also one of China's few remaining walled cities.

Although no longer the greatest capital city on earth, it remains the capital of Sha'anxi province. Having become one of China's top tourist destinations after the country began reopening to travelers in the late 1970s, Xi'an had state-of-the-art infrastructure much earlier than most other cities. It continues to serve the visitor—for both business and pleasure—at a higher level at least as well as any other city in the western part of China, if not better.

Xi'an is one of China's top sources of new technology talent. An estimated 400,000 students are enrolled at its universities, with about 65,000 new graduates per year, based on 2003 figures.[35]

In 2000, the city launched Digital Xi'an, an initiative designed to establish itself as a center for technological research and development. With support from the local government and alignment with China's drive to develop the western provinces, Digital Xi'an focuses on infrastructure, education, and commercial developments, while promoting the establishment of an information-based economy and culture in Xi'an.

Digital Xi'an is a forward-thinking initiative. Xi'an was once the greatest city in the world, a hub of trade and technology. The Xi'an Information Center and the Xi'an government are working to establish Xi'an as a key hub for future technology and trade.

Along with forward-thinking government support, one of Xi'an's greatest advantages is its talent cost structure. A software engineer in this city earns, on average, approximately half what his or her compatriot in Beijing does.[36]

In September 2006, Xi'an declared itself "China's Service Outsourcing Capital," and in 2005 had total software export revenue of US$42 million, indicating room for significant growth in this sector.[37]

The following month, Xi'an Mayor Chen Baogen vowed to make the city the heart of China's BPO industry. "The modern BPO industry is vital to Xi'an's economic development. As an inland city, Xi'an does not enjoy the geographic advantages when competing with southeast coastal cities in terms of the industries in traditional sense," he said. Chen added, "But we are in the same footage in terms of BPO development. The service outsourcing based on software and Internet technology will bring about the change in the current international trade pattern."[38]

JINAN

Population   5.9 million[39]

Software Parks or Technology Zones   Qilu Software Park. Founded in 1997, the park established sister-park relations with Bangalore Software Park in 2001. It has cooperated with multinational corporations including Microsoft, IBM, Sun, Hewlett-Packard, and Oracle.[40] No salary info.

Top University or Universities   Jinan University. The top university of Shandong province, it also operates a campus in Guangdong province.

International Air, Rail, and Road Connections   Jinan is probably the most isolated of China's software bases, despite being the capital of a major coastal province. International flights connect it only with Korea, although Shandong Airlines, based at Jinan International Airport, flies to Los Angeles, Frankfurt, Tokyo, and San Francisco, all via Beijing.

Jinan is a major rail junction for Shandong province, as it is its capital and is located geographically in its middle. Although not a national rail hub in itself, it lies on the main north-south Beijing to Guangzhou/Hong Kong corridor and therefore receives significant rail traffic in both directions. The same is true for road access, with highways linking it both north and south to Beijing and Guangdong, and similarly to the other major Shandong cities of Yantai and Qingdao (Tsingtao).

History and Description Jinan and the area surrounding it is one of the oldest cradles of Chinese civilization. Neolithic sites from more than 6,000 years ago have been found in the area, and political entities resembling Jinan have existed for more than 2,600 years.[41] The state of Qi existed in and around Jinan during China's Warring States Period (475–221 BC). It was during this time that the philosopher Confucius lived in Qi and developed his philosophy. Of the various kingdoms that existed at that time, Qi was the last to surrender to Qin Shi Huang, China's first emperor.[42]

The city is a jumping-off point for two major Chinese historical sites: Qufu, the birthplace of Confucius, a tiny town that is one of the great showcases for classical Chinese architecture; and Mt. Tai (Tai Shan), one of China's five sacred mountain peaks. The city of Tai Shan also has the distinction of being the hometown of one of modern Chinese history's most despised figures: Jiang Qing, the wife of Chairman Mao Zedong and a member of the Gang of Four.

Jinan today is Shandong's provincial capital, although it is overshadowed by other Shandong cities that have capitalized on coastal locations for trade and tourism. Qingdao and its counterpart on the Shandong peninsula's northern coast, Yantai, see more visitors, and Qingdao is the province's richest city. Qingdao is home to three major Chinese companies: Tsingtao Beer, Haier Electronics, and Laoshan Mineral Water.

Named a software industry base in December 2001, Jinan seems the least likely of cities to receive the honor. Unlike the other cities, including Shanghai, Beijing, Xi'an, and Chengdu, Jinan is not generally renowned for being international, as an inland city in a coastal province. That said, it was cited at the time of the creation of the software industrial base initiative for having 51 companies involved in the software business, with a combined 920 million yuan (US$118.8 million) in revenue in 2000.[43]

Jinan's main attraction for ITO will be its cost advantages, with engineering talent and office space costing a fraction of operations in larger Chinese cities. However, Jinan's talent pool is somewhat limited, as will be the level of experience of such engineers, and therefore may need time to mature before it can compete with other big outsourcing destinations.

HANGZHOU

Population   6,428,700 (2003)[44]

Software Parks or Technology Zones   Hangzhou Hi-Tech Industry Development Zone and Hangzhou East Software Park.

Top University or Universities   Zhejiang University, Hangzhou University, Hangzhou University of Commerce, and Zhejiang University of Technology.

International Air, Rail, and Road Connections   Hangzhou Xiaoshan International Airport lies to the north and slightly east of the city center. Modern and efficient, its main drawback is that it can take an hour to reach by car from the city. Hangzhou receives daily international flights from Japan and Hong Kong. Regularly scheduled air service also connects Hangzhou with South Korea and Macau. All major provincial capitals and financial centers can be reached by air from Hangzhou.

Hangzhou's location gives it easy access to other nearby cities in Zhejiang and Jiangsu province by both rail and road. Shanghai lies just under two hours away by either car or train, as do Ningbo in Zhejiang, and Suzhou and Wuxi in Jiangsu. Wenzhou on Zhejiang's southern coast can be reached in less than three hours. Major highways connect Hangzhou to all of these destinations. Hangzhou in itself is not a rail hub, but via its two train stations one can connect to almost every major city, especially Beijing, Shanghai, and Guangzhou, directly.

As one of the main cities on the Grand Canal, a man-made waterway that stretches from Beijing to Shanghai, it is also possible to reach Hangzhou by boat, although this would be of greater interest to tourists and would largely be impractical for business travelers.

History and Description   Visit Hangzhou and many of your local hosts will repeatedly share the local marketing slogan, which comes from a line of ancient poetry: "Above there is paradise; below, there is Suzhou and Hangzhou." That said, in fairness to Hangzhou, perhaps no other city in China can offer this level of business opportunity and acumen coupled with scenic beauty.

That couplet is traced back to the time of the Southern Song Dynasty (1127–1279 AD), which made Hangzhou its capital city after fleeing Genghis Khan's Mongolian forces as they drove farther south into China. The Southern Song was the only dynasty ever to use Hangzhou as its capital. They eventually fell to further Mongol incursions in 1279 AD.

Built around the West Lake, one of China's most famous scenic attractions, Hangzhou is a model of modern Chinese urban planning. From a small city in a beautiful setting, Hanghzou has grown into a modern city and a prominent provincial capital.

Seeing the need for increased infrastructure and growth, the city chose to retain mostly low-rise architecture around the lake, and reserved new construction for other areas of the city. The result is a city that has kept most of its original charm and attraction, and a rare site in China where tourism and business travel can exist side by side.

Considered a second-tier city, in 2004 and again in 2005, Hangzhou garnered an impressive distinction: *Forbes Magazine* named it the best city in China for business.[45]

For technology companies, this is not really news. One of China's homegrown stars, Alibaba.com Corp., is based there, helped by the fact that founder and CEO Jack Ma hails from the city. However, with offices in Shanghai and Hong Kong, Alibaba had other choices and yet chose to remain in the city by the lake. Alibaba also now operates Yahoo in China, following a 2005, US$1 billion investment from the search giant.

Hangzhou likes to portray at itself as China's Silicon Valley, and while the weather is certainly pleasant, Hangzhou is not quite there. That is not to take anything away from the city. Zhejiang University is well known as a source of technology talent, both for the province and the rest of the nation. Zhejiang is also the country's second-largest mobile market. A major advantage for Hangzhou is its proximity to Shanghai, but without Shanghai's top-tier prices in terms of real estate and talent.

The city is one of ten national software bases. Outsourcing services in 2006 were valued at 6 billion yuan (US$774 million).[46] Tata Consultancy Services, India's largest IT company, first opened a Hangzhou office in 2002[47] as one of its own outsourcing bases in China, with some of its 800 consultants split between there and Shanghai.[48] In particular, Tata operates an outsourcing center for General Electric in Hangzhou.

GUANGZHOU

Population   12 million (2007)[49]

Software Parks or Technology Zones   Tianhe Software Park, Guangdong Software Science Park, Nansha IT Software Park, and Guangzhou New & Hi-Tech Industrial Development Zone. Tianhe Software Park has the distinction of being named a China Software Industry Base.

Top University or Universities Zhongshan University and Guangzhou University.

International Air, Rail, and Road Connections Guangzhou is a major transportation hub for southern China, for all transport methods. Guangzhou Baiyun International Airport, relocated and expanded in 2004, is one of the region's busiest airports and has significant international connections, many via China Southern Airlines, the country's largest air carrier, which uses Baiyun as its home base. Guangzhou is connected to international capitals and financial centers through daily or regular air service, including Tokyo, Seoul, London, Los Angeles, San Francisco, Singapore, and Paris. Destinations as far-flung as Lagos, Nigeria, and Moscow, Russia are served by Baiyun, along with every major airport in China.

Guangzhou is also southern China's primary rail hub, with fast connections to and from economic powerhouse Shenzhen and just beyond it, Hong Kong. With direct trains as fast as 90 minutes to 2 hours, the run between these two Pearl River Delta economic powerhouses is now down to the time of a commuter train in most major metropolitan areas. Guangzhou is at the southern end of China's most traveled rail corridor, from Beijing to Guangzhou and Hong Kong, with the trip now completed in less than 24 hours. Guangzhou Railway Station is one of the nation's top stations in terms of passenger volume.

Guangzhou is one city served well by regular bus service to nearby cities, including Shenzhen, Hong Kong, and other Pearl River Delta cities including Dongguan, Shunde, Zhuhai, and Macau. Bus departures are available directly from both Baiyun Airport and from stations in Guangzhou.

As a port, Guangzhou also serves Hong Kong, Zhuhai, and Macau with regular fast ferry service.

History and Description Guangzhou's history as a top China trading port dates back to China and the West's initial commercial contacts in the seventeenth century. At the time, Guangzhou (perhaps known better to Westerners by its historical name, Canton) was the only city in China authorized by the Qing Dynasty emperors (1664–1911) to conduct trade with foreigners.

In 1842, the Opium Wars led to Guangzhou and other coastal cities being forced open to trade with the West, following the capitulation by the imperial government in the face of a series of military actions in Guangzhou and elsewhere by Western nations.

Guangzhou also served as a base for China's anti-imperial revolutionary movement, and the formation of the Republic of China in 1911 was proclaimed there,[50] although Nanjing served as its capital. Zhongshan University is named for Dr. Sun Yat-sen, the Chinese revolutionary leader.

Since China began reopening to foreign trade in the late 1970s, Guangzhou's traditional linguistic and cultural ties and geographic proximity to Hong Kong have made it one of southern China's primary economic engines. Seen as more freewheeling than northern rivals such as Beijing, Guangzhou is the commercial hub and political capital for Guangdong province, China's richest, although it is challenged by its southern neighbors Shenzhen and, of course, Hong Kong.

The city's ties with Hong Kong and use of the same Chinese dialect—Cantonese—has made Guangzhou a prime outsourcing center for Hong Kong's IT demands, and also for customer service and call centers. Both Hong Kong and Shanghai Banking Corp. (HSBC) and PCCW Ltd. use Guangzhou as an outsourcing center.

City software officials are hoping to leverage Guangzhou's designation as a national software base to build software export revenues to US$1.2 billion by 2010.[51]

ITO and BPO in Guangzhou will be influenced by two major factors: the availability of talent, and its cost. Although Guangzhou's universities are excellent, it does not have as many as Beijing or Shanghai, and therefore will have to attract talent away from university cities. That will also increase the price of such talent, both in attracting and retaining it. However, the domestic outsourcing business and continued support for IT services, especially in banking and finance, from Hong Kong represent significant opportunities for the pearl of the Pearl River Delta.

NANJING

Population   6.4 million[52]

Software Parks or Technology Zones   Nanjing New and High-Tech Industry Development Zone,[53] Pukou High and New Technology Development Zone, Jiangning Economic-Technological Development Zone.

Top University or Universities   Nanjing University of Science and Technology,[54] Nanjing University, Southeast University, Nanjing University of Aviation and Aeronautics, Hohai University, and Nanjing Normal University. Nanjing is one of the four concentrated areas of tertiary education in China and has 37 general universities and colleges.[55]

International Air, Rail, and Road Connections   Nanjing Lukou International Airport lies over 35 km southeast of the city center.[56] It is served by regular international flights to and from Seoul, Osaka, and Singapore, along with flights to the Special Administrative regions of Hong Kong and Macau. Flights also serve every major domestic provincial capital and financial centers.

Nanjing is not a major rail center, but is connected via express trains to nearby cities including Shanghai, Hangzhou, Suzhou, and Wuxi, and regular service takes passengers to all other major destinations in China.

Highways crisscrossing Jiangsu province give travelers more options to arrive at and depart from Nanjing. Shanghai, Hangzhou, Suzhou, and Wuxi are all easily accessible via regular bus services, taxis, or private cars.

Because it lies on the Yangzi River, travel by boat downstream to Shanghai, and upstream to Wuhan and Chongqing, are both possible, although these are not likely to be the first choices for business travelers. Travel time to Shanghai by boat is about four hours, double what a similar journey would take by rail or road.

History and Description   Nanjing (which means "Southern Capital") is the only other city in China besides Beijing to serve as the capital in more than 600 years, and has done so twice, first upon the establishment of the Ming Dynasty (1368–1644). The Ming emperors, however, stayed in the southern capital for less than half a century before moving north to their permanent base in Beijing.

Nanjing became the base for a religious-influenced uprising against the Qing Dynasty (1644–1911) called the Taiping Rebellion, led by Hong Xiuquan, who believed he was the Chinese incarnation of Jesus Christ. The rebellion lasted 13 years before ultimately being put down by Qing troops.

Again in 1911, Dr. Sun Yat-Sen overthrew the imperial system and, in nationalistic homage to the Ming emperors, also chose Nanjing as the capital for the Republic of China. The capital remained there until the defeat of the Nationalists in 1949 at the end of the Chinese Civil War. Nanjing remains the capital of Jiangsu province. Under the Wade-Giles Romanization system, the city was known as Nanking. Its current spelling, based on China's official Pinyin Romanization system, more accurately reflects its Mandarin Chinese pronunciation, which has never changed.

Nanjing was also the site of one of the most notorious war crimes of the World War II: the Nanjing Massacre. Between December 1937, when the Nationalist government fled west in advance of the Japanese Imperial army, and February 1938, between 100,000 and 300,000 citizens of Nanjing were killed, a message from the conquering Japanese to other Chinese cities not to resist. Hundreds of thousands of women in the city were raped by Japanese forces, giving the incident its alternate name, "The Rape of Nanjing." The incident is still a point of tension in Sino-Japanese relations, and as such, Nanjing will not likely be a center for Japanese outsourcing.

Today Nanjing remains one of China's few walled cities, with its city almost entirely intact except for spots where it was damaged during the war and during construction and development since then. However, as capital of lush and prosperous Jiangsu, Nanjing is a solid second-tier city that has benefited greatly from its proximity to Shanghai and other major urban areas in China's central coastal area.

The city is also a major stop on the Yangzi River, giving it another outlet for trade and goods heading to Shanghai or upstream to China's interior.

Nanjing is one of ten national software bases, as designated by the Ministry of Commerce, and received the title in December 2006.[57] In February 2007, Nanjing announced it would host Satyam Computer Services Ltd.'s largest outsourcing service facility outside of India.[58] The center, to open in Nanjing Software Park, will employ 2,500 software engineers, and increase Satyam's headcount in China from 400 to around 3,000. Satyam is India's fourth largest outsourcing service company.[59] The move is a huge and legitimizing step for Nanjing's outsourcing industry and may serve to attract other large outsourcing enterprises.

SHENZHEN

Population   Over 10 million[60]

Software Parks or Technology Zones   Shenzhen Hi-tech Industrial Park; Qianhai Industrial Park, Liuxiandong Industrial Park, Shiyan Industrial Park, South Guangming Industrial Park, Guanlan-Longhua-Banxuegang Industrial Park, Baolong Industrial Park, Shenzhen Grand Industrial Zone (including Export Processing Zone).

Top University or Universities   Shenzhen University, Shenzhen Polytechnic, Shenzhen Institute of Information Technology, Guangdong Jianhua Polytechnic, and Shenzhen Senior Technical Institute. Also in Shenzhen is the University Town, completed and opened in 2003. It is used by Qinghua University, Beijing University, and Harbin Institute of Technology as Shenzhen campuses for nearly 2,000 full-time students enrolled on a private basis.

International Air, Rail, and Road Connections   Fortune and politics smiled upon Shenzhen when they placed it just north of Hong Kong's border with the rest of China. Although during the 1990s, especially prior to Hong Kong's return to China in 1997, travel in and out of Hong Kong was very difficult for People's Republic citizens, movement back and forth to

Hong Kong is now a simple administrative procedure, backed with superb transportation infrastructure on both sides of the border.

To solve the problem of travel eligibility into or out of Hong Kong, Shenzhen Huangtian International Airport has grown into a regional air hub in its own right. Part of its appeal is to residents of Hong Kong, especially those already living in the New Territories, closer to the border, who use Huangtian to reach other destinations in China for 50 percent or less what it would cost to fly from Hong Kong International Airport. Travelers from the rest of China enter the Hong Kong SAR in the same manner, making use of ferries, buses, and light rail to reach destinations in Hong Kong via several border posts.

International flights link Shenzhen with regional destinations in Japan, Korea, Singapore, Thailand, and even to Macau. International travelers from North America or Europe can land in Hong Kong or Guangzhou and then make their way by road or rail to Shenzhen.

Shenzhen is the end of the line for China's busiest rail link, from Beijing to the border station at Lo Wu in Shenzhen, although a daily through train in each direction serves Beijing and Shanghai from Hong Kong. Shenzhen serves all major destinations within China by rail, almost always via Guangzhou. Lo Wu is a short walk over the Shenzhen River and a straightforward border clearance to reach the respective side. Hong Kong–bound travelers may board the Kowloon-Canton Railway (KCR) and now connect to Tsimshatsui at the end of the Kowloon Peninsula, just across the harbor from Hong Kong Island. The journey takes about one hour. Travelers can also switch from the KCR to the Mass Transit Railway (MTR), Hong Kong's swift and efficient subway, to reach numerous destinations around the SAR.

Those taking the direct train to Hong Kong will arrive at Hung Hom Station in East Kowloon.

Bus service from Shenzhen to neighboring cities, including Dongguan, Guangzhou, Zhuhai, and Hong Kong runs a continuous basis.

Shenzhen also offers ferry service to destinations in the Pearl River Delta, including near the airport, which offers a convenient sea route to Hong Kong. Hong Kong, Zhuhai (the SAR just north of Macau), Macau, Dongguan, and Guangzhou are all served from Shenzhen.

History and Description   If the phrase "You've come a long way, baby," applies to any city in China, that city is Shenzhen. In May 1980, the small fishing village of Shenzhen, then with a population of about 30,000, hit the geopolitical lottery: it became one of China's first Special Economic Zones (SEZs), the first of a series of designated areas where the communist giant would experiment with capitalism. Shenzhen was different from the other choices of SEZs in that it had no history of foreign trade prior to the establishment of the People's Republic in 1949.

Shenzhen is now China's second-richest city, having only recently been passed by Shanghai, and is also one of its most densely populated. Unlike most of its rivals, Shenzhen's history is rather short. It does mean, however, that it is not saddled with any historical baggage.

The city remains a magnet for talent, which makes up in part for its lack of a significant university structure. Also, with the possible exception of Beijing, Shenzhen has one of China's most diverse populations in terms of people from all over the country, and therefore enjoys an egalitarian spirit that is freer from regional and linguistic rivalries than other cities. Being just north of Hong Kong, Shenzhen is also a refuge for young and talented people seeking a better life away from some of China's colder climes.

Since the mid-1990s, the city has focused on the development of seven major industries including computer software, IT, microelectronics and components, video and audio products, electro-mechanical integration, and key of light industry and energy projects. Meanwhile, new industries such as pharmaceuticals, medical equipment, biotechnology, and new materials have grown rapidly.[61] Shenzhen is the only city that we have included that does not hold the distinction of being designated a national software base. However, this has not in any way detracted from its attractiveness as an outsourcing center, nor has it hindered outsourcing growth in the city.

Shenzhen is home to some of China's most successful high-tech companies, such as Cisco Systems' rival Huawei Technologies and ZTE and has representation of more than 400 of the world's 500 largest companies.[62] Shenzhen also hosts 15 percent of China's IT industry and has the highest per capita income in the country.[63]

The high technology sector has become the driving force behind the local economy. High-tech output value soared to 320 billion yuan (US$4.1 billion) in 2004, an increase of 28.8 percent over the previous year, accounting for 49.2 percent of the total industrial output. The development of IT is prominent in the city with a total output value increase by 30 percent, laying a solid foundation for economic growth.[64]

IBM operates a global services delivery center in Shenzhen along with its global procurement center.[65]

While these are currently the primary destinations for outsourcing services in China for the time being, there are certainly others that will develop their outsourcing landscape for the IT services field over time.

Close to Beijing, the city of Tianjin, also administered directly by the central government, is a talent center that offers lower costs than those in the capital, and has been a center of high-tech manufacturing for years. Specifically, the Tianjin Economic and Technological Development Area

(TEDA) is home to corporations including Motorola, Samsung Hyundai, and LG, and is now entering the high-end engineering services market. TEDA has been a model technology zone, and we expect to see more in outsourcing there in the future.

Near Shanghai are two smaller cities, Suzhou and Wuxi. Both lie between the coastal giant and the Jiangsu provincial capital of Nanjing. Known as much for their scenic beauty as for their industrial might, both are offering lower-cost facilities, and therefore may even receive outsourced subcontracts from their larger neighbors. Although the two lack local university communities, their pleasant surroundings may serve to attract talent put off by life in big cities.

Finally, Chongqing, China's largest city and the fourth such municipality directly administered by the central government, is entering the outsourcing arena. Significant direct investment from the central government in making Chongqing an inland port—one of the aims of the Three Gorges Dam project—is also leading high-tech service outsourcing in its direction. Its Sichuan province rival Chengdu has already demonstrated that inland cities can successfully adopt the outsourcing model, and there is ample evidence that Chongqing will follow suit.

ENDNOTES

1. www.chinadaily.com.cn/english/doc/2005-01/07/content_406996.htm.
2. www.sourcingmag.com/content/c050926a.asp
3. www.zparkworld.com/tenants.asp?menuid=ps6
4. Ibid.
5. www.china.org.cn/english/BAT/195642.htm
6. Ibid.
7. www.chinadaily.com.cn/en/doc/2003-12/05/content_287714.htm
8. www.emporis.com/en/wm/ci/?id=100223
9. www.dlhitech.gov.cn
10. http://2003.dl.gov.cn/i18n/en/investment/2203_16139.jsp
11. www.dlut.edu.cn/dutn/dut-e/main.htm
12. www.lnnu.edu.cn/english/english.htm
13. http://english.dlmu.edu.cn/
14. http://english.people.com.cn/200603/15/eng20060315_250672.html
15. http://2003.dl.gov.cn/i18n/en/investment/
16. www.deloitte.com/dtt/section_node/0,1042,sid%253D10721,00.html
17. Ibid.
18. www.china.org.cn/english/BAT/156122.htm
19. http://invest.chengdu.gov.cn/english/detail.asp?id=105&ClassID=
    020301

20. www.cdht.gov.cn/tzfw1/en/en-01.htm
21. www.answers.com/Chengdu
22. www.cdairport.com/cdairport/en_front/index.jsp
23. http://wccdaily.scol.com.cn/2006/12/29/20061229415414171321 8.htm
24. http://english.people.com.cn/200610/26/eng20061026_315185.html
25. www.managementconsultancy.co.uk/itweek/news/2158617/eds-double-chinese-outsourcing
26. http://english.people.com.cn/200610/30/eng20061030_316355.html
27. www.zdnetasia.com/news/business/0,39044229,61974725,00.htm
28. www.answers.com/Chengdu
29. Ibid.
30. Ibid.
31. http://sie.xjtu.edu.cn/xa_intro_en.php
32. http://resources.alibaba.com/book/industrypark/detail/31247/ Xi_an_High_tech_Park_including_Xi_an_Software_Park_Xi_an_ University_Science_Park_.htm
33. www.china.org.cn/english/BAT/32476.htm
34. Ibid.
35. http://resources.alibaba.com/book/industrypark/detail/31247/ Xi_an_High_tech_Park_including_Xi_an_Software_Park_Xi_an_ University_Science_Park_.htm
36. www.sourcingmag.com/content/c050926a.asp
37. http://english.people.com.cn/200609/13/eng20060913_302413.html
38. http://english.people.com.cn/200610/27/eng20061027_315764.html
39. http://en.wikipedia.org/wiki/Jinan
40. www.qilusoft.org/english/introduction.asp
41. www.jinan.gov.cn/20050808/column/1842.htm
42. http://en.wikipedia.org/wiki/Qi_(state)
43. http://english.people.com.cn/200112/10/eng20011210_86300.shtml
44. http://english.hangzhou.gov.cn/english/context/Population& Employment/userobject1ai21.html
45. http://members.forbes.com/global/2005/0919/024.html
46. www.zhejiang.gov.cn/zjforeign/english/node491/userobject1ai10241. html
47. http://offshoringmanagement.rediffblogs.com/2005_19_06_ offshoringmanagement_archive.html
48. www.panasianbiz.com/2007/02/indian_outsourcing_king_outsou.html
49. www.chinadaily.com.cn/china/2007-02/12/content_807703.htm
50. www.infoplease.com/ce6/world/A0858513.html
51. www.china.org.cn/english/BAT/190633.htm
52. http://english.nanjing.gov.cn/cps/site/English/2006/jrnj1.htm

53. www.njnhz.com.cn/english
54. www.njuct.edu.cn/english
55. http://english.nanjing.gov.cn/cps/site/English/2006/jrnj8.htm
56. http://en.wikipedia.org/wiki/Lukou_International_Airport
57. http://english.people.com.cn/200612/04/eng20061204_328182.html
58. www.networkworld.com/news/2007/020807-satyam-sets-up-new-facility.html
59. Ibid.
60. http://english.sina.com/china/1/2005/0821/43131.html
61. http://english.sz.gov.cn/economy/200509/t20050930_506.htm
62. www.answers.com/Shenzhen
63. www.deloitte.com/dtt/section_node/0,1042,sid%253D10727,00.html
64. http://english.sz.gov.cn/economy/200509/t20050929_478.htm
65. http://english.people.com.cn/200603/27/eng20060327_253810.html

IT Outsourcing, Business Process Outsourcing, and Knowledge Process Outsourcing in China

T he growth in outsourcing since the 1980s is the result of the increased development of the global economy, accompanied by a shift in business philosophy. With changes in political and economic conditions globally, there has been an emergence of a global labor pool. China's labor pool and its availability to the global marketplace is a significant example. Prior to this period, companies sought to diversify their business in order to reduce risk brought on by limited talent choices, locking companies into higher costs and little choice among service providers.

This diversification of labor was achieved in a number of ways (e.g., organic growth by adding new lines of business to produce new products and services. However, diversification was perhaps more commonly achieved through mergers and acquisitions). The intention of building highly diversified businesses was to reduce risk by having an overall portfolio of lines of businesses or distinct business entities themselves. Many industries are cyclical in terms of demand and production, impacting their profit cycle. The intention of increasing company diversification was to balance the timing of industry cycles within diversified businesses and thereby offset risk and maximize profit.

Companies discovered, however, that there were significant challenges to running a group of highly diversified businesses. One need only look back at the number of unsuccessful large-scale mergers of the 1980s. These mergers failed to produce the significant results predicted from the synergies of the combined businesses. With acquisitions, companies were not always able to successfully incorporate the new businesses for maximum results. In many cases the companies retained nearly the full structures of acquired businesses in a decentralized business model. However, the decentralized business model then resulted in duplicate activities and business processes, often on the administrative side, which negatively impacted overall costs. In these cases companies did not successfully redesign their value chains to take advantage of their capabilities as a whole.

With diversified products, services, and industries, companies found it challenging to manage the overall entities successfully and synergistically. Companies struggled to focus their management and organizational energy on the right business priorities, issues, and products to deliver maximum value for shareholders. Without experience or in-house expertise in the new industry areas, companies struggled to maintain the success of merged or acquired business lines. In addition, some companies had achieved success based on branding related to their core products and services, and the diversification or merging of their businesses negatively impacted their brands. Executive management of companies underestimated the power of branding of not only products and services but the companies themselves, in the eyes of consumers, the larger corporate marketplace, and the financial markets.

Many of these diversified companies began to dismantle or sell acquired businesses and business lines. In some cases businesses or activities that were not considered part of the company's core competency were eliminated or outsourced. The companies refocused their efforts on their original or most successful business areas. This is often referred to as their core business, and typically represents the products or service brands most closely associated with the company's success. Companies redefined their mission, vision, product and service offerings, and business models based on their perceived best chance of success in the marketplace. For public companies, the role of shareholder pressure to deliver regular, increasingly successful business results also contributed to this business shift. It should be noted, however, that some major global diversified business entities are still highly successful with a diversified decentralized model due to superior management and captive market share.

Eventually companies learned from history and, rather than just divest, they began to proactively plan their functions within their supply and value chain and transfer functions when appropriate. This process of adjusting not only the product and service models but the business model and supporting activities themselves is now a reality of competing in today's global marketplace. This reality is contributing to the dramatic growth of outsourced business, and more specifically, business processes.

Outsourcing occurs when a company purchases products, services, or both from an outside supplier in order to achieve some type of business advantage. Typically, the company was previously performing the work in its own facilities. Today, outsourcing is a common part of a global business model, carried out by companies of all sizes and many different industries. Initially, the outsourced functions were transactional and administrative processes that the company had difficulty successfully carrying out. In some cases companies did not have the appropriate investments in IT to carry out the activities successfully, such as the payroll process. Outsourcing vendors, by focusing on business processes as part of their business model, provide better service enforced by contracts and with appropriate management oversight.

Outsourcing can be a considerable undertaking for a company because it involves changing the company's business or value chain model. Although outsourcing can be done on a small scale, typically companies make a significant initial investment in order to fully take advantage of the outsourcing capabilities and economies of scale. Once a business area has been outsourced, if unsuccessful, it can be extremely costly, time consuming, and difficult for a company to take back its business functions. Even the planning and implementation of outsourcing takes considerable management time, resources, and focus as well the opportunity costs of not developing other projects.

The benefits of outsourcing depend in part on the reason a company chooses to outsource. The development of the global economy has now made available a global workforce. Due to different economies and living standards, the cost of various workforces around the world covers a wide spectrum. This gives companies the choice of the cost of labor. Along with that comes the risk that the labor cannot deliver the products or services needed at the quality required by the outsourcing company. Initially, cost reduction has been a dominant driver for outsourcing although other benefits are realized. Cost savings based on labor alone in lower cost countries can be dramatic. Estimates are that IT workers in China get 20 cents on the dollar compared to U.S. employees. However, customers outsourcing to lower-cost countries have also complained that cost savings are somewhat offset by internal costs to successfully manage the relationship. Along with outsourcing is the significant risk of a loss in control over the product or service. This risk is in relation to the value of the business process to the outsourcing company.

In addition to cost opportunities, there are many reasons that companies seek outsourcing. Common drivers for outsourcing are well documented and surveys are conducted annually to reflect the changing market. For example, companies seek to be closer to global markets they serve or new markets they hope to serve. The emergence of a middle class with purchasing power in China is bringing businesses to the Asia market. Companies want to reduce process backlog, an example of which may be application fix requests. Companies seek to improve service delivery to end customers; this can be satisfied through the implementation of an outsourced call center. Companies want to reduce their focus on back office processing, which they may not be successfully carrying out in their own company. With changing technologies, companies may have difficulty hiring IT workers with the right range of technology skills to support the companies' changing technology environment. In some cases, outsourcing is a me-too phenomenon, where companies are aware other large companies including competitors are outsourcing. Companies believe they must also do this to be successful in the global marketplace.

Successful outsourcing requires a strong executive management understanding and consensus of a company's mission, vision, strategy, and current capabilities. In other words, "Company, know thyself." Decisions regarding outsourcing are among the most strategic that can be made by a company. They address the difficult questions of why a company is in business, what it means for a company to be in business, and which activities a company wants its own employees to carry out. The answers to these difficult questions can depend on the point of the company in its development, the executive management team in power, and its current financial status. There can be negative repercussions of outsourcing for companies that lay off workers and close plants in order to produce products and services more cheaply in other countries. Studies are unclear as to the long-term impact of outsourcing on the host country, with some studies showing an actual increase of jobs in the host country due to improved company performance.

SCOPE OF OUTSOURCING

When one thinks of outsourcing, the outsourcing of manufacturing to low-cost countries is typically what comes to mind; the outsourced activity is a business process that produces a product or service. These business processes can be of nearly any type in the business model, but are often classified as IT outsourcing (ITO), business process outsourcing (BPO), and knowledge process outsourcing (KPO). There are other variations by process type as well. In the case of some outsource vendors, they differentiate not by classification of business process, but by functional practices. Vendors may classify what types of business processes they can manage for clients by functional categories such as finance and accounting and sales and marketing. Some vendors specialize by vertical markets such as financial services, manufacturing, telecommunications, and healthcare. The specialization of outsource vendors will continue to develop as vendors seek to fill market niches. In addition, the generalization of some outsource vendors will continue to grow as vendors invest in infrastructure and technology. These larger vendors will then be able to support increased scale and scope of business processes. The large vendors can leverage their current investments but may become less appealing to smaller and midsize companies that need to ensure they receive adequate focus from a potential outsource vendor.

In terms of scope, outsourcing can be undertaken to varying degrees, ranging from total outsourcing to selective outsourcing. Total outsourcing may involve dismantling entire departments or divisions and transferring the employees, facilities, equipment, and complete responsibility for a product or function to an outside vendor. In contrast, selective outsourcing may target a single, time-consuming task within a department, such as preparing payroll or manufacturing a minor component, that can be handled more efficiently by an outside specialist. This can be referred to as outtasking. Outtasking in general refers to business process activities or tasks that are smaller in scale than outsourcing. The term outtasking helps companies to limit what they are outsourcing to a manageable size.

Vendors providing outsourcing services are generally grouped into two models: BPO and application service provider (ASP). In the BPO model, major resources and assets are transferred from the company to the vendor. Under the ASP model vendors concentrate on providing selected services for multiple clients. Many variations exist within these two models. Vendors originated from the need to fulfill a specific market demand and therefore range widely in their models and service offerings. In some cases outsource vendors themselves were businesses spun off of larger companies and therefore retain services from their historical composition and parent ties. There is a wide range of pricing models, options, and services, which makes it difficult to compare vendors. When comparing vendors the same services and measurements are not presented uniformly. While some classic measurements are used, the vendors have their own measurements unique to their culture, products, and services. This requires companies investigating outsourcing to define their own measurement models for evaluation based on their own strategy, priorities, and internal measurement criteria.

Information Technology Outsourcing

There is no shortage of acronyms in the outsourcing environment. As the outsourcing marketplace changes, so too does the scope of the term information technology outsourcing. ITO is defined differently by different vendors but in very general terms refers to the outsourcing of IT processes to produce IT-related products and services, for example, an IT product could be a custom-developed application. Commonly outsourced information technology processes are software development, testing, and quality assurance. Infrastructure management outsourcing (IMO) is another classification of IT-related services. Another relevant term is infrastructure outsourcing (IO), which is a subset of ITO.

Background on China   The movement in business is toward improving the company's performance through the application of globally recognized standards and practices. ISO 9000 and the Capability Maturity Model for Software (CMM for Software) were two recognized initiatives that have gained widespread acceptance around the world. The first versions of both ISO 9000 and the CMM were originally developed around the same time, 1987. ISO 9000 was created as a model for establishing a quality system that was general enough to be used by all industries and all disciplines. The initial CMM was created to be a model for improvement for organizations that perform software engineering development and maintenance, based on best practices that should be implemented. In China, you will find many organizations that have applied ISO 9000 in general. You will also find many more organizations that have adopted the CMM for Software as the guiding model for improving their software engineering practices. But time does not stand still. While the use of CMM for Software has grown significantly on a global basis, it is now also growing in usage dramatically with a focus on how to help the expansion of a business in the newly emerging economic bases of power, such as China.

The need for improvement of process capability is recognized quickly when organizations grow rapidly. Rapid expansion requires the use of more robust and mature processes to operate effectively and efficiently. A solid process foundation and principles will support the core needs of any organization regardless of their current or future size. The ability to change scale and complexity is being challenged in a new way in China today. Some companies are expanding their workforce by double or triple within one year. Without a cohesive process foundation their operations will be much more likely to be in chaos. The need for following proven standards is very high. The intent of CMM for Software and the more recently enhanced model CMMI is to instill discipline, which is precisely what companies in China needed for them to be recognized as competitive in the global marketplace today.

Growth of CMMI in China   Along with China's phenomenal economic and business growth comes the need for more complex and reliable applications and systems to support that growth. It was only natural that many companies in China would look to the future to see where they needed to be. When the

Software Engineering Institute (SEI) announced the "sunsetting" of CMM for Software and moving to the enhanced CMMI model, it was inevitable that companies in China would get on board quickly. Companies in China are frequently looking for the newest concepts and latest ideas to help them improve. Furthermore, achieving higher levels of capability, whether it would be maturity levels or capability levels, will gain their company recognition, which is the focus of their efforts. Now, not only has the CMM for Software been sunsetted, but the CMMI product suite is evolving as well. The original sunset date for v1.1 of the CMMI Product Suite was December 31, 2007. That date was accelerated to August 31, 2007 because of the policy changes and model changes that have been made. What this means is that no more appraisals for v1.1 CMMI Product Suite will be recognized by the SEI after August 31, 2007.

This growth and expansion of companies using the CMMI model is encouraged and supported by various city governments in China. The city governments offer incentives for the companies to achieve higher levels of maturity applying the concepts of CMMI. This support from the government is part of the overall strategy of establishing China as a global hub for outsourcing. With the significant growth of outsourcing centers in the world, the support of the Chinese government in promoting standards will assist and help to drive the improvement for companies in China. Other governments around the world have created similar incentives. This support will certainly have an impact and is intended to increase the role and developing influence for companies from China in the outsourcing market.

Process Maturity Levels in China   The implementation of an improvement model such as CMMI within organizations is complex, and there is no short path to success. The progress of implementation of CMMI in companies based in China is increasing all the time. Just as most companies all over the world, companies in China implementing CMMI typically start at the lower levels of capability and work toward higher levels of maturity. Many companies in China have progressed to Maturity Levels 2 and 3. Some have even achieved Maturity Levels 4 or 5. If the company gives its authorization, the SEI will publish their appraisal results on its Web site: http://sas.sei.cmu.edu/pars. In 2006, two of the 20 organizations (10 percent) that published their achievement of Maturity Level 4 were in China. Likewise, in 2006, ten of the 60 organizations (16 percent) that published their achievement of Maturity Level 5 were in China. The improvement of the overall industry around the world utilizing CMMI will take a long time, but progress is being made and some organizations can demonstrate their improvement quantitatively.

These companies in China, and elsewhere in the world, that are implementing CMMI practices, see the value and the benefit of not only the recognition of the capabilities they have developed, but also the discipline infused into their organization and processes. Culturally, if Chinese employees are told to follow a process, in general they are compliant. This is perhaps in contrast to other cultures in countries supporting outsourcing hubs that have different cultural forces influencing local workers. The companies in China that have achieved Level 3 and above have had significant changes in the way their employees operate. The Maturity Level truly does reflect implementing better practices not likely to be found in organizations with lower levels of maturity. The compliance of Chinese employees in implementing standards, the willingness to learn, and the resultant business success can be seen as critical success factors in the growth of outsourcing hubs in China.

Be a Knowledgeable Consumer   The Standard CMMI Appraisal Method for Process Improvement (SCAMPI) process is considered to be a self-evaluation technique. It can be utilized in a source selection process, but most appraisals are initiated by the organization itself for the purposes of improvement. The results are determined by an Appraisal Team, which is led by an Authorized Lead Appraiser. The Authorized Lead Appraiser is authorized by SEI to lead such appraisal activities. All Authorized Lead Appraisers go through an extensive training and experience requirements process and review to receive their authorization. Because of the nature of a self-evaluation mechanism, some appraisal results have been questioned for their accuracy and validity. SEI has taken this issue very seriously. It has conducted quality assurance reviews and interviews in some cases and reserves the right to review any appraisal utilizing the SCAMPI Appraisal Method. This increased activity with regard to review of Authorized Lead Appraisers and appraisal results provides much more assurance that the results are reliable and trustworthy. All companies considering whether to use the services of an organization that claims to be at a specific Maturity Level or Capability Level should follow some simple guidelines:

- Know what should be expected of an organization at each Maturity Level
- Understand the difference between capabilities at each Maturity Level
- Know how Capability Levels differ from Maturity Levels
- Ask probing questions to validate the claims of specific levels of achievement
- Ask to see the Findings Report, not just the certificate hanging on the wall

With a few key questions you can find out whether the organization really understands what it means to be operating at a high level of maturity. This is good advice regardless of where the company is located. To further enhance the reliability of the appraisal results, SEI has made some significant improvements to the SCAMPI appraisal process in the upgrade to version 1.2.

One significant improvement has been the creation of an expiration date for the appraisal results. Previously, the results of an appraisal were good indefinitely. They were only intended to be a snapshot, indicating the capabilities of an organization at that particular time. But organizations would claim to be a particular level of maturity even though the results may have been several years old. The danger there was that an organization could tell you they had been appraised at Maturity Level 5, but the appraisal actually occurred five years ago. Their processes most likely changed dramatically in the past five years. Now, all appraisals completed using SCAMPI v1.2 have a three-year expiration date. After that three-year window the results are not accepted as being reflective of their organization without conducting another appraisal.

Another significant difference is the level of detail the Authorized Lead Appraiser must report to SEI. This includes much more detail about the planning activities prior to the appraisal happening. This more detailed reporting also supports a more reliable and trustworthy process in developing the results of the appraisal. All SCAMPI appraisals completed after August 31, 2007 will have to follow SCAMPI v1.2 and the new Appraisal Disclosure Statement; v1.1 SCAMPI will no longer be supported.

Furthermore, starting in October 2006, SEI is certifying High Maturity Lead Appraisers. The High Maturity Lead Appraisers are accepted to have the required knowledge and experience to understand the intricate and complex details of the higher levels of maturity. So, any organization working toward the higher levels of maturity need to make sure their Lead Appraiser is recognized as qualified by SEI.

SEI has also created the policy that all SCAMPI appraisals following v1.2 that will become public record (e.g., announced in a press release, published on an organization's Web site, or posted on the published SCAMPI appraisal results Web page) must be led by an SEI-authorized SCAMPI Lead Appraiser from an external, third-party organization.

It is not acceptable that an Authorized Lead Appraiser lead an appraisal of the organization where they work. It must be led by an Authorized Lead Appraiser from a separate organization. The third-party organization may be within the same company—being from a different division would satisfy this requirement. This policy, however, does not seem to go far enough.

Internal forces within the same company may still represent a conflict of interest. The most reliable way to eliminate conflicts of interest would be to require the Authorized Lead Appraiser be from a completely separate company, not just a third-party organization.

SEI has also considered other steps to further add credibility to the overall appraisal process. Some steps are in the works but not yet complete at the time of the writing of this book, including changing the Lead Appraiser authorization process to become a certification process. There are subtle but significant implications in saying a Lead Appraiser is certified. This may be coming shortly. The bottom line is that you need to be a knowledgeable consumer when you consider using the services of an outsource provider. Know what you should expect and ask a lot of detailed questions.

Development of CMMI to Benefit Customers   While CMM for Software was focused on processes that were predominantly Software Engineering, SEI saw the need to expand the model to the CMMI. CMMI encompasses not just Software Engineering but Systems Engineering as well. The intention was to add more benefit to the end customer of the products and services because the systems created today are rarely just software. In previous years of IT development, software was custom developed for homogeneous IT environments that were not integrated with the world outside a company's great walls. However, in today's environment software is often acquired, modified, and integrated with other software in heterogeneous and complex technology environments. What is considered the development of a system might include software but could also include hardware and systems engineering components. CMMI is a broader model that addresses all of these types of issues. CMMI v1.2 has also incorporated changes to the model to better reflect the learning of how the model has evolved and improved.

Assurance of Results for Customers with CMMI   With CMMI, the results indicate a level of performance that becomes predictable so the buyer should better understand what can be expected from the supplier. In the ITO world this can be very important to a customer selecting an ITO vendor/partner. It seems all outsourcing vendors make claims of product and service quality and low cost. However, with the implementation of CMMI practices the performance of a product/service should now be able to be better understood. Depending on the Capability Level or Maturity Level that a company achieves they can be expected to be following certain specific best practices. For example, for Maturity Level 2, Project Management practices are the foundation. For Maturity Level 3 the organization establishes standards and processes that are common across the whole organization. For Maturity Level 4 the company utilizes the historical data collected from the standard processes in order to start applying statistical techniques to manage quantitatively instead of anecdotally. The benefit of Maturity Level 5 is that the company has firmly entrenched their knowledge, skills, and statistical methods so they can make improvements in the process based on the actual performance in the organization and the plans they have put in place. At Maturity Level 5 the plans are based on the needs and expectations of the customer. To implement a model this robust and sustain the practices requires significant leadership on the part of management as well as follow up by lower levels of management and trained operational staff.

The impact on the customer of the IT services company is predictable. In lower-maturity organizations, the customers receive whatever the organization happens to produce. At higher levels of capability the organization is focused on needs of the customer and provides assurance they can achieve those goals. The spectrum of maturity levels move from repeatable, to organizational, to quantitative, to institutionalization of improvement. The benefit to the end customer may be significant in time and cost savings and ultimately higher quality of products and services received.

Role of Standards in Selecting an IT Outsourcing Vendor   In outsourcing IT services to an IT services company, customers may be transferring IT processes such as application development, package selection, project management, requirements management, integration, quality assurance, configuration control of the system, engineering practices from requirements analysis, design, verification, and validation through to product integration. These processes can carry a great deal of risk. If a customer selects an IT services company that is using CMMI, and the customer understands the model, then they know what to expect from that supplier. This gives the customer a better understanding of the capabilities of that supplier in regards to the business needs the customer plans to outsource. This enables the customer to jointly plan better with their outsourcing partner. Note, in many cases if the ITO partner has implemented CMMI the outsourcing partner may have more rigorous processes, practices, and standards than the customer had in their originating organization. This may then actually yield a higher quality level than the customer was producing with their own processes.

Benefits of Outsourcing to a Company using CMMI   In addition to understanding the level of process performance and the resultant level of product and service quality of a company utilizing CMMI, there are other benefits to outsourcing to a service provider who is utilizing rigorous standards. Following the principles and practices of CMMI, companies have a variety of mechanisms with which they can have interfaces with the customer. Once they look at practices that have been employed, customers of the organization have established communication vehicles directly with management and also through the Configuration Management area and the Quality Assurance function. There are multiple avenues of gaining insight into not only the status but the quality characteristics of the project being performed by the IT services provider. By using a model like CMMI, the IT service provider gives much more value to the client. For example, there are controls in place to ensure the process produces the right results, with minimum of rework, and there are channels for communication and involvement. Process performance measurements within CMMI are involved in every level of maturity (General Practice 2.8 Monitor and Control Process) and provide the customer with information about the performance of the process performed on their behalf in an outsourcing agreement.

Business Process Outsourcing   BPO is the usage of specialist process vendors, often offshore, to provide and manage a company's enterprise processes and applications. BPO typically refers to certain types of business processes that are more commodity based than strategic. Business processes can be classified in a number of ways; one of these is the value of the business process to the company, which is the outsourcing customer. If a business process is strategic in nature or delivers strategic value to the enterprise, for example, the Strategic Planning process, it is referred to as a strategic process. Commodity business processes may be higher-volume processes, and may be lower-margin processes in terms of profitability to the enterprise. The focus on commodity processes is typically to produce them at lower cost. Specific types of processes are selected by companies for outsourcing; examples of these are IT processes, human resources, accounting, and payroll processes. The delivery of these processes or the services they produce are often provided through a call-center channel. BPO refers to all of the effort needed to support and enable the business process. This would typically include the software, the process management, and the people to operate the service. Typically BPO is dependent on IT.

Knowledge Process Outsourcing

KPO is the promise of the future of the BPO industry. Knowledge processes are those that require more thought, decision making, and specialized knowledge. Once commodity business processes are successfully outsourced, the vision is that knowledge processes can be outsourced as well. In KPOs, business processes are high-end processes like valuation, research, patent filing, legal and insurance claims, medical diagnoses and reports, and other processes depending on the industry the KPO pursues. Typically, these industries include pharmaceuticals, biotechnology, financial services, research and analytics, technology research, computer-aided simulation and engineering, business research, legal services, and financial analysis.

The goals and advantages in outsourcing knowledge processes are the same as those for business processes: cost savings, operational efficiencies, improved quality, and access to a large and skilled workforce base. Outsourced knowledge processes will bring higher profit margins to outsourcing vendors than commodity business processes, but will still result in lower costs to the outsourcing customer due to labor differentials globally.

The promise of KPO is the delivery of business expertise rather than just process expertise. The types of processes that are considered knowledge processes demand advanced analytical and specialized skill of the knowledge workers who will carry them out. A highly skilled and talented workforce is needed including MBAs, master's, or Ph.D. holders, engineers, doctors, lawyers, and accountants, for example. In addition to these new labor requirements, increased training and management oversight are needed. The outsourcing of knowledge processes faces more challenges than BPO. Some of the challenges involved in KPO will be in maintaining higher quality standards, investment in the necessary infrastructure specific to the KPO industries, the need for the development of the appropriate talent pool, the requirement of a higher level of control, the assurance of confidentiality, and enhanced risk management practices.

Today, some believe that the successful outsourcing of knowledge processes on a large scale is still hype. However, it is inevitable as the skills in the global marketplace continue to develop, that eventually the processes that are outsourced will continue to move up the scale in complexity and knowledge required. India is currently considered to be the most successful market for KPO; however, China is again expected to be a strong player in the long term. While the promise of KPO has yet to be globally proven, it has the potential for enormous growth but will require even more rigorous adherence to business process performance standards. With knowledge processes there will be no room for error and the standards and certifications of the outsourcers will need to be specific to the industries and processes they are supporting.

This market is currently an immature market but one certainly to watch in the global field.

GLOBAL OUTSOURCING OPTIONS FOR CUSTOMERS

For companies seeking to outsource business and knowledge processes, the choices of service providers and countries to source to have never been richer. With the rise in economic development and business ventures in many areas of the world it seems every newly developed country is now a potential outsourcing hub. Business entities in major markets of the world all offer outsourcing capabilities to companies that are seeking to change their business models. Classifications of markets that provide outsourcing are commonly:

- Asia: India, China, Malaysia, Philippines, Vietnam, Thailand, Singapore
- Europe: Ireland, Hungary, Romania, Bulgaria, Czech Republic, Poland, Ukraine, Russia
- Middle East: Israel, Egypt
- Africa: Ghana, South Africa
- The Americas: Canada, Mexico, Costa Rica, Brazil, Argentina

However, with this potential is the challenge of selecting service providers who are the right match for a customer's current and future needs. There have already been significant failure stories of outsourced efforts that resulted in tears and lost revenue for the optimistic outsourcing customer. How can companies make sense of the options when the potential outsourcing service providers all make similar service promises?

ADVANTAGES OF OUTSOURCING TO CHINA

While labor arbitrage was the initial business driver for shifting work, the locations for lowest-cost labor continue to shift as new markets emerge. It is not economically feasible for companies to continue to chase the lowest-cost market. Companies will want to outsource to lower-cost markets, but other drivers will become more dominant. In terms of global competition for outsourced business, India appears to have a clear lead over other global players. China, however, is emerging as a significant player that could eventually challenge India. While any presentation from an outsourcing provider will show their company and country as the best solution, clearly there are advantages and disadvantages to any locale that must be considered and weighed against a company's specific strategic needs.

Advantages to outsourcing in China include:

- A workforce of undisputable size that is educated and skilled
- Low wages—China is not yet experiencing the wage inflation that is impacting India's outsourcing model
- A large university system and an increasing cultural emphasis on university-level education

- Relatively low unemployment and less employee turnover than India
- Rapidly improving telecommunications and business infrastructure
- Chinese government has had success in modernizing the economy and these efforts appear to be continuing
- An undisputed large domestic market with growing purchasing power
- Outsourcing in China brings access to other markets geographically
- Culturally, Chinese employees are hardworking, dedicated, and eager to learn and satisfy their customers' expectations

DISADVANTAGES TO OUTSOURCING TO CHINA

There are barriers to outsourcing to China as well. A key barrier to outsourcing knowledge processes to China is concerns about security and protection of intellectual property (IP). Language is a barrier due to still developing English language capabilities, although this barrier is expected to decrease in the future as language skills improve. There is a lack of management experience and Western management business practices. There are barriers to entry into business in China. There is a lack of understanding of Chinese culture by Western companies. There is also a perception of bureaucracy and the potential for corruption in China. For companies located far away from China such as the United States, the geographic and time differences could require the customer to adapt their business practices.

SELECTION OF VENDOR PARTNERS

Each country offers its own competitive and comparative advantage to offshore outsourcing. Beyond the obvious there are certain risks to be considered. As the world changes newer risks emerge. Companies should develop their own risk models specific to their business and the processes to be outsourced. Once the risks have been identified, they should be assessed and programs should be put in place to mitigate those risks.

While there are many factors influencing the cost of outsourced business process activities, such as the cost of doing business in a specific country such as China or India, there are hidden costs that can dramatically impact the customer. For example, if a customer chooses a service provider that cannot or does not provide the appropriate level of quality of the outsourced business process, this can result in increased and repeated costs for the customer to resolve the business issues. Poor business process results by the outsourced provider can actually result in lost customers of the sponsoring organization's business. A trend of lost customers over time can result in significant business loss to the outsourcing customer. As with any new business model, there have been stories of work unsuccessfully outsourced to other countries, which then had to be reabsorbed back into the customer's business model at a significant financial loss.

DUE DILIGENCE OF THE CAPABILITIES OF VENDORS

Whether it is BPO or, ultimately, KPO, customers, in addition to weighing other significant capabilities, should look carefully at the capability of the outsourcing vendor to produce business process results of the appropriate quality level. All business processes should have an expected result within a specified performance range, depending on the process. The level of quality expected in the business processes should be documented in a service level agreement as part of the contractual agreement. Customers should perform a rigorous verification of the standards and certifications outsourcers claim in their marketing materials. With the fierce competition between outsourcers in low-cost countries there has been an inflation of capabilities of these providers through exaggerated claims. For some low-cost countries or newly formed companies there may not have been enough of a history of process execution to support claims of particular maturity levels. For example, for the Malcolm Baldrige criteria, the performance must have been demonstrated over time.

A thorough understanding of the outsourcer's capabilities in regard to the standards they follow should include not only an examination of certification documentation and reports, but an on-site review of processes and practices with special focus on the end results of the business processes. If necessary, customers should consider paying for an external, objective review. For all significant processes, the outsourcing vendor should be able to provide a variety of automated metrics demonstrating the performance of the process within acceptable levels. The customer will then have assurance that the performance results of their outsourced business or knowledge processes will equal or exceed the customer's quality and performance expectations.

IMPORTANCE OF BUSINESS PROCESS STANDARDS

The claims that outsourcing service providers make include an expansive variety of benefits and each outsourcing provider has its own comparison reports showing their superiority. Many of the claims related to business processes focus on providing lower cost and higher quality than other outsourcing providers. Ultimately, the customer must choose their outsourcing provider based on a realistic knowledge of their own company's needs. Customers must also make their decision based on trust that the outsourcing provider can truly deliver the required and promised business process results. Regardless of the due diligence that will be done, in the end there is always some element of risk, a leap of faith based on the trust that the outsourcer will deliver what they promise to deliver, and trust in part in the relationship developed with the outsourcer's management representatives.

Because business processes are the service (providing a product) to be outsourced, the performance of the business process itself has to be a factor highly scrutinized. The business process results produced from the service provider must be repeatable, measurable, and reportable. One of the ways to achieve business process repeatability, effectiveness, and measurability is by producing them in an environment in which processes, practices, and management are standards compliant and driven. The management of the outsourcing organization must be relentless in its pursuit of certification and standards to continue to raise the performance of its own organization. Without a clear and proven focus on standards, there will always be variation in business processes produced by the outsourcer, and the receiving customer cannot rely on the results produced by the outsourcer.

IMPORTANCE OF STANDARDS IN BPO

If the intention of outsourcing business processes to another company is to reduce costs and improve quality, then the customer needs to ensure that the outsourcing provider has in place stringent processes, practices, measures, and standards that will produce the desired business process results for the customer's company. While many outsourcers tout trained employees and the quality of English language skills as major selling points of the outsourcer's capabilities, these alone are not enough. Outsource providers can have very highly educated employees; however, if those employees are not following repeatable processes, according to proven process standards, this can only result in variability of the business processes. Variability of business processes results in lower quality, rework, increased cost, and decreased customer satisfaction. Education, training, language skills, and good intentions do not guarantee high-quality business process results. Clear industry and globally recognized standards must be implemented, monitored, and maintained in the outsourcing organization. These standards need to be those applicable to the types of business and knowledge processes being performed on behalf of the customer.

APPLICATION STANDARDS TO DIFFERENT PROCESS TYPES

Different industry and global standards apply to different types of processes. There is a wide variety of quality management systems, industry-specific quality standards, and industry-specific regulations. Examples of standards briefly touched upon include: CMMI, ISO 9000, ITIL, PMI, Re-engineering, Six Sigma, Lean, SAS 70, and BS7799. These represent a small but significant set of standards to which outsource vendors should aspire to.

CMMI supports processes related to the software and systems development. ISO 9000 is an international quality management framework that can be applied to a variety of industry types. The Information Technology Infrastructure Library (ITIL) standard also applies to IT-related processes; however, those are more focused on support and infrastructure. The ITIL processes include: incident management, change management, problem management, service-level management, continuity management (disaster recovery), configuration management, release management, capacity management, financial management, availability management, security management, and help-desk management. The Project Management Institute (PMI) standards apply to project management across all industries. In addition to standards that are applied to organizational processes, there are certifications also relevant to types of business process that should be obtained by individuals in the outsourcing company. IT-related certifications are abundant and should be specific to the work being performed on behalf of the customer. Process Management (re-engineering), Six Sigma, and Lean are quality management systems that drive process improvement with a continuous focus to exceed its customers' expectations in the quality of services and products provided. SAS 70 is an internationally recognized auditing standard developed by the American Institute of Certified Public Accountants (AICPA). An SAS 70 audit is widely recognized because it represents that a service organization has been through an in-depth audit of their control activities. The BS7799 certification is an internationally renowned certification for data security and integrity created by the British Standards Institute.

PROCESS SELECTION FOR OUTSOURCING

Identifying Candidate Processes for Outsourcing

It is important that the customer seeking to outsource first clearly understand and define which business processes they plan to outsource. While this sounds simple in theory, the customer should not choose to outsource processes just because the outsourcer's model provides that capability, or based on volume discounts offered by the outsourcer. The customer should carry out this not-insignificant exercise by developing a business process model (BPM) of not only their enterprise, but their entire value chain. A BPM of their value chain would include business processes that are shared with other partners in their business chain, such as other customers, joint venture partners, suppliers, and other relationships. This will give the customer a total view of all processes they are carrying out on behalf of their mission and vision. In addition, many business processes that are shared with other partners in a value chain may be processes that should be improved through outsourcing, or which may require input from other partners in the value chain. A BPM is a drill-down model that starts with mega processes (level 0), such as "generate demand" and drills down to processes at levels very specific to the customer's unique operations.

Developing a Process Model of the Extended Enterprise

Depending on the nature of the customer's business, there may be relevant industry models to assist the customer in developing a total BPM; for example, for manufacturing businesses there is the standard SCOR model (Supply Chain Operations Reference Model). This model can be used as a template to develop an overall BPM of the customer's business entity. After developing a BPM the customer should then identify and rank its candidate business processes for outsourcing. These can be ranked by a variety of factors such as type of process, strategic value, and cost to carry out the process, current process performance, and applicability for outsourcing. A sophisticated outsourcing vendor will be able to partner with the customer during this exercise in order to provide valuable input or even offer consulting services to assist and provide actionable output. Sophisticated outsourcing vendors should be able to show standard industry process models, for example, for the IT industry. Within those process models they should be able to demonstrate in which areas they provide outsourced process coverage for their customers.

Understanding the Processes to Be Outsourced

After a thorough understanding of the customer's own business, and identification and ranking of business processes for outsourcing, the customer should evaluate their potential outsourcing vendors based on the customer's established and ranked criteria. Customers should establish a ranking system for vendors based on criteria significant to their business objectives for outsourcing. This criterion should not be developed based on presentations provided by courting vendors, but developed independently based on items deemed of importance to the customer's unique business needs.

Understanding Vendor Capability Related to Processes

A significant criterion for outsourcing of business processes should be the ability of the outsourcing vendor to provide evidence of business process excellence. This should be demonstrated through certification in standards appropriate to the business processes to be supported. For example, if "manage IT projects" is a process to be outsourced, then the outsourcing vendor should demonstrate competence in project management as evidenced by practices from the PMI global standard.

This will require that the customers seeking to outsource research and understand which standards are relevant and most significant to the business processes to be outsourced. In some cases, the customer's organization may or may not have certification in standards themselves. If customers are following a specific methodology already, such as CMMI, they may seek to ensure the outsourcing vendor is following the same methodology at the same maturity level if not higher. However, it should be noted in many cases if customers choose to outsource processes in order to provide improved service delivery, these processes may currently be unsuccessful processes in the customer's organization. In this case, the customer may not have insight as to why the process is not successful in their own organization, but the customer must seek new solutions for improving the process through the outsourcing vendor.

Process Representations

Whether in the process of selecting an outsource vendor or overseeing an already outsourced business process, outsource vendors should be able to produce documentation of the business processes. This documentation is required by many of the implemented standards and will vary according to the standard followed and the documentation system of the vendor. For business processes, process documentation should be available, for example, process mapping such as integrated computer-aided manufacturing (ICAM) definition languages (IDEF), swim-lane process maps, and value stream mapping.

An example of a process mapping specific to a quality management system is Value Stream Mapping. Value Stream Mapping is designed to document manufacturing processes that are to be improved using Lean manufacturing methods. Lean manufacturing methods remove waste and nonvalue-adding activities from processes so that organizations can produce and deliver the products customers order more rapidly and at lower cost. Companies that are already following lean manufacturing methods and outsource processes to outsource vendors may wish to see the outsourced processes represented in a language they understand. In addition they may wish to synchronize these outsourced processes with their own lean process representations within the value chain.

CHAPTER 9

China's Legal Framework

For legal purposes, outsourcing can be defined as a transaction or process in which the supplier of outsourced services is based in a distant country, meaning in a country other than the one where the products or services will be sold or consumed. Today, outsourcing is a common practice throughout the technology industry and IT is the function most likely to be outsourced. With the increasingly rapid pace of technology development, many outsourcers are trying to keep up with the latest advances and prefer to shift the responsibility or risk to a firm that specializes in IT. While being evaluated with the strongest growth potential, China has been the country to watch in the global outsourcing market. According to the Offshore Location Attractiveness Index provided by A.T. Kearney, China is one of the most preferred outsourcing destinations.

Why outsource to China? Considering such complex issues as cultural differences, IT advancement, and legislative framework, the United States, Europe, and Japan have been the most popular destinations for outsourcing services in the past few years. Nevertheless, total investment scales on global offshore outsourcing are showing an upward trend. China, India, and other Asian countries are becoming more attractive and competitive as outsourcing service providers. Fast growth in those Asian countries, however, has raised a number of legal, political, and social concerns in the actual practice of outsourcing.

Because the benefits and impact of offshoring tend to vary widely, most foreign investors are still learning how to do it well. Although any given company can be initially attracted to China by its cheap labor resource, cost is not the only motive. Government support, infrastructure, risk mitigation, and the legal and policy formation process, among other things, are also essential elements for outsourcers' consideration.

MARKET ENTRY AND ESTABLISHING A BUSINESS IN CHINA

China has seen a surge in foreign investment over the past decade. As previous restrictions on foreign investment have been eased, they are being replaced with legal and regulatory frameworks, composed of Company Law, Foreign Trade Law, and other relevant laws or provisions, which encourage investment so that China can compete effectively with other countries in the Asia-Pacific region.

How can an outsourcer start their business in China? They may consider buying into an existing Chinese local company or establishing a new foreign invested enterprise (FIE) in China for captive operations, or collaborating with local Chinese companies.

For a captive operation, in order to retain overall control, the investor may establish an FIE, which is subject to project-by-project examination, approval, and registration by the government. According to the Company Law of the People's Republic of China (PRC), at least 25 percent of shares should be held by foreign investors to enjoy the favorable treatment permitted for FIEs. The major types of FIE are: Equity Joint Venture (EJV), Co-operative Joint Venture (CJV), and Wholly Owned Foreign Enterprises (WOFE). EJVs and WOFEs are all required to be incorporated in the form of a limited liability company, while CJVs can be established as an entity without legal person status.

Market Entry Policies

As a centrally planned economy, China has historically set entry barriers against foreign investors in specific industries. The Ministry of Commerce (MoC) and its forerunner, the Ministry of Foreign Trade and Economic Cooperation (MOFTEC), laid out this policy through the promulgation of a periodical Foreign Investment Industrial Guidance Catalogs (the Catalog), categorizing foreign investment projects as "encouraged," "permitted," "restricted," or "prohibited." No barrier exists for industries under the "encouraged" category, and few for "permitted" ones. Up along this scale gradually restrictive policies are imposed on the entry of foreigners, in terms of specific type of FIE permitted, the control party of the FIE, and so forth. The currently valid Catalog was promulgated in 2004.

In accordance with China's commitments made upon accession to the World Trade Organization (WTO) in 2001, industry entry barriers for FIEs have gradually been lifted. Previously restricted, and even prohibited industries such as trade and distribution, commercial wholesale and retail, franchise, advertisement, freight transportation, banking, and so on, have been completely opened to foreign investors. However, in several areas like news agency, publishing, and the like, barriers still exist to foreign investors.

FIEs enjoy various preferential treatment compared to pure domestically invested enterprises, as long as the foreign investment accounts for more than 25 percent of the registered capital. The most conspicuous ones include: an income tax exemption for the first two years of establishment and a 50 percent reduction of the income tax for the following three years, if the FIE has any taxable profit; an import customs duties reduction or exemption for equipment imported by the FIE; special preferences for an FIE's foreign borrowing and foreign exchange management, and so on. However, there is a tendency to decrease and remove these preferential treatments as the barriers to entry against foreign investors are lowered.

Foreign investors can also choose to set up a representative office in China, which can explore the market and introduce its products and services in China but is prohibited from conducting direct business activities. The threshold for setting up a representative office is substantially lower than setting up an FIE, and therefore it is a good vehicle for the early stages of business.

Foreign investors often transfer technology and intellectual property such as trademarks, patents, and copyrighted material to the FIEs in which they invest. While the technology and intellectual property are contributed as part of an FIE's registered capital, the FIE will then become the owner of the technology and the foreign contributor will have to request approval from the FIE if it wants to use the technology and intellectual property.

Pursuant to the Regulation on Administration of Technology Import and Export, technology contributed as capital is required to be appraised upon importation and should also be registered with the MoC. The supplying party to a technology import contract shall ensure its legal ownership of the technology supplied. The receiving party shall be under obligation to keep confidential the undisclosed part of the technology within the scope of the confidentiality and time limit thereof as agreed in the contract.

A foreign party may also license technology to unaffiliated Chinese companies by way of contracting to an independent service provider. Unlike joint venture contracts, such service contracts can be governed by foreign law. For contracting to an independent service provider in China, the investor may enter into (1) an outsourcing contract for outsourcing its entire IT department, or (2) a partial outsourcing contract, with its specific need on software development, or software maintenances, for example.

INTELLECTUAL PROPERTY RIGHTS PROTECTION

Although the preceding foreign investment vehicles have been practiced successfully in China for years, the government is still seeking a gradual and evolutionary reform of the foreign investment legal system, especially in some specific areas such as IT. As such, China has established the legislative framework on technology services over the past few years, and effected several legislative changes in copyrights, trademarks, patents, trade secrets, and other issues. In 1998, China established the State Intellectual Property Office (SIPO), with the vision that it would coordinate China's Intellectual Property Right (IPR) enforcement efforts by merging the patent, trademark, and copyright offices under one authority. SIPO is responsible for granting patents (national office), registering semiconductor and integrated circuit layout designs (national office), and enforcing patents (local SIPO offices), as well as coordinating domestic foreign-related IPR issues involving copyrights, trademarks, and patents. These measures have drastically reformed PRC laws on intellectual property.

Undoubtedly, how to protect IPR has been one of the major concerns for investors. The IPR law under the PRC's legal framework consists mainly of copyright law, trademark law, patent law, and some provisions provided in civil, contract, and labor law on confidentiality, trade secret, unfair competition, and so forth.

For the purpose of protecting and securing IPR, it is necessary to prepare a technology development contract. The technology development contract includes a commissioned development contract and a cooperative development contract. According to the Regulations on Protection of Computer Software, for the commissioning contract, two parties shall enter into a written agreement on ownership rights with freely negotiable clauses. If there is no written contract or if the matter is not clearly stipulated in the contract, the IPR shall be enjoyed by the person undertaking the commission. It is also provided in the Contract Law of the PRC that IPR ownership belongs to the party that undertakes the research and development (the service provider), except as otherwise agreed upon by the parties. While the service provider is granted IPR, the commissioning party may exploit the patent for free. In the event that the service provider transfers the right to apply for IPR, the commissioning party shall have the preemptive right in acquiring such rights on the same conditions.

The Contract Law was influenced to a great extent by the United Nations Convention on Contracts for the International Sale of Goods, especially regarding the formation of contracts and the liability for breach of contract.

Under the Contract Law, a contract can be reached in written or oral form. The written form refers to not only a typed contract, but also any other form in which the contract's content is visibly recorded, including telegrams, telexes, facsimiles, electronic mail, and so forth. Using such terms as offer, acceptance, revocation, and withdrawal, the process of contract formation is divided into two separate stages: the offer and the acceptance. A contract is concluded at the time the offering party receives a valid acceptance from the offeree.

Like the contract laws of most other countries, contracts reached contrary to state mandatory law and public policy, through a process tarnished by substantial mistakes, fraud, duress, conspiracy, or by persons without capacity are void or voidable. For a contract with standard clauses proposed solely by one party without a bargaining process, if disagreements arise regarding the meaning of these clauses, the Contract Law mandates an unfavorable interpretation against the contract maker.

The breaching party to a contract shall remedy its breach by resuming performing duties under the contract, taking steps to repair any damage resulting from the breach, or paying monetary damages. The monetary damages shall include the anticipated benefits the nonbreaching party would have obtained were the contract duly carried out, but shall be limited by the amount that is foreseen or reasonably foreseeable by the breaching party at the time of the contract's conclusion.

The Contract Law also recognizes liquidated damage, or damages to be paid upon breach as stipulated in the contract. If the court or tribunal deems the liquidated damage as stipulated in the contract to be too little or too great, it has the authority to adjust the amount.

In addition to the aforementioned general principles, the Contract Law also contains provisions addressing various specific types of contracts. Most of them are applicable only when the contract between parties does not otherwise stipulate.

Contract Law and Intellectual Property Rights

Under the agreement of joint development of technology, the IPR ownership can also be decided by both parties therein. If there is no written contract or if the matter is not clearly stipulated in the contract, the right to apply for an IPR shall be jointly owned by the parties who participated in the cooperative development in accordance with Contract Law of PRC. While one party transfers its part of the jointly owned right to apply for an IPR, the other party or parties may have the preemptive right in acquiring such rights under the same conditions.

In the event that one party renounces its part of the shared right to apply for IPR protection, the other party may apply for it alone or the other parties may apply for it jointly. While a patent is granted to the applicant, the party that renounced its right to apply for it may exploit the patent for free.

Provided that the jointly developed software cannot be used in separate parts, the co-developers shall enjoy the copyright jointly and exploit the copyright by consensus. If consensus cannot be reached, and in the absence of any unusual circumstances, no party may prevent the other parties from implementing the exclusive rights, with the exception of the right of transfer to a third party. However, any benefits earned shall be fairly distributed among the co-developers.

Apart from these, occupational inventions have also been raised as a concern under IPR protection. In the event that the occupational invention is generated from the technology development by the employees, according to the Contract Law of the PRC, IPR ownership shall be deemed to vest with the employer. The occupational invention is defined as a technological achievement accomplished in the process of carrying out the task of employer, or mainly through using the materials and technological means thereof. In this regard, the employer shall pay a certain percentage of technology license or transfer fee to the employees as reward or remuneration. The employees shall have the preemptive right in acquiring occupational inventions under the same conditions while the employer transfers the right.

What mechanisms in China will be constructed to ensure protection of intellectual property? The newly amended Foreign Trade Law of the PRC, effective as of July 1, 2004, contains a new chapter on the protection of intellectual property rights in foreign trade. The power of IPR judicial protection has been increasingly intensified, and the level of protection has been enhanced constantly. Such newly amended law also permits the foreign trade authorities to intervene if an intellectual property rights owner abuses its power. When any party violates another's IPR, the victim could choose and execute at their discretion three kinds of possible solutions, namely civil litigation, administrative litigation, and criminal litigation, under the respective procedural codes. To protect relevant right owners' legitimate interests and maintain the order of the socialist market economy, the People's Courts at each level around China settle IPR disputes and severely punish IPR crimes in accordance with the law.

There are two parallel approaches available in IPR enforcement in China: administrative and judicial measures. In case of infringement, the rights holder may either file a lawsuit or apply to competent authorities for administrative measures.

Protecting IPR through administrative means is an important enforcement feature in China in terms of its rapid crackdown on infringement and low cost. By implementing of copyright law, for instance, the National Copyright Administration is set up at China's central level and local administrations in various provinces, municipalities, and autonomous regions, and even in relatively big cities. Therefore, the right holder can protect his or her rights through the administrative approaches other than judiciary means. As for acts infringing IPR, the right holder can complain to the competent administrative authorities and the authorities can also investigate and handle cases in light of their duties. During this process, they can seal up, sequester infringed goods, and take such remedies as order of stopping infringement and fines.

As far as the judiciary aspect is concerned, special judicial tribunals for intellectual property cases have been established at courts at all levels in China. The courts at all levels have continuously strengthened work in IPR-related civil and criminal trials under the principle of "justice and efficiency." Through handling a large number of IPR-related cases, they have protected the legitimate rights and interests of right holders and punished acts of IPR infringement criminal IPR infringements in fairness and justice. During the process of litigation, a court can take such temporary measures as preservation of evidence or property. Such measures as, for instance, the pretrial provisional judicial measure, similar to the preliminary injunctions seen in the United Kingdom, United States, and certain European countries, are made in conformity with the enforcement requirements of Trade-Related aspects of Intellectual Property Rights (TRIPS). In the case of torts, the People's Court, in accordance with the law, cannot only order the undertaking of such civil liabilities as infringement cessation, negative influence elimination, apology, and loss compensation, but also give him or her such punishments as illegal income confiscation, fines, and detention. In civil cases, the rights holder can receive timely compensation for their financial losses. In the event of an intellectual property crime, an intellectual property wrongdoer will be given a penal punishment in accordance with the law. As a judiciary measure, it will be beneficial to the enhancement of the domestic enforcement level of intellectual property, to the intensification of crackdown on IPR infringement crimes, and to the improvement of the penal protection of intellectual property.

For the purpose of better fulfillment of its international commitments and promotion of IPR protection for software in China, the State Council issued a document in 2000, requiring governmental organs and state-owned enterprises to use legitimate software and establish a regular inspection system. To this end, the Chinese government has conducted a check among various ministries and departments of the State Council. At present, the government is concentrating on encouraging governments at local levels to strictly implement relevant provisions and has made significant progress in this area.

The Chinese government constituted the Mechanism of Regular Communication and Coordination with Foreign Invested Enterprises to further improve the foreign investment environment, reinforce the crackdown on infringement, fakes and inferior products, and protect intellectual property. The mechanism includes the relevant government authorities, such as the Ministry of Commerce, State Intellectual Property Office, and others. They have been acting as coordination or communication offices for foreign investment enterprises in terms of IPR protection, improving the foreign investment environment, and maintaining a unified, open, fair, competitive, and orderly market. Through this mechanism, the enforcement authorities have intensified their cooperation in infringement crackdowns with FIEs and have attained remarkable results.

Actively Fulfilling International Obligations to Protect IPR

China has taken an active approach to joining major international conventions and agreements on IPR protection. It has joined more than ten international conventions, treaties, agreements, and protocols, such as the Paris Convention for the Protection of Industrial Property, the Patent Cooperation Treaty, the Budapest Treaty on the International Recognition of the Deposit of Microorganisms for the Purposes of Patent Procedure, and others. While strictly executing its international obligations in IPR protection, China has devoted great efforts to adjusting and improving international rules regarding IPR protection in order to let all countries of the world share the fruits and benefits brought about by the progress of science and technology.

In addition, the Chinese courts have continuously enhanced international exchanges and cooperation in the field of IPR-related adjudication, learning from the useful experiences and successful practices of foreign countries. The Supreme People's Court actively cooperates with the World Intellectual Property Organization and European Union, and has hosted several seminars and training courses on IPR, the results of which have been encouraging. These seminars and training courses have effectively promoted the enhancement of China's IPR judicial protection, and continuously pushed the level of its IPR-related judicial work to a new high.

Secured Interests Law

The Secured Interests Law of the PRC lays down five forms of security a creditor may require: guarantee, pledge, mortgage, lien, and deposit. To minimize risk for the creditor, the creditor may require a debtor to provide one or more guarantors. A guarantee agreement shall be in written form.

A creditor may also require the debtor to mortgage immovables to the creditor by signing a written contract and conducting registration with the relevant authority, or to pledge movables or rights (including negotiable instruments, securities certificates, and intellectual property rights) to the creditor upon delivery of chattels/instruments or due registration. In the event of default by the debtor, the creditor can ask the guarantor to perform the debt obligation, or can ask the court with jurisdiction to sell the mortgaged or pledged properties through auction to clear the debt.

Unlike the aforementioned three forms of security universally applicable to any transaction, liens and deposits only apply to specific types of transactions. A lien refers to the case where a creditor is entitled to sell relevant movables in its possession but owned by the debtor to get compensated from the proceeds, if the debtor fails to fulfill its obligations under a storage contract, transport contract, or processing contract. A deposit refers to a sum of money deposited by one party of a contract to another to demonstrate good faith and safeguard performance.

EMPLOYMENT ISSUES

When global outsourcers enter China, on the one hand, it helps in creating new employment opportunities; on the other hand, it results in short-term reductions in domestic jobs within countries doing outsourcing. In addition to this, it also raises issues pertaining to the quality and confidentiality of specialized and sensitive work that gets outsourced to a foreign country. In this regard, the employer shall enter into a nondisclosure agreement (NDA) or confidentiality agreement with the employee in terms of the scope and period of confidentiality, prior to the business execution. The employer is, of course, obliged to warrant the title to the technology or trade secret as well as its quality, effectiveness, and technology objectives.

It is also provided in the Labor Law of PRC that noncompetition clauses can be negotiable and included in the labor contract. For posttermination, noncompetition clauses should be limited to a reasonable geographic area and time limit. Compensation is also required to be paid during the period of noncompetition.

Although China recognizes the work-for-hire principle, the labor contract should clearly assign ownership of intellectual property created in the course of employment; otherwise IPR may prove practically impossible to enforce against an employee who creates an IPR-related work for hire.

Currently, probation periods are limited by the length of the labor contract, not by the type of job. To prevent employers from prolonging the probation period, probation shall apply to employment contracts with a term of longer than three months. It is provided that the probations for nontechnology jobs, technology jobs, and highly skilled technology jobs shall be as follows:

- No more than one month for workers in nontechnical jobs;
- No more than two months for employees with technical jobs; and
- No more than six months for senior technical professional jobs.

Labor Contracts

PRC law requires all employers and employees to sign labor contracts in Chinese that clearly define the parties' rights and obligations, including the term and nature of the job, remuneration, safety and working conditions, disciplinary actions, welfare benefits, and conditions for termination and breach of contract. Employers may also consider including confidentiality and noncompetition covenants to protect the employer from former employees divulging trade secrets to competitors. Probationary contracts do not free employers from their obligations, and will be considered a formal contract in the case of a dispute.

Remuneration and Benefits

Employers must provide a minimum wage as determined by provincial law. Employers must also provide housing subsidies and medical treatment allowances, as well as enroll employees in the social insurance system for pensions, unemployment benefits, work-related injuries, and medical and maternity care.

The standard work week is five eight-hour days with an allowance for one hour per day of overtime (no more than 36 hours of overtime per month), though approval can be obtained for more flexible work schedules. Increased overtime wages shall be paid upon the performance of overtime work. Employers must provide annual leave to employees after one year's service, and must also provide home leave for employees to visit their spouse or parents.

Termination of Labor Contract

Under PRC law, an employer may not terminate an employee without just cause. Generally employers may dismiss employees with 30 days notice if the employee is not competent for their assigned work. A dismissal without notice by employers is only permitted in special situations such as when an employee seriously violates laws or workplace regulations. When the employee suffers from work-related sickness, injury, or is pregnant, they cannot be dismissed.

Employees may resign at will; however, they are typically required to give at least 30 days notice. Resignation without notice by the employee is again only limited to special cases.

Labor unions begin to play a more and more important role in labor issues, especially when FIEs are involved. Major labor disputes are often resolved through unions. Labor disputes must go through a labor arbitration procedure before a court can hear the case.

Hiring Requirements for Representative Offices and FIEs

For a representative office of a foreign business to hire Chinese nationals, the representative office must first obtain registration. The hiring then must be completed via a designated employment agency, which may also serve as a labor-relations liaison between the employee and employer, provide welfare benefits to the employee (depending on the arrangement agreed to with the representative office), as well as manage personnel files, residence permits, and passport and visa applications.

Joint ventures and WOFEs have much more flexibility and autonomy in hiring matters. If they would like, the joint ventures and WOFEs can also hire employees through the employment agencies.

Foreign nationals must obtain Employment Permits and Residence Certificates prior to working in China, except in several specific cases. Foreign nationals hired by a company residing in China shall pay taxes for their income in China according to China tax laws.

GOVERNMENT POLICY

In 2006, the Ministry of Commerce (MOC) initiated the "Thousand-Hundred-Ten Project" in Outsourcing Services and "The Circular on Implementation of 'Thousand-Hundred-Ten Project'" (the Circular) has been promulgated and becomes effective as of October 16, 2006, which gives investors a clear picture of how to do business in the context of China. Meanwhile, the Department of Trade in Services has been established by the MOC, specially designed for outsourcing services. The government will be providing RMB100 million in financing each year to build up outsourcing service infrastructure in China. Technology services, such as IT and software, will be on the top of the list to be supported and promoted. Shanghai, Xi'an, Dalian, Chengdu, and others have been accredited as National Outsourcing Service Cities.

It states in the Circular that the local IT outsourcing service provider may enjoy financial support for technology development from national funds set aside for that purpose. An eligible outsourcing service company may apply for 80 percent of the necessary technology development investment from the government's special fund within five years from the date of its establishment. The government is also supporting human resource training and international credential certification by way of reimbursement of fees and costs used for those purposes. The company may, in the meantime, enjoy tax incentives and other related benefits from the government. In the event that the company is low on cash flow and applies for a loan from a bank, a 20 percent loan interest subsidy is provided basis of the published bank interest rate.

Doing foreign exchange in and out of China is still being tightly controlled, and as such, the outsourcing service company may want to keep a certain amount of foreign currency outside China for the purpose of business development only.

CURRENCY AND TAXATION

The renminbi (RMB) is not a fully convertible currency yet. The PRC regulator exerts different degrees of regulation upon the conversion between foreign currencies and RMB, depending on whether the transaction is on current account or capital account. As a general principle, a conversion under current account transaction shall go through the verification procedure with the handling bank, while a conversion under capital account transaction is subject to the approval of the Administration of Foreign Exchange (AFE).

An RMB account can be opened on shore only. An enterprise can only open one basic RMB account to withdraw cash and pay salaries and bonuses. Opening foreign currency accounts used to be strictly regulated in China; now a company residing in China can open foreign exchange accounts upon filing with the AFE. Foreign exchange current accounts always have a maximum amount permitted; amounts exceeding the limit shall be sold to the designated bank.

In order to carry out exchange receipts and payments under current account, a company need only go through a verification procedure with the handling bank or AFE (depending on the amount involved) upon production of relevant documents. With regard to capital accounts, both the opening of an account and account transactions are subject to strict regulation.

Intercompany loans in RMB are generally forbidden in China, except when an enterprise conglomerate sets up a financial company providing financial services, including loans, to its members. For those companies not belonging to an enterprise conglomerate, intercompany borrowing can only be arranged through an intermediary bank using an "entrust loan" scheme.

To encourage FIEs to introduce advanced foreign technologies and equipment, the Chinese government has stipulated in recent years a series of favorable tax policies for encouraging foreign investment in high technology industries.

The income tax on FIEs is levied at the rate of 33 percent. The income tax on FIEs located in special economic zones, state high-tech industrial zones, or economic and technological development zones is levied at the rate of 15 percent. The income tax on foreign-invested production enterprises located in coastal economic open zones, special economic zones, or in the old urban district of cities where economic and technological development zones are located is levied at the rate of 24 percent.

FIEs may further enjoy tax exemption through deduction policies, such as a newly established enterprise in state high-tech zones may, upon approval by the tax authorities, be exempted from income tax for the first two years of operation.

Foreign invested production enterprises that have an operation period exceeding ten years shall, from the year they begin to make a profit, be exempted from income tax for the first two years and allowed a 50 percent reduction for the following three years. In addition to the two-year tax exemption and three-year tax reduction treatment, FIEs producing for export shall be allowed a reduced income tax rate of 50 percent as long as their annual export accounts for 70 percent or above of their sales volume.

FIEs that adopt advanced technology shall be exempt from income tax for the first two years and allowed a 50 percent reduction for the following six years.

The foreign investor of an FIE who reinvests its share of profit obtained from the enterprise in a project with an operation period of five years or above shall, upon approval by the tax authority, be refunded 40 percent of the income tax already paid on the reinvested amount.

The Chinese government levies value-added tax, consumption tax, and business tax, and other circulation-stage tax on the enterprises in China. FIEs may enjoy preferential policies, for instance:

- Exemption of import tariff and import-stage value-added tax of the self-use equipment and supporting technologies, parts and spares imported that are encouraged and supported by the state;
- Exemption of business tax for the incomes obtained from advanced technology transfer or technology transfer with favorable terms.

If the expenditure on technology development of foreign invested enterprises increases by 10 percent or more over that of the previous year, the taxable income of the enterprises for the current year can, with the approval of the tax authority, be set off by 50 percent of the actual amount spending on technology development.

Turnover Taxes

A turnover tax system consists of value added tax (VAT), consumption tax, and business tax. They are indirect taxes charged on the gross turnover of businesses and enterprises operating in China.

Under the PRC turnover tax system, VAT is levied on the sales of tangible goods, processing services, repair and replacement services, and the importation of goods within the PRC. The general rate is 17 percent on products and imports. A lower rate of 13 percent is levied on certain specific products. A business tax, ranging from 3 to 20 percent depending on the category of business concerned, is applicable to enterprises in service, transport, and other nonproduction industries, as well as to the transfer of intangible assets or immovable properties. Business tax paid is deductible for foreign enterprise income tax purposes because it is deemed as cost to the enterprise.

The PRC taxation system contains measures to prevent double taxation and evasion of taxes incurred in territories outside of China. China has taxation treaties and arrangements with most economically developed states around the world. FIEs are allowed to make deductions for the foreign income tax already paid abroad for income derived from sources outside of China.

Income Tax on Nonresident Enterprises

Profits, dividends, interest, rental fees, and royalties gained from the rental or sale of buildings and structures located in China or from the assignment of land use rights within China, as well as other China-sourced incomes, used to be liable to a withholding tax of 20 percent. The withholding tax rate for interest, rental fees, royalties, and other income was later reduced to 10 percent. For after tax profits distributed to foreign investors, and for some royalty fees from the transfer of advanced technology, the withholding tax is totally exempted.

Individual Income Tax for Foreign Nationals

A foreign national should pay individual income tax on incomes derived from sources within the territory of China. For foreign nationals working in China for more than 183 days annually whose remuneration is borne by a foreign employer without a permanent establishment within the territory of China, the income paid by the foreign employer is also regarded as income from within China for tax purposes. For those working in China less than 183 days annually, the individual income tax should only be levied on the income paid by the enterprise within the territory of China. These provisions are adjustable from time to time according to the new rules of State Administration of Taxation.

Outlook on China Outsourcing Services

In view of the rapidly growing economy and accompanying policy reforms in China, potentially huge commercial opportunities have been recognized and subsequently created. And yet, technology outsourcing in China is at a nascent stage that plays the role of providing back-office support in neighboring Asian countries. Piracy fears, relatively insufficient English, and a lack of high-level international quality certification have held Chinese startups back. But with training and experience, such obstacles are not insurmountable. By honing skills in the burgeoning markets close to home, China's ITO industry is sure to get up to speed fast. Northeast China and east China will become the main drivers of the China software outsourcing market in the next few years. Southern China currently has a smaller market size but is rich in resources, such as software talent, and, therefore, its rapid growth will soon be noticeable. According to Research in China, which reports on a wide range of Chinese industries, the Chinese software outsourcing industry will grow annually at a rate of over 30 percent for the next three to five years.

PRC law is enacted based on the continental European legal system, whereas many nations, including the United States and India, base their legal systems on the English common law tradition. That would always cause some unexpected conflicts and impingements upon transaction between two legal systems. The best way to ensure the application of a particular legal system to international contracts is to choose a particular law to govern the contract. The courts can hold the law which the parties have expressly or impliedly chosen, or which is imputed to them upon the doctrine of the most significant relationship.

Outsourcing is not a risk-free business process, although it can bring the investor favorable returns and strategic success in the Asia market. Transparency and IPRs remain as the main concerns of foreign investors doing business in China and a large majority of them would hope for better enforcement of IPR law and regulations. A complete IPR protection system, however, cannot be established overnight. At present, there are still IPR infringements in certain areas and fields in China, some of which are very serious. Awareness of the importance of IPR in Chinese society as a whole needs to be further enhanced. Meanwhile, China's IPR protection work is facing new challenges in the course of economic globalization and rapid development of science and technology worldwide. In accordance with the requirements of the concept of scientific development, the Chinese government will adopt more effective policies and measures in building up a sound system and environment favorable for IPR protection worldwide. The outlook for a strong IPR legal system in China is a very hopeful one and may indeed be stronger than our current expectations. There is reason to be confident that IPR will contribute greatly to the flourishing economic future of China.

The financial issues of company loans, reinvestment, foreign exchange, as well as a successful exit are also problematic due to administrative ambiguity. Regulatory approvals can be required at various stages. Today, the Chinese administrative system functions are being gradually improved by the principle of simplicity, unity, and efficiency. The same or similar functions shall be undertaken by a single administrative organ so that the administrative procedures can be simplified. In the meantime, a one-stop agency for the promotion of ITO service would also be helpful for foreign investors on good understanding of PRC law and policy. The Chinese government has been working on various proposals on tax exemption issues on outsourcing business recently. The tax proposal may vary from different service products and tax models, such as exemptions on business tax and tax refund policy on VAT. These proposals could have a greater impact on outsourcing activities than any of the legislative proposals to moderate the amount of IT and back-office work being outsourced. These moves are leading to reassessments of global strategies by both clients and competitors of China's growing IT sector. Undoubtedly, China will benefit from recent events showing it as a preferred outsourcing destination in the world.

DISPUTE RESOLUTION AND LITIGATION

China International Economic and Trade Arbitration Commission

Arbitration through the China International Economic and Trade Arbitration Commission (CIETAC) is the most popular manner of dispute resolution among foreign investors. Based in Beijing and with two subcommissions in Shenzhen and Shanghai, CIETAC enjoys a reputation for of its expertise in resolving foreign-related disputes and its expedited and flexible procedural requirements. In 2005, CIETAC published its most updated arbitration rules, which govern the arbitration conducted by CIETAC and its subcommissions.

CIETAC arbitration may be triggered by one party bringing a written claim to CIETAC based on a written arbitration agreement between the parties either prior to or subsequent to the occurrence of the dispute. The parties may choose Chinese or foreigners to represent them during the arbitration. They may also choose the language of the arbitration and the place of the hearing. Generally the arbitral tribunal for each case will be composed of three arbitrators, with each party independently appointing one, and with those two arbitrators jointly appointing the third or entrusting the Chairman of CIETAC to appoint the third from CIETAC's Panel of Arbitrators. For simple cases, the option for having a sole arbitrator and a summary procedure is available.

The claimant can also apply for preservation of property or evidence prior to the final award, for which the application will be forwarded to the People's Court with jurisdiction for its interlocutory rule. The arbitral tribunal will decide on whether to hold an oral hearing. If an oral hearing is held, the manner and style of the hearing, its evidentiary rules, the active or passive role the arbitrators will play, and other factors, will be decided under the broad guidance of the arbitration rules of CIETAC.

The tribunal shall issue the arbitration award within six months after commencement of the arbitration. The arbitration award is enforceable by the People's Court, which may also exercise its discretion in regard to evaluating the validity and fairness of procedural issues and of the arbitral award's compliance with public policy. The arbitral tribunal can decide the allocation of fees, such as arbitration and lawyers' fees between the parties as it deems appropriate.

Besides its general arbitration rules, CIETAC also adopted arbitration rules specific to governing financial disputes. CIETAC may also hear other special types of disputes, including Internet domain name disputes.

Other Arbitrations

Besides CIETAC, there are other arbitration institutions in China whose arbitral awards can be enforced by the People's Court. However, the court exerts a wider review power over these arbitral awards than the CIETAC case. It has power to scrutinize both the procedural and the substantive issues of these arbitrations before it decide to enforce the awards.

As China has acceded to the New York Convention, an arbitral award made by an arbitration tribunal of another country that is party to the New York Convention shall be recognized and enforced by the relevant court of China. Therefore a party can choose arbitration outside the territory of

China as a dispute resolution mechanism. Generally Hong Kong,[1] Singapore, and Stockholm arbitration institutions are favorable to foreign investors.

Litigation

The last resort is to seek redress via the court system. The People's Court system, despite its poor reputation for cronyism and judges with little expertise, is improving its performance continuously, especially since China's accession to the WTO in 2001.

China has a four-level court system: the basic level court is situated in every county and city district; above them every municipality has one or more intermediate courts; every province has a sole higher court; and the final tribunal is the People's Supreme Court located in Beijing. As a general rule, every case will reach the final judgment after proceeding through two levels of courts. The court with jurisdiction over the first instance will be determined depending on the disputed amount, as well as the nature, complexity, and influence of the dispute, the domicile of the defendant, and so forth.[2] Both the substantive judgments and procedural rulings can be appealed. If the losing party of the first instance fails to appeal within 15 days after the service of the judgment, it is by default forfeit its right to appeal, and the judgment of the first instance becomes final. In rare cases, the losing party of the second instance or the procuratorate is allowed to institute a special third instance.

A case can be tried in the first instance using ordinary procedure or summary procedure, depending on the complexity and nature of the case. There are also several other special procedures applicable to specific cases like bankruptcy, repayment, and declaration of ownership of properties. The evidentiary rules are relatively simple in China compared to the Anglo-American system, considering its lack of complex exclusion rules. In addition, PRC courts more often adopt documentary evidence, rather than oral testimony.

Many complain that even if a favorable judgment is obtained in China, the enforcement of the judgment is plagued with pathologies like prolonged delay, cronyism, corruption, and unfair treatment of creditors. In spite of the Supreme Court's recognition of this problem and its consistent attempt to solve it, enforcement procedure remains the most agonizing part of China's civil justice system.

Mediation and Conciliation

Besides arbitration and litigation, mediation and conciliation are also used often to solve disputes. Mediations can be presided over by a neutral third-party institution. The arbitration institutions and the courts, prior to entering into official procedure, will also play the role as a mediator for the parties in dispute. The court will not directly enforce a mediation agreement; however, it will give a quick, enforceable judgment based on the mediation.

In order to be successful in China, it is imperative for the global out-sourcers to design and adopt a sound entry strategy as well as clear guiding principles for the execution of strategy, thus fully utilizing this new and emerging outsourcing trend. Just like in any business endeavor, outsourcing of course has its own uncertainties and therefore carries potential risks. If not handled appropriately, outsourcing can damage corporate image, create sour relationships with clients, and lower quality of services. How-ever, the reward can indeed be satisfying and overshadows any potential risks. Toward that end, ultimately it is again an issue of understanding the trend, knowing the local market, designing the appropriate action plans, and executing properly.

Prospects

Since its adoption of its economic opening policy in the early 1980s, China has been undertaking a great shift from a centrally planned economy to a market-oriented economy. While China has yet to meet several of its com-mitments for liberalization made upon its accession to the WTO, including the opening of its cultural and communications industry, granting national treatment to foreign companies, and full compliance with international intel-lectual property standards, it has simultaneously been facing an increasingly urgent demand for more effective and fair regulation. While the efficiency of a laissez-faire economy is widely acknowledged by the whole nation, people are gradually recognizing the necessity of managing pure market forces that could result in disarray of market order, drastic inequality in wealth and status, violation of human rights and dignity, deterioration of the natu-ral environment, and balkanization of the society as a whole. Intentional remedial policies have been adopted or are under legislative deliberation to counteract the aforementioned trend, including the imposition of more strict environmental and labor compliance obligations upon enterprises; tilting of the playing field in favor of less developed districts, especially the rural areas; easing the burden on disadvantageous groups of society by lifting policy barriers and filling income gaps through tax reform; and campaigning against corruption, monopolies, and other activities corrosive to a healthy market.

This new trend of regulation does not change the basic movement and direction of China's economic development, however; nor are China's environmental, labor, and other regulations likely to surpass the extent of those adopted in Europe and North America. The ultimate outcome of China's reform is likely to be merging into the international economic and legal order.

ENDNOTES

1. Arbitral awards in Hong Kong are not subject to the New York Convention, but are still enforceable according to a special arrangement between mainland China and Hong Kong.
2. Significant foreign-related cases will be tried by an Intermediate Court as the first instance court according to the *Civil Procedure Law of the PRC*.

CHAPTER 10

China 2020

While there are several scenarios that provide various outlooks for the global economy in 2020 and how the China market will be a part of it, this chapter assumes that the basic model for sourcing technology and related support services holds as it is known today.

The year 2020 is not that far away, yet making a leap forward to envision what the technology outsourcing industry environment will look like then, takes a lot of analysis, reflection, and modeling.

The next 12 years will witness an unprecedented buildup of a giant technology and information processing-related services industry in China, both to fuel its rapidly growing domestic market, but also to satisfy the vast demand for global offshore talents. Why?

PILLAR OF THE ECONOMY: FOCUS ON THE HIGH-TECH SECTOR

Earlier in this book, we touched on the priority that the government has given the technology sector. We also covered the education emphasis of the Chinese culture and how the Ministry of Education restructured its curriculum ten years ago to ramp up the output of technology-related majors.

This started to gain momentum and became clear in 2003, when the world saw the numbers for computer sciences and software graduates in China go over the 100,000 annual graduates mark, currently reaching 140,000. For the first time, a second market emerged to supply a large pool of tech talent, with figures above 100,000 tech graduates per year.

Just how amazing is it that just three years later, 2006 saw that number double and exceed the 300,000 computer science and software graduates per year mark? That now makes China the largest provider market of tech graduates in the world.

It is difficult to predict at which point the output for annual computer sciences and software graduates will start to plateau, but one thing is sure, we have not yet reached that point. It is a reasonable projection that, by 2012, China will see annual numbers of tech graduates soar close to, if not above, 500,000. Most of the current figures are based on universities and technology institutes graduates. To add to these numbers, the so-called blue-collar programmers are in the ramp-up phase as well. That will see a large number of low-cost high-school graduates enter the work force at even lower labor costs.

So, when anticipating what 2020 might look like from a tech talent annual output perspective, expect a qualified output of fluent English-speakers (taken as computer sciences—software and related fields) between 500,000 and 1 million per year. It is very realistic to take an outlook of 2020 with 800,000 graduates a year (white and blue collar).

GROWTH OF THE SERVICES SECTOR

Paving the way for the technology outsourcing services, the growth of the services sector all together is yet another milestone of the China market transformation, which is accelerating. For years the concept of service in China was either not getting much recognition, or was in its embryonic stage. The market, consumers, and decision-makers saw value only in tangible goods, and had little understanding for what service meant, nor wanted to be bothered with having to pay for it.

Paying for a product, hardware-oriented goods and tangible materials was the primary mode of doing business. Obviously, the manufacturing sector blossomed in such an environment. Trying to promote or sell a service in such an environment was really hard, many times impossible.

The history for services in China is recent. Sporadic attempts by various players in different sectors started in the mid-1990s with a wild range of mitigated results or success. The turn of the millennium marked an improvement toward some services awareness, and by 2005, China had made huge progress toward adopting services with a growing expectation for them. Today the services sector is growing fast, and with it the technology-related support and development services.

China has reached a crossroads where it no longer is considered just a market that can provide only low skill-sets and cheap labor for manufacturing-only usage, but it has now tapped into the upper value chain segment of the economy, that of value-added technology services.

Now strong in both low- and high-tech industrial and engineering skills, its economy is going to undergo another transformation, shaping its workforce and structuring its rapid demand for services.

SATISFYING A FAST-GROWING GLOBAL IT AND BUSINESS PROCESSES SERVICES DEMAND

Domestic Demand

The demand for tech talent is greatest within China, when compared to any other country. The economic boom, bundled with the expansion of all industry sectors and affluence of overseas investments has put a major push to information systems and intelligent electronic means of handling a large number of consumers, users, corporate needs, and government initiatives. By 2010, the China market is expected to reach a leadership size for just about every world economic sector. It already holds that flag for some of those, like the mobile-phone sector, with an expected figure to surpass 500 million mobile users sometime in 2007. The rate at which each sector gains momentum is truly unique in China, and that accounts for massive business growth, which in turn converts into high demand for support services and related educated technical workforce.

It is obvious that by 2020 a large portion of the tech talent workforce in China will be serving its own domestic demand. Just how large a percentage is up to the various type of economic scenario that one decides to take for the future of the market. In making a prediction, expect that by 2020 at least 50 percent of the China tech talent workforce will be engaged in its own domestic industry-related activities. That contrasts steeply with other key competing markets.

Offshore Demand

Looking at the projected growth for tech talent, globally, it does not take long to understand that the business process outsourcing (BPO) sector is a much larger business economic stake when compared to the applications development and maintenance sector (IT outsourcing [ITO]). Historically, though, the greater portion of offshored talents has been in the ITO segment.

With the current leading offshoring market currently unable to fulfill the demand for tech talent that exists, while facing soaring turnover and steep salary increases, it is not surprising that international offshoring needs have turned to China.

Most of the initial concerns linked to outsourcing to China will vanish by 2010, as success stories and more key players aggressively move in the market. Historically, some 60 percent of all China-based offshore IT services were geared toward Japan. By 2020, a forecast would see a reverse of this trend. While obviously IT and related tech export services will continue to grow with the Japan market, by 2020, China will most probably offshore less than 40 percent to Japan. More that 60 percent of the offshore-focused numbers will service Western markets and the Asia-Pacific region.

While at present senior technical skill-sets in China maybe be hard to find, such as systems architects, by 2020, China will hold a varied and multitalented workforce, all around, and with specialization in different markets and languages.

OVERSEAS PROMOTIONS LEAP FORWARD

While China holds a number of large, impressive trade shows, international exhibitions, and seminars within its own borders, it is interesting to note that it has really only just begun to promote its outsourcing exports services at overseas events. These overseas promotion efforts are the likely engines to positively impact and support a formidable expansion of the outsourcing sector to overseas markets. This new trend coincides also with recent expansion by China-based companies to conduct business overseas and engage partnerships with partners in their own foreign markets.

In the recent past, technology-focused trade shows on the international scene were mostly dominated by vendors from other markets with little to no participation from China-based suppliers. This long-awaited participation is also at the root of the selection of market and vendor. It is easy to understand why buyers and executive decision makers made decisions where to go, on the basis of the overwhelming attendance by vendors from other countries.

The year 2004 saw for the first time a coordinated approach to organize a pavilion outside of China. That effort was led by the TORCH agency under the Ministry of Science and Technology (MOST). Although relatively simple in its form, that participation of a group of companies at the London-held OutsourceWorld trade show was the start of a new era.

Since then, overseas promotions are gaining momentum. In April 2006, a significant step took place with the Beijing Ministry of Commerce (MOFCOM)-led China Sourcing pavilion organized at the Gartner Outsourcing Summit in Orlando. That pavilion was a true success and also the result of a well-planned strategy. It was followed in the same year by the October 2006 China Software and Integrated Service Platform (CSIP)-led

China Sourcing pavilion, at the Gartner ITXPO Symposium, also held in Orlando.

It is no surprise then that the momentum is building in size and importance with the participation of the China Sourcing pavilions at the March 2007 Gartner Outsourcing Summit in Dallas. For the first time, a central government agency, MOFCOM, led the efforts in promoting and introducing China and its main outsourcing industry players at an overseas trade show (Gartner Outsourcing Summit—Dallas). Participation in Gartner events is a start, and one can expect participation in many other leading events with similar industry-focused trade shows, primarily in North America, Europe, and Japan.

By 2012, it is realistic to anticipate overseas trade shows well attended by solid, regular representation from China. An outlook for year 2020: expect representation by China-based vendors to become a given, reflecting China's implantation as the global leader.

In addition, there are currently many subsidies being structured and rolled out to support China-based company efforts to promote sourcing from China and from those companies, specifically. This is another major new trend that is motivating more players to expand their reach to active direct participation abroad. This is a long-awaited push that was needed, in order to match similar promotion and subsidies sponsored by government, agencies, and organizations from other countries.

Eventually, an association of IT and related services in China will materialize with a chance to succeed in supporting its national players with proper access to overseas and international promotion events. Such an organization will also supplement its members' overseas efforts and cost by advertising to international markets and offering subsidies to its expanding qualifying members.

STABLE CHINA MARKET ECONOMIC PROSPECTS

The stability of the China market is one of the most significant assets that supports its booming outsourcing sector. China is a stable market, and has managed to undergo phenomenal changes over the past 15 years, without any negative outcome. The solid economic outlook for China in 2020 gives every confidence in a prosperous era of continued positive business and market reforms.

With 2020 expectations that China's gross domestic product (GDP) overall will more than quadruple from its current level to over $4 trillion, it is no surprise that a sustained GDP growth forecast provides an annual growth average of 7.2 percent. As for the GDP per capita, it is earmarked to more than triple and surpasses $3,000, up from the $1,000 current level.

Economic stability is critical in providing the outsourcing industry with a sound framework for growth. China has seen positive results since its accession to the World Trade Organization (WTO), with the Beijing 2008 Olympics around the corner, and the upcoming World Expo 2010 in Shanghai, the global marketplace is waking up to a new business face of China, where conducting professional, trade, economic, but also cultural, social, and athletic activities of all kinds take place, like nowhere else.

This is the type of climate; these are the kind of indicators that investors and business executives all around are looking for in firming their strategies and making decisions as to which market they need to offshore with for the long run.

If you recall the motto of "country before company," which was covered earlier, most corporate and international enterprises are moving to China, as it represents the key strategic market of expansion for their own core business. Because most players are pouring into the market to take advantage of the largest industry sectors under construction, it is no surprise that they also settle on sourcing from this strategic expansion market all products and services they can get, especially when those are better, faster, and cheaper than anywhere else.

China has demonstrated that it can implement change and progress in a stable fashion and at a rapid pace. That is why its economy continues to flourish and it also explains the fact that more businesses are taking the step to offshore with China, with a long-term vision.

RISE OF GLOBALIZATION: IN THE FRONT ROW

The world's largest companies are constantly on the move, looking for new business opportunities in all corners of the globe. In the face of increasingly complex global operations and a fast-changing business environment, companies will continuously try to optimize their global networks to minimize the cost of doing business, grow revenue and profits, and manage the associated risks. China represents the cornerstone for market expansion, across industry sectors. By 2020, companies that do not have a firm footstep and market share in China will get earmarked for extinction, downsizing, or merger-and-acquisition activities.

Creating the capabilities to ensure that existing and new network investments—in sourcing opportunities, production locations, product development, and markets—are holistically and continuously optimized is crucial for addressing the challenges created by the rise of globalization.

Offshoring represents an important part of globalization, and the ascension of China to take the lead in that sector is inevitable.

Companies must stay competitive (e.g., revenue growth and cost management targets, and innovation) and compliance (e.g., global and local regulatory constraints and opportunities imposed by regulatory, taxation, and other issues) drivers in mind.

The outlook for 2020 puts China on the map as a driver, no longer of manufacturing goods, but also of engineering and high-end development and business support services of all kinds.

To boost growth and attract high-value-added activities, dozens of countries offer companies tax credits on research and development activities, not only for laboratory research but also for other innovations. China has in every way matched and currently leads those incentives. Software exports from China are tax free. That already provides another five percent competitive advantage to offshore services to China, as opposed to costly India.

Intellectual property, intellectual assets, and intellectual capital are an integral part of how China is shaping up to be an outsourcing world leader. While every decision maker attaches high importance on these factors, different countries treat the valuation and returns on those assets very differently for regulatory, tax, and other purposes.

China is implementing international standards in every one of these key areas. It is only fair to ask that one should not confuse intellectual-related values with occasional tourist-aimed cheap counterfeits on the streets. The government has been driving massive awareness campaigns to educate its people as well as conducting stringent regular crackdowns on counterfeit street shops and countryside factories. One can envision China in 2020 as a counterfeit-free market, with mature and ample means to control, prevent, and remove such goods.

With globalization in full swing, there are today no more risks to offshore to China, as compared to developing in one's own backyard. As long as the basics for security and related processes are in place (physical, logical), as long as networks are properly managed and users segregated with restricted access to authorized space(s), as long as access is properly regulated and protected, China is as safe as building a development center in the United States or the European Union.

To ensure not just episodic, but also continuous optimization, companies must holistically build their infrastructure, aligning people and organizational structures, business processes, and technology platforms. China offers a major advantage to its corporate citizen: the market provides for a state-of-the-art infrastructure. In other countries and other markets, companies have been forced to build around themselves the critical infras-tructure in order to conduct business with other domestic centers and with overseas partners. Expect China to continue to drive the leading edge with every part of its infrastructure until 2020 and beyond.

Entering new markets and accessing new sources of supply around the world often creates new silos of operation. These seldom adopt the same systems and processes of the rest of the company because during their creation they focus on seizing new opportunities. China-based companies have made vested improvements in accessing international standards, at least those that have started to engage in doing business overseas.

International mergers and acquisitions activities are currently vivid proof of how globalization is touching China and its players because they create even larger constellations of values with players leveraging world-class, market-provided infrastructure.

To obtain continuous network optimization off the ground, companies must carefully consider their investment in the needed people, organiza-tional, process, and technology capabilities. Access to the China market and its tech talent is of obvious critical importance to all.

By 2020, expect a truly global China, in advance of so-called considered first world markets, in many ways, constantly reviewing and expanding its business and contact networks.

CHINA 2020: WILD CARDS

There are obviously wild cards that sit on the side of the road, in the shadows, when making forecasts of where China might be with its outsourcing industry, by 2020.

Here is a short summary of those and their likelihood to become an issue:

- **Changes in Regulations.** Changes in regulations can be expected—in every market. China has demonstrated clear business intelligence in structuring regulations that support and are conducive to doing business in China, and with China-based companies. It is likely that this will continue and nothing really can suggest that it will change. Factor: LOW.
- **English and Foreign Language Communications.** There is already ample English-speaking fluent talent and professionals in the market. Bundle that with large amounts of graduates expected to increase the ranks of the largest outsourcing supplier's market and you have a prime working environment. Whereby there may be differences in cultural awareness

and understanding by tech talent in China dealing with overseas clients, expect that by 2020 cultural awareness will be achieved. Factor: LOW.

■ **Aging of China's Population.** The aging of the population in China typically results in forecasts that the number of people over 60 years of age will double by 2025. So, what happens to the young? There is no shortage of graduates to replenish regularly the growing needs for quality and low-cost talents. Besides, there has been talk and rumors of a "two-child policy," although nothing at the moment suggests that the one-child policy is ready to be changed. So, obviously, there are many options toward assessing how the aging of China's population might or might not affect the volume of qualified tech talent from which to source. Factor: LOW.

■ **Currency: Open Trading and Fluctuation.** The revaluation of the Chinese currency, the renminbi (RMB), is a potential factor that deserves some consideration. The RMB was pegged to the dollar in its recent history. Changes in how the RMB is pegged is part of how it is getting ready to eventually be traded as an open currency everywhere. It has managed to revaluate to under RMB7.8 per US$1. Some say that this will help to match the Hong Kong dollar with a unique currency merger. Revaluation of the RMB has a negative impact on the competitiveness of all its goods and services for export. Obviously, when offshoring to China, this is a factor that needs to be taken into consideration. It is unlikely that the RMB will be revalued significantly before 2012. It is unclear what the picture may be beyond that point and what the RMB looks like in 2020. Factor: LOW to MEDIUM.

■ **Rural and Poverty-Linked Social Unrest.** This is the one wild card that most people see as a question mark. According to the United Nations Development Program (UNDP), there are an estimated 100 million people in China living in absolute poverty or on less than US$1 per day. That obviously contrasts negatively with the highly developed, modern, and opulent urban environment.

China and its leaders are fully aware and focused on solving this important challenge. Although the numbers may look a bit different by their standards, Chinese leaders all unanimously agree that this is the "most most important of the most important" (zhong zhong zhi zhong) task that they have to solve. With that in mind, and knowing how rapidly China undertakes and implements change initiatives, it at least gives a positive feel that its leaders' awareness is on high alert, and that solving it is within reach. Although it is not an easy challenge to solve, China is well aware of this challenge and will find an approach to harness it without tumultuous results. Factor: LOW to MEDIUM.

- **Improving the Environment.** Of the wild cards on the outsourcing industry's radar screen, this is the least likely to have any effects. Obviously, it has a high impact on the world and I have received on several instances comments by people that said they were not interested in offshoring in a country that pollutes the rest of the world. The country and its leaders are making vested, aggressive steps toward major environment-focused initiatives. While in the eyes of Western critics, these environment-focused initiatives are never enough, one has to give credit to the leadership of China for what it has already started to accomplish and one must encourage them to continue with a positive outlook and increased momentum by 2020. Factor: LOW.
- **International Protectionism Measures.** With more complex international economic and political environments—changes in regulations, environmental protection, international trade and investments, and currency rate fluctuations—compounding possible future scenarios, protectionism may be the most critical potential trade situation that China faces.

  Some developed economies and Western countries may undergo a rise in unemployment, which may lead to a premature reaction and generating some level of protectionism. Protectionism could affect the global outsourcing industry by 2020 only during a very brief moment, should it take place. Why? It is obvious that ultimately such measures are detrimental and harmful to the very economies (or countries) that would consider inflicting such measures on them in a global marketplace. Factor: LOW.

Exclusive Survey of Selected Cities in Cooperation With MOFCOM

T he following survey was conducted exclusively for I.T. UNITED by the Ministry of Commerce. Participating were the administrations from China's most important software and technology parks, in 11 different cities throughout the country. This is one of the first such looks at the growth and perspectives of software and technology park administrators regarding their own plans to promote technology adoption and encourage investment by both foreign and domestic technology firms.

QUALITATIVE RESULTS: OPEN FORMULATED QUESTIONS

City	Is One of the Following an Issue for Your High-Tech Park? What are You Doing About it?	How Do You Plan to Control Rising Salary/Rapid Turnover?	How Do You Plan to Support the Software Outsourcing Industry in Your City/ Province? What Will You Do?	Is Anybody in Your High-Tech Park in Charge of Overseas Relationships?
Beijing	Employee turnover	Different company has its own culture	Training resources, international development, and cooperation	Yes
Chengdu	Rising salaries Employee turnover	Educating the resources Enhance the company culture training	Training good talents, enhancing the market development	Yes

City	Is One of the Following an Issue for Your High-Tech Park? What are You Doing About it?	How Do You Plan to Control Rising Salary/Rapid Turnover?	How Do You Plan to Support the Software Outsourcing Industry in Your City/Province? What Will You Do?	Is Anybody in Your High-Tech Park in Charge of Overseas Relationships?
Dalian	Rising salaries Employee turnover Attracting technology talents	Enhance the benefits, life, and working environment. For the senior talents, Dalian government will pay them more compensation to file their own income tax.	Will release official policy like "how to promote outsourcing development in Dalian."	Yes
Guangzhou	Rising salaries Employee turnover Attracting technology talents 1. Industry rule 2. Industry association restriction 3. Government rewarding	N/A	Training good talents, market development, provide technical support	Yes
Hangzhou	N/A	Policy support Better services Improving the environment	N/A	Yes
Ji'nan	Rising salaries Employee turnover Attracting technology talents Frame the policies to support the company's association to keep the salary level	Because Jinan is near the ancestral home of Confucius, people are simple and honest, we have naturally low turnover. Via the international cooperation association, could keep the salary level.	N/A	Yes

City	Is One of the Following an Issue for Your High-Tech Park? What are You Doing About it?	How Do You Plan to Control Rising Salary/Rapid Turnover?	How Do You Plan to Support the Software Outsourcing Industry in Your City/ Province? What Will You Do?	Is Anybody in Your High-Tech Park in Charge of Overseas Relationships?
Nanjing	Rising salaries Employee turnover Attracting technology talents The salary level should match the local economic development level; it should be related to the staff's work performance. The turnover should be solved based on the "labor law," but the key way is to improve the working & living environment. Regarding resources, we should work with the universities to train more senior resources.	Establish the company culture to let the employee know the company's future. Improve the working and living environment.	Aggressive promotion, frames the related policies, and enhancing the communication internationally, encourage the companies to pass CMM/CMMI.	Yes
Shanghai	Employee turnover	N/A	Training Market development Establish public technical services platform	Such plans exist but require the support of economic and financial policy. support.

City	Is One of the Following an Issue for Your High-Tech Park? What are You Doing About it?	How Do You Plan to Control Rising Salary/Rapid Turnover?	How Do You Plan to Support the Software Outsourcing Industry in Your City/Province? What Will You Do?	Is Anybody in Your High-Tech Park in Charge of Overseas Relationships?
Shenzhen	Rising salaries Employee turnover Attracting technology talents	Control management, enhance efficiency, and improve the development process. Establish the company culture.	Enhance international communication; establish the image of outsourcing city for Shenzhen. Unite the companies to control the salary to avoid turnover. Give more training on software resources.	Yes
Tianjin	Employee turnover Attracting technology talents	We have plenty of software/ computer talents and low turnover.	We have established relevant policies to encourage and promote software outsourcing industry.	Yes
Xi'an	Rising salaries Employee turnover Attracting technology talents	Get more training and job promotion opportunity to the employees.	Xi'an has abundant resources in software industry. Will release related policies to support the industry.	Yes

HOW MANY SOFTWARE/COMPUTER SCIENCE MAJOR STUDENTS (BACHELOR'S OR MASTER'S DEGREE) GRADUATED IN YOUR CITY IN THE LAST 3 YEARS?

		2004	2005	2006
1	Beijing	18,100	24,900	33,000
2	Chengdu	n/a	n/a	n/a
3	Dalian	n/a	n/a	8,000
4	Guangzhou	n/a	n/a	38,000
5	Hangzhou	12,000	18,000	20,000
6	Ji'nan	5,000	5,500	5,000
7	Nanjing	4,500	6,000	8,000
8	Shanghai	n/a	n/a	n/a
9	Shenzhen	1,500	2,000	3,000
10	Tianjin	2,464	2,925	3,489
11	Xi'an	22,000	26,000	30,000
	SUM	65,564	85,325	148,489

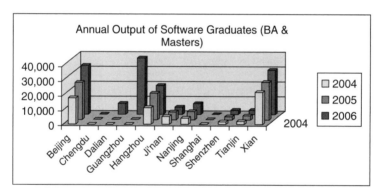

EXHIBIT A.1 Annual Output of Software Graduates in Top Chinese Cities (B.A. and Masters)

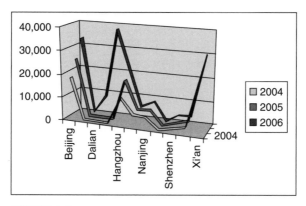

EXHIBIT A.1   (continued)
Source: Ministry of Commerce of the People's Republic of China

Case Studies

As we know, theory and practice in business are very different. To this point, this book has discussed a lot of what it is like to outsource to China, of course, based on more than a decade of experience in the China business environment and in outsourcing specifically.

However, perhaps the best way to demonstrate the value of what outsourcing partners in China can offer is through a series of case studies involving different companies, both in terms of clients and the outsourcing companies they chose.

In the following cases, the clients had opportunities to outsource to other countries and companies, but instead chose the partners noted here. Overall, these case studies demonstrate the wide range of services available from outsourcing firms in China, and the cost savings and advantages in quality they can offer.

Going for the Chinese Choice

The client initially contacted one of the best-known Indian-based outsourcing companies to handle the project. However, the client was not satisfied with the progress of the project and that company's attitude. The client was not big enough for the Indian corporation, junior management handled the client and the company's response to the client's needs was slow and insufficient. Therefore, the client decided to check options within the Chinese market as they wanted to localize their product to ten languages (Simplified Chinese, Traditional Chinese, Japanese, Korean, Russian, Spanish, German, French, Portuguese, and Turkish). For that purpose, the client required a partner who would set up the test plan and test case development, and conduct all functional and localization testing in all ten languages.

Not long after turning to China, the client chose Beyondsoft (after an initial study of more than ten service suppliers in China) as their new outsourcing provider. Client's decision was based on service provider's track record, service quality, and workforce professionalism, especially senior

BEYONDSOFT GROUP

For questions concerning this case study contact:
Name: Anita Lee, Business Relationship Manager, Sales and Marketing Department
E-mail: anita@beyondsoft.com
Phone: 86 (10) 8282-6100 (ext.) 8203

Overview
Client: A leading global company in Business Performance Management (BPM) software. The company's main function is data warehousing, which enables its clients to collect, organize, and analyze data, then distribute it throughout their enterprise using a rich, unified workspace that makes business performance management easier. The company was named one of the Fortune 100 Best Companies to Work For (2004) and serves global customers in more than 90 countries. The company generated revenues of US$765 million for the fiscal year that ended on June 2006.

Client Industry: Business intelligence.

Service Line: Testing and localization services.

Project Description: Full functionality and localization testing for a Web-based budget planning system, widely used by many large enterprises. Testing was performed on a multiple platforms and in conjunction with multiple database engines.

Technology/Platform:

- MS Windows 2003 (x86/Itanium)
- AIX 5.3, HP-UX 11i win64, Sun Solaris 9
- MS Windows 2000 (Client only), DB2, Oracle, SQL server, Websphere, Weblogic, Tomcat, IE, and Firefox

Number of staff involved in China: 1 Project Manager, 25 testers during peak period, 1 test lead.
Project Size: Over US$500,000

management team's commitment to long-term relationships with clients, flexibility, and cost savings. The client's choice was based on Beyondsoft's excellent performance demonstrated through most of the aforementioned perspectives, and finding that Beyondsoft received better references from their previous clients in comparison to the references given to the other suppliers.

For companies with a limited budget for outsourcing projects (around US$5 million annual spending with one supplier or under), China provides an attractive alternative to the outsourcing establishment. Add the fact that China is also a strategic market for most companies and you have got the perfect case for building a business network with China-based providers to establish technical expertise support market entry and/or expansion. In this case, the client received a level of management attention that was a far cry from what had been going on before. Beyondsoft guarantees a 24-hour response to any client requests and also arranges meetings with the client for detailed requirement discussions that also include quantity of Full-time Team Extensions (FTEs) and cost effects before the project got underway.

Key Challenges...

The project team identified the following challenges before project kickoff:

- A very tight schedule for the completion of the project.
- Short ramp-up time for personnel recruitment and staffing.
- The project's complexity rendered it difficult for the client to configure a structured, coherent test strategy and test plan, resulting in faulty implementation during the software development cycle.
- The high-level test requirements from the client were unclear. It soon also emerged that the offshore team had to cope with changing demands.
- The China-based offshore team lacked knowledge of the client's complex product: the testing team's knowledge and understanding of the localized product was insufficient due to limited access to product information. This generated problems in the nondefect reporting, which proved to be ineffective and overly time consuming.
- As the client was located in a different time zone, real-time communication was required during this project.

... And How They Were Addressed

To address the needs of the client as stated previously, the Beyondsoft team took the following action:

- The Beyondsoft team initiated the project using internal staff and teams. Beyondsoft's Human Resources team assisted staffing more than 15 experienced testers within one month. Because the Beyondsoft teams are composed of both local and international engineers with extensive experience in working in bilingual environment, they easily communicated with the client's team in English throughout the whole process
- The offshore team developed and implemented a complete testing methodology for the project and provided a one-stop solution for the whole software test life cycle.
- With the client's help, Beyondsoft conducted a series of training sessions for the project team members: system installation training and financial knowledge training was given to team members before and during the project. The Beyondsoft team also consulted the client frequently on ambiguous issues to avoid reporting nondefects.
- Team analysis helped track defects that were potentially nondefects (e.g., specific parts which were not supposed to be localized). The team also discussed potential defects of this kind with the client before officially delivering a defect report to the client. This way, the team could provide accurate bug descriptions and log files to help the client's team reproduce the reported bugs in order to eliminate them all.
- As the client was located in a different time zone, and in order to streamline communication with the client's team, Beyondsoft used conference calling and Remote Desktop/VNC/Telnet for daily communication and troubleshooting

The Results

The Beyondsoft team was able to meet the client's needs, and as demonstrated by these results, the client has continued and expanded its relationship with Beyondsoft:

- Working with a China-based company enabled the client to achieve an over 30 percent cost savings compared with their previous Indian provider, both in terms of FTEs and working hours dedicated to the project.
- The Beyondsoft test and project management practices improved the quality testing process for the client. This resulted in Beyondsoft reporting 320 defects that are over 30 percent of the client's expectation and successfully managed to eliminate them.
- In the wake of the successful completion of this project, the client decided to migrate their software development to Beyondsoft's Offshore Delivery Centre (ODC).

About Beyondsoft

Established in 1995, Beyondsoft is one of the biggest software outsourcing companies in China. Its focus is on end-to-end software engineering services, providing its global clients with software development services, full quality assurance and testing services, multilingual localization, and Business Process Outsourcing (BPO) services in different industries, such as IT, telecom, finance, and insurance.

Beyondsoft is an International Data Corp. (IDC)-ranked top three U.S. and Europe-oriented IT outsourcing and China (CCID)-ranked top ten software outsourcing company in China. It was recognized by the Chinese government and expert panels as the key software enterprise of 2005.

Challenges

The client in this case study is a leading commercial bank with fast growth and a strong reputation for innovation in the industry. Although a relatively new player in this sector, the client operates through a network of 370 branches in 36 major cities in the Asia Pacific region and has one of the most highly regarded credit-card operations in the industry. However, the client was also faced with unprecedented challenges both in terms of market competition and diversified client requirements, given its relatively small size and short operational history.

With the recent deregulation of the banking sector in the region in general and China in particular, banks have witnessed the fastest growth in their history. In an industry crowded already with global giants like Citigroup and HSBC and regional players such as the Bank of China, small and medium-sized banks without a massive network and robust back office capabilities must be very agile and innovative to win their niche in the market.

The key challenge for the client was to offer similar or better products and services at lower cost, yet with higher efficiency and shorter turnaround time—and without significant change impact on the day-to-day operation of their business. To this end, the client first engaged a management consulting firm to redesign its business processes and come up with recommendations on where processes could be optimized. The study found out that many middle- and back-office functions were repetitive and labor intensive in nature and added little value to the client's total value chain. In the meantime, they represented a disproportional percentage of the client's headcount and management headaches.

CHINA DATA GROUP

For questions concerning this case study contact:
Name: Roc Yang
E-mail: roc_yang@chinadatagroup.com
Phone: 861089451251

Overview

Client: An innovative and fast-growing commercial bank in the Asia Pacific region.

Industry: Financial services.

Service Line: BPO-credit card applications processing

Project Description: A leading Asia Pacific-based commercial bank outsourced its middle and back office credit card application processes to China Data Group (CDG). The end-to-end solution covers mailroom processes, screening, scanning, archiving, credit reference checking, data capturing, and physical document storage, as well as contact center services.

Technology/Platform:

- Technology: Delphi, .NET, J2EE, JSP, XML, HTML, PGP (for Encryption)
- Platform: Linux, Windows Server 2003

Number of staff involved in China: 200 people in five locations, including process experts, software engineers, hardware engineers, and process operators.

Project Size: US$2 million P.A.

Selecting the Right Partner

This message was very clear and well received by the client in late 2004 when new management was sworn in. The client decided to focus on the most value-added processes and capabilities and offload noncore hassles to a third-party provider. A lengthy vendor selection process followed. Not surprisingly, instead of a low-cost vendor, the client was looking for a long-term strategic partner who could grow with them over time. CDG's investment in quality and security over the years paid off when faced with demanding clients.

EXHIBIT B.1 CDG's credentials vs. client's requirements

Areas Measured	What CDG Had to Offer
Industry and process domain knowledge	Nine years systems integration and business process outsourcing (BPO) experience in the Banking, Financial Services, and Insurance (BFSI) sectors
Technological capability	Strong IT team with third core member meeting (CMM3) capability
Solutions maturity	End-to-end credit card application processing solution for close to 20 BFSI clients, among six credit card issuers
Delivery capability	On-site, near-site, and off-site delivery capability, multiple languages delivery capabilities for the Asia-Pacific region
Data security practice	Sophisticated data and information security policy and infrastructure consistent with BS17799 standards
Financial strength	Funded by four reputable global funds

Compared with the long selection process, the decision was a quick one. Exhibit B.1 shows a number of reasons why CDG stood out.

Price had been an issue at the early selection stage, however, the client's concern for quality, reliability, and data security quickly imposed itself over the need for pure cost cutting. As reflected in the Service Level Agreements (SLAs), the client put high priority on turnaround time, quality of the services, and data and information security, which were more mission critical to them.

Project Scope

The project scope included all typical noncore functions such as mailroom processes (anything from receiving and sorting incoming credit application forms and basic statistics), to screening, scanning, indexing, quality checking, credit reference checking, data capturing, and storage of the physical documents. As an additional complication, while some processes such as data capture could be done remotely against the scanned images at the vendor's site, there were also some tasks that had to be conducted on site. This also meant that a Business Process Management (BPM) system had to be put in place at three different client locations to run all the processes and data interfaces with the client's core system.

CDG therefore had to deploy the right combination of process experts, software and hardware engineers, and process operators. What made the task even more demanding was that the client wanted the project to go live within two months time to meet with its business target of a major milestone promotion event. The sheer logistics behind the project were daunting.

Solutions and Delivery Model

CDG came well prepared. Within four weeks, the team was halfway through CDG's Project Implementation Methodology (see Exhibit B.2) leveraging on its industry templates for the Analysis and Customization Stages. CDG took into full account all the stumbling blocks in a typical transformation project, for example, people, process, facility, system, and project management.

The Pilot Stage kicked off the business transformation. The approaches were quick but not at all dirty. CDG's team took over most of the client's staff from the three key locations and put in place its own management, processes, and software system to get things going before the target due date for the operation stage.

The transformation of the on-site portion was much smoother and less painful than the client had foreseen, given that CDG was using the same people in the same premises, only under different project management.

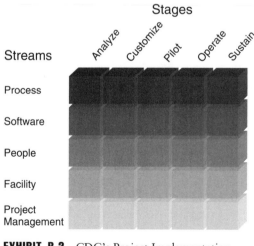

EXHIBIT B.2 CDG's Project Implementation Methodology

For the off-site portion, CDG leveraged its existing large-scale transaction processing facility in Beijing to handle the volume.

However, just six months into the normal operation of the project, the team ran into a bottleneck. Because the back-office data capture capability at CDG was way too efficient for the client, the on-site staff in those three locations simply could not meet the requested throughput to feed the data processing team. So, CDG had to come up with something more radical and innovative for the client and proposed a seemingly drastic solution: to consolidate all the middle-office processes such as screening, scanning, archiving, and credit reference checking to a centralized location in Shanghai and to manage those processes very much like several parallel assembly lines with real-time video monitoring access to the client.

Because the benefits were obvious, this plan received an immediate green-light from the client and went live within three months (see Exhibits Exhibit B.3 and Exhibit B.4 for the Delivery Model Migration). Bar-coding technology and Kanban technique, which were widely used in the manufacturing sector to better manage transparency and improve productivity, were also introduced at the facility, resulting in significant improvement in processing throughput and information transparency during the whole process.

Project governance did not come as a challenge because CDG had already put in place the mechanism of a project steering committee and project management team for two-way communications at different levels.

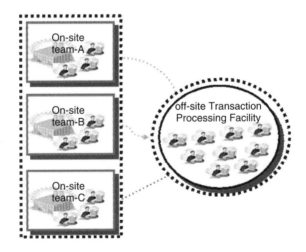

EXHIBIT B.3 Initial Delivery Model

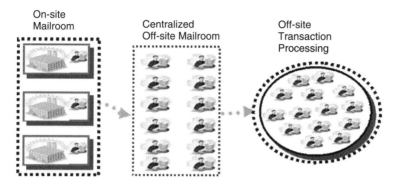

On-site
Mailroom

Centralized
Off-site Mailroom

Off-site
Transaction
Processing

EXHIBIT B.4 Improved Delivery Model

Its operations staff was also very familiar with the reporting mechanism, regular client quality checks, and random surprise visits.

The Results

Two years into the project, the client has become one of the award-winning credit-card operators in the region, constantly rolling out new products and services at no extra fixed assets investment. The savings were apparent in almost every aspect of their operation: office rental, headcount, hardware investment, software development, recruiting and training, as well as per head operations cost. In some areas, the savings could be as high as 30 percent year on year. All the while, the client's customer satisfaction levels have been climbing thanks to the much improved service quality and product-to-market turnaround time. In the client's organization, managing SLAs instead of managing the hassles of daily operation became a much-appreciated fact of life and management efforts are devoted solely to their core business. No more complaints from their staff about overtime and no more worries of having to juggle between business peaks and troughs.

As a result of the very satisfactory development of the partnership, the client has decided to outsource additional areas to CDG, which will be opening up a call center for the client very soon. Many other opportunities for cooperation are yet to unfold down the road as the partners tackle an increasing number of business challenges together in good faith.

About China Data Group

Founded in 1998, CDG is the leading BPO provider in China, specializing in the banking, financial services, and insurance (BFSI) sectors and finance and accounting outsourcing (FAO) services. Its unique operations model combines state-of-the-art business process management (BPM) solutions to enable clients to reduce costs, standardize internal processes, and focus on their core business.

CDG was founded and is currently managed by experienced professionals from the leading financial services institutions, such as HSBC, Citigroup, and ICBC, and premier service providers, such as PricewaterhouseCoopers, Capgemini, Deloitte Touche Tomhatsu, and Satyam. This unique combination of talents assures a real partnership spirit between CDG and its clients.

Headquartered in Beijing, CDG operates through 1,200 staff capacity in three key locations of Beijing, Shanghai, and Guangzhou in China. For more information about CDG's BPO solutions, visit www.chinadatagroup.com.

Localization and Product Testing: Be Global, Act Local

The client in this case study (hereafter referred to as "the corporation") needed support in China for localization and testing of their existing PLM application.

Meet the Client

The corporation, a proven PLM solution in the industry, is used by original equipment manufacturers throughout the supply value chain. The corporation's solutions allow companies to manage the day-to-day changes of product content throughout development, prototype, manufacturing, support, and retirement phases. Customers leverage the corporation's application suite to coordinate an array of product contact configurations across different partners, daily changes in product content, and product content communication across multiple parties. Key functions of the application include access control, product structure, and change control.

Initial Engagement and Project Outline

The corporation and DarwinSuzsoft began working together in 2004 for localization and testing of the corporation's latest and most advanced PLM series product. DarwinSuzsoft was selected after a formal, competitive evaluation process based in part on domain knowledge and English-speaking skills. In 2005, after the initial engagement was successfully completed, DarwinSuzsoft was awarded responsibility for developing and maintaining the PLM series in China, covering the entire life cycle of the product.

DarwinSuzsoft

For questions concerning this case study contact:
Name: Jonathan Myerov
E-mail: jmyerov@darwinsuzsoft.com
Phone: 781-213-7143

Overview

Client: DarwinSuzsoft's client (the corporation) is a NASDAQ-listed software corporation that makes a broad suite of enterprise-class product life-cycle management (PLM) solutions to help companies manage the entire product lifecycle and leverage maximum business value from their products. Over 11,000 customers in the automotive, aerospace and defense, consumer packaged goods, electronics, high tech, industrial products, and life sciences industries have licensed solutions by the corporation.

Industry: PLM software solutions.

Service Line: DarwinSuzsoft provided full life-cycle software product development and maintenance.

Project Description: DarwinSuzsoft is responsible for the development and maintenance of the corporation's PLM series in China.

Technology / Platform:

- OS: Windows Server 2003, Windows XP
- Database: Oracle 8i, 10g
- CASE Tools: Rational Rose, PowerDesigner 10.0
- Development Tools: Visual Studio 6.0, JBuilder X, PL/SQL Developer 6.0, InstallShield DevStudio 9.0, Visual Build 5.4 Professional, Ant, BoundsCheck 7.2, Identify AppSight, XML SPY 2004 Enterprise, CrashFinder
- Testing Tools: Parasoft C++Test, JUnit, Rational Robot 2003, WinRunner 7.6, LoadRunner 8.0

Number of staff involved in China: 54 full-time employees.
Project Size: Approximately US$2 million annually

The product—that is, the application suite—consisted of several components: Administrator, Windows Client, Web Application, Program Management, ChangeCAST, Import, eXpress Professional, Scan, Dataload & Fileload, Viewer, ACSU, Database Utilities, SDK (JAVA & COM), Distributed iFS, and Web Service. The application suite also covered more than eight solutions, including product record management, document management and control, view and markup, quality management, product sourcing, engineering integration, and enterprise integration.

The DarwinSuzsoft team undertook the following responsibilities:

- Analysis and design
- Implementation and integration
- Testing & deployment
- Internationalization
- Maintenance and support

Team: Structured for Success

DarwinSuzsoft set up a team consisting of 1 Development Manager, 3 Project Managers, 2 Quality Assurance Managers, 2 Sustaining Managers, approximately 30 Engineers (support, C/C++, and JAVA), 16 QA/Testers as well as Designers and Architects. The team was set up in a separate physical space on DarwinSuzsoft premises. The overall organizational structure, on an ongoing basis, has consisted of both crossfunctional and product line teams that have also been highly flexible.

With three product lines and the sheer number of components, it was imperative to set up a clear structure and build in-depth product knowledge for the dedicated team. DarwinSuzsoft therefore organized the team by product line. A project manager responsible for all related project activities, including resources, scheduling, and communication, headed each product-line team. Depending on the number of activities for the product line, there would be team lead for each track, reporting back to the project manager. Leads would come from development, sustaining, localization, quality assurance (QA), and so on.

On the corporation's side, there was a counterpart (ranging from director to manager level) that was responsible for engaging with DarwinSuzsoft at the project team level. At the project level, the project managers communicated with their corporation counterparts on an as-needed basis. Depending on the track, this communication would occur several times a day, once a day, or less frequently. However, DarwinSuzsoft's project managers met with their corporation counterparts at least once a week to monitor team activities. English was the primary language of the project team.

Building the Partnership...

After successfully delivering the corporation's application service packs in May 2005, DarwinSuzsoft's team provided ongoing support by resolving issues or questions from customers—approximately 40 per week. On average, DarwinSuzsoft's team was able to resolve single issues within two days. For major enhancement requests, the team developed plans with a minimum of two recommended solutions, including an estimated implementation schedule for each solution. Together with human resources (HR), the team also planned ahead the number of staff required to cover any contingencies such as new enhancements, so as not to affect ongoing maintenance work (Service Packs and Hot Fixes).

While individual DarwinSuzsoft engagements with the corporation have been anywhere from two months to a year in duration, DarwinSuzsoft has maintained a stable core corporation team and deployed additional skilled resources as required. For example, as offshore engineering needs increased, DarwinSuzsoft rapidly scaled its teams in China. Team scalability and skills availability had been primary reasons, in addition to cost savings, why the corporation selected DarwinSuzsoft for China-based development work.

... Based on Tangible Results

The corporation benefited directly by working with DarwinSuzsoft, particularly in gaining the capability to scale up their team at short notice, which was crucial in completing all projects on time and within budget. Currently, the DarwinSuzsoft team includes more than 50 core members, and the corporation's savings on engineer salaries along has totaled approximately US$2 million, not including facility and HR costs.

Over the years, DarwinSuzsoft has supported several of the corporation's product lines by providing development, localization, sustenance, QA testing, and maintenance, and has become a valuable member of the client's partner team. The chosen engagement model was a result of DarwinSuzsoft's accumulated knowledge, continual improvements, and commitment on the part of both the corporation and DarwinSuzsoft. As China's importance keeps growing and more and more U.S. companies are getting accustomed to working with China-based IT services providers, this deployment model is also becoming more common in China.

This model has particularly benefited the corporation by having their knowledge bases continually built up in product and PLM domain intelligence. DarwinSuzsoft is responsible for retaining and managing this knowledge base and growing the team, which allows the corporation to focus on developing intellectual capital without compromising standards in team management and project execution.

About DarwinSuzsoft

As the first U.S. IT services company with 100 percent ownership of a major Chinese software engineering firm, DarwinSuzsoft provides technical project support and China-based development services to more than 300 blue chip clients globally. DarwinSuzsoft's fully integrated United States-China services include project management and technical implementation; offshore software application development, enhancement and maintenance; offshore development centers; business process outsourcing; software product support; and strategic staffing. Celebrating a 20-year company history, DarwinSuzsoft employs more than 1,000 people based in its Boston headquarters and cities including San Francisco, Shanghai, Beijing, Hong Kong, and Dalian, China. For more information, visit www.darwinsuzsoft.com.

Introduction

This case study is about hiSoft's first and most challenging long-term commitment in Europe and North America, which was to provide qualified services and solutions for the purpose of maintaining the U.S. energy firm's support system.

The U.S. Energy Firm — A Revitalizing Dive into China's Offshore Tech Market

The client is a world leader in the utilization and control of water, and has been supplying equipment to the hydropower and water-control industries for over one hundred fifty years. The client provides services to power stations and water-control installations all over the world, and has designed and manufactured some of the world's largest and most technologically advanced hydro turbines, hydraulic gates, generators, and valves. In China, the client is heavily involved in the Three Gorges Project, with the responsibility for the hydraulic design of all the machines, as well as the supply of turbines and generators.

Being a leading Fortune 100 corporation, the client companies frequently audit such matters as security, network, processes, and resources to ensure that their vendors maintain the same level of quality they do at home. When the client's vendor in Canada experienced problems in implementing its global delivery center standards (GDC standards) for the client's support system, the management decided to discontinue the contract and started looking at outsourcing providers in Asia, anticipating a more cost-efficient solution system.

The support system is the platform for all core functionalities and processes for the client's outlets in the United States, Canada, Europe, Asia, and Australia. Its functions range from finance to enterprise resource

hiSoft

For questions concerning this case study contact:
Name: Meg Luo
E-mail: meg.luo@hisoft.com
Phone (ext.): 021 5467 0508 (810)

Overview

Client: U.S. energy firm.

Industry: Energy.

Service Line: Packaged solutions, which include IT outsourcing/business-process outsourcing (ITO/BPO), testing, and application development.

Project Description: This case study is about hiSoft's first and most challenging long-term commitment in Europe and North America, which was to provide qualified services and solutions for the purpose of maintaining the U.S energy firm's support system.

Technology / Platform:

- AS400 related (Cobol/JCL/VSAM)
- DB2, Oracle
- ERP
- Java

Number of staff involved in China: 15
Project Size: US$2 million

planning (ERP) to manufacturing resource planning (MRP). For the client, the GDC means IT software application and maintenance outsourcing from GE to third party IT vendors.

Finding the Right Partner

In March 2004, the U.S. energy firm launched its project in China, looking for a partner who could offer solutions including program development, application testing, system maintenance, and 24-hour technical support.

The U.S. firm expected the new provider to fully meet its quality standards and started looking for a medium-sized team that could manage one of the most complex and advanced technical systems in the world of hydropower and water-control installations. The required technological skillset included:

- Application server (BEA Weblogic)
- DB (DB2, Oracle, MS SQL Server, MS Access)
- DB related technologies (Data Warehouse, Data Mining, Data Mart, performance tuning)
- Programming languages such as C/C++, Java/J2EE, Delphi, VB, COBOL/JCL

hiSoft—Pitching the U.S. Energy Firm

The most critical question for the U.S. energy firm was: "How can we ensure that the outsourcing software company is qualified?" The firm started the selection process by sending out the request for proposal (RFP) to major IT outsourcing providers in India and China, expecting them to submit a proposal that responded to all 68 survey questions. The questions explored the matrix of on-/offshore with onsite support modules, ERP/MRP, staffing planning, highly complex skillsets, risk/quality/process management methodologies, and communication planning.

For hiSoft, a China-based provider, this was an excellent opportunity to cut into the European and U.S. markets. However, there were several challenges—among them, the fact that China is perceived to be at a much lower level than the mature Indian outsourcing market. Records showed that all the major partners the client had worked with in the past were located in India. Companies like Tata, InfoSys, and Birlasoft had mature and integrated systems coupled with profound experience in working with high-profile industry leaders. How would hiSoft—or any other China-based company for that matter—be able to beat such competitors? Second, meeting global delivery standards for all three modules—onsite, onshore, and offshore—at once, represented a major challenge.

In April 2004, the client retained hiSoft's proposal for the two-year contract, which promised to achieve the results expected by the client, within budget. HiSoft's onsite-offshore delivery model was aimed at optimizing quality and cost-of-project delivery through the use of proven project-delivery methodology, and taking advantage of available global voice/data connectivity.

Rolling out the Plan

hiSoft took the initiative in staffing and deployment, trying to build a team to support the project in terms of integrating offshore and onsite modules. After a meeting in Montreal, the headquarters of the client, five consultants (one delivery manager, four senior consultants [called business analysts], ERP/MRP, a data-warehouse analyst, and a database administrator) were assigned to the onsite support group in Montreal. Meanwhile, the offshore team was formed in Dalian, a leading second-tier outsourcing city. The offshore team included several different technical groups:

- AS400 Solution team
- DB (DB2, Oracle, MS SDL Server Solution team, Data Warehouse Solution team)
- ERP/MRP Solution team
- Java/J2EE Solution team
- C/C++ Solution team

To provide support to the client's business applications, offshore team members were then grouped into the following three teams:

- Client's Application Maintenance and Support PSA AS 400 team
- Client's Application Maintenance and Support PSA AS 400 team
- Client's Application Maintenance and Support team

Once the staffing platform was set, the hiSoft client's teams then started breaking down the plan into process steps of quality/risk/communication and project management. At the same time, the core team developed the communication plan for the client/hiSoft, set up the onsite/offshore teams, as well as the development and Quality Assurance teams.

The Takeover

The project in this case study was special, insofar as part of the system had originally been designed by the client's vendor in Canada. To fully take over all design concepts and efficiently take the system to the next level, the hiSoft client's teams went through four planning stages before the real takeover took place.

The first step was a meeting with the client's previous vendor. The meeting allowed the new team to collect and restore all the functional and technical documents for further development, obtain access to the current applications, and to finalize the knowledge transfer (KT) plan for business process.

The second step was to prepare for the skillset applied to the system. The hiSoft client's teams succeeded in the knowledge acquisition of the third-party software, third-party packages, and tools required for the project. Along with the process of business analysis of criticality and functionality of applications, they quickly decided on the front- and back-end components, interfaces, and system input/output. Special attention was also paid to source-code elements and the documentation used by the application.

The third stage was testing pilot support services. In view of mitigating future proces risks, the hiSoft client's teams designed a pilot system that could be used for test runs. With the client's and the previous vendor's approval, hiSoft dedicated a significant amount of time to selecting and testing sample cases. Meanwhile, the team also designed a toll-gate process for the client to regularly review the pilot, and continued testing its 24/7 support model, which was intended to cater to the client's needs for around-the-clock system maintenance. The official support began after the pilot had been signed off on, and transition approval was received from the client.

The fourth and final takeover stage was conducted in a flow of constant software deployment, application testing, service execution, and result reporting. Communication between the client and hiSoft client's teams was ongoing and the service level agreement (SLA) review took place on a biweekly basis.

The Results

Twenty-four months into the project, hiSoft migrated the concept of Six Sigma to their project-management group right after the testing period. The group significantly improved its services with the evaluation of CMM five standards, and it received very positive feedback from the client. Statistics from the client's teams show that the first-time right (FTR)—new features and the first-time release are correct—was above 98 percent, the on-time delivery (OTD) above 99 percent, and the on-time response (OTR) above 98 percent. These statistics represented top-service levels not only for China, but also in comparison to the global IT outsourcing industry.

The two-year project was completed in January 2006. Since the client's expectations of a more cost-effective solution were fully met, the partnership has since evolved to the next stage, with a new three-year project being put into motion. With a proposal already 20 percent less expensive than the bidding price from Indian vendors, hiSoft enabled the client to cut the previous vendor's budget nearly in half.

Last, but not least, the fact that hiSoft managed to move up the value chain by successfully providing services that matched demanding global-delivery standard marked yet another milestone in the rapid development of China-based tech outsourcing.

About hiSoft

With more than 2,000 IT resources, a comprehensive solutions platform, and mature delivery model, hiSoft has established itself as one of China's largest and leading IT service providers. Dedicated to innovation, superior quality, and customer satisfaction, it continues to lead the way and deliver unparalleled services to its clients worldwide.

As one of the pioneers to have a large, scalable team of IT professionals in China with front-end local experts in both the Japan and U.S. markets, hiSoft is positioned to become the largest global IT services company based in China. For more information visit www.hisoft.com.

Offshore Software R&D in China within HP

Early in May 2002, HP set up its Shanghai-based China Delivery Center (GDCC) as an application services provider of choice for customers. This organization has grown more than 20-fold and has become the second largest global delivery hub for HP in Application Services. With competitive complement country capabilities in delivery of services across applications life-cycle, GDCC is capable of helping:

- Improve HP differentiation through solutions, IP retention, and reuse
- Reduce risk and improve quality through uniform, consistent tools and processes across delivery value chain
- Reduce cost of software development, integration, and support by leveraging global delivery model

In 2005, GDCC was successfully certified with CMMI ML5. At that time, GDCC had more than 1,000 professionals and the number is expected to double by the end of 2007.

The GDCC started executing an effective ramp-up strategy for supporting the HP R&D initiatives from 2004. The first program in GDCC started with a five-member team in mid-May 2004, which expanded very fast over the last three years owing to increasing business needs, and it has now becomes an extended offshore R&D resource pool with always improving competency.

Strong support from the HP and GDCC leadership team has progressively moved GDCC forward as a worldwide Center of Expertise (CoE) on system administration software solutions. With strong commitment to customer satisfaction, extensive training, and cooperation with other CoEs, GDCC has been developed into an extremely rigorous, agile, and effective implementation team, with the following critical success factors:

- Fast growing APJ market
- Capabilities in skills, processes, methodologies, infrastructure, and scalability
- Competitive unit labor cost
- Best TCE—high intimacy with internal customers
- Software intellectual property (IP) harvest and reuse
- Highly creative, enthusiastic, dynamic, and motivated workforce
- Organization maturity and teamwork

Shanghai Team

The R&D Shanghai team is composed of various product domain groups with focuses on software R&D, application development, product CPE (Current Product Engineering), testing, as well as software support and services. The operational focus is to build and implement a sustainable

HP GLOBAL DELIVERY CHINA CENTER

For questions concerning this case study contact:
Name: Ouyang Jiezi
E-mail: jiezi.ouyang@hp.com
Phone: 86 (21) 3889 8102

Overview
Client: HP Internal
   Client Industry: System Administration Software
   Service Line: Offshore software R&D
   Project Description: Offshore software R&D, provides R&D delivery with core development, current product engineering, testing, etc.
   Technology / Platform:

- ITSM, J2EE, C/C++, .net, XML/SOAP, Oracle, SQL DB, C#
- MS-Windows, Windows Platform SDK, Unix (HP-UX, Solaris, Linux)

task force to provide consistent and well-managed workflows for software development.

Dedicated Resource Provision Model

Focusing on enabling software R&D to become a more comprehensive CoE in GDCC, Shanghai R&D team launched its operations from November 2005 as a dedicated resource pool for its sponsoring partners.

   The primary principle driving the dedicated resource provision model is to leverage the synergy and trust relationship between the sponsoring partner(s) and the delivery unit. With a proven track record of high-level performance and engagement, this model demonstrates development of a very healthy relationship between GDCC and its sponsoring partners. By merging and embracing its customers' objectives, GDCC R&D team has proved itself to be a trustworthy extended team of overseas R&D organizations.

Integrated Development and Delivery Operating Model

As a unique strategy, the "integrated development and delivery operating model" helps GDCC team bring into full play its strong backend development capacity and rich front-line delivery experiences.

By learning and receiving feedback on customers' real needs and experiences timely and accurately, the delivery team helps the development team to get closer to customers and the market. Also, they help to adapt to market changes quickly, meet individual customer's needs and consequently achieve greater timeliness of development and lower development cost. Meanwhile, close cooperation with the development team enables the delivery team to improve delivery efficiency, quality, and service capability as well as resources and cost saving. Therefore, the delivery team is capable of serving customers more competitively by grasping knowledge on products and technologies more quickly, accurately, and thoroughly, as well as receiving full support from the development team. The development team and the delivery team support and benefit each other by fully sharing and exchanging people, information, and knowledge, in addition to continuing self-improvement, thus forming a stronger team.

Through close cooperation between the development and delivery teams, the GDCC team offers quality and cost-effective delivery services. The following section is a typical case of successful project leveraging integrated development and delivery operating model.

Project Delivery: Maximize Customer Satisfaction

The customer is one of the largest mobile communication service providers in the world. HP applied ITSM (IT Service Management) disciplines to help the customer streamline its IT process management.

A specific requirement from the customer was that one of the key enabling products running on an operating system platform that was not previously supported. The project delivery team in GDCC passed the request to GDCC R&D team. After some investigation and discussions, GDCC R&D team was approved to help the delivery team by providing source code, consulting, and support for the porting process. This way, the GDCC team successfully helped HP win a very large and strategic customer deal. Later on, the GDCC software support team was also involved in this project to offer 24/7 on duty support as committed in a long-term service and support contract.

Road Ahead

With significant progress on this offshore R&D collaboration project, GDCC is also facing some challenges like:

- A 7/24/365 SLA (Service Level Agreement) is very often required
- Robust and flexible IT infrastructure
- High visibility of security and IP protection
- Difficulty getting the right software engineers and architects

Aiming to address these challenges, GDCC developed a proactive working plan in order to be competitive in the marketplace which includes:

- Build scalable, flexible and cost-competitive workforce
- Build just-in-time resource supply chain
- Align and leverage resources from 3rd-party business partners, especially local small and medium software companies
- Continuously improve overall cost structure
- Build worldwide service standard
- Consistency with other region/country
- Continuous improvement of culture and practice
- Build robust and flexible service delivery infrastructure
- Service capability 7/24/365
- Business continuity and contingency handling plan
- High standard of service and IP protection for HP and external clients

About GDCC

HP Global Delivery China Center (GDCC) was established in 2002. With the center's establishment, investment of HP in China has grown from product manufacturing and selling into a much more specialized field in product R&D and application delivery services. It also represents the commitment HP made to China. In May 2004, the GDCC was brought into HP Global Service Organization. It is now the second largest global delivery application service center of HP with 2000 + employees and customers across Europe, America, and Asia. GDCC's headquarters is located in Shanghai, four service centers are located in Dalian, Beijing, Chongqing, and Guangzhou. GDCC was certified as CMM level 3 in March 2003, CMM level 5 in April 2004, and CMMi ML5 in September 2005, ISO9001 in June 2006, and PCMM3 in September 2006. It marks one of the fastest growing organizations around the world.

GDCC business covers the whole software life cycle from R&D to customization and packaging, which addresses user requirements at the onset, subsequently software framework engineering and in the latter phases the simulation environment, programming, integration, testing, and introduction into the market. Presently, GDCC provides services primarily to HP customers in the Asia-Pacific region and China. By making use of China's advantages in low labor costs and competitiveness in rich human resources, GDCC creates the best software solutions for telecom, financial services and manufacturing industries.

GDCC is now a world leader in terms of software quality control and engineering management.

I.T. UNITED

For questions concerning this case study contact:
Name: Doris Li, Assistant to the CEO
E-mail: doris.li@ituc.com
Phone: 86-10-6599-2288 ext. 801

Overview

Client: Dell—A Fortune 100 company with a unique direct to market business model

Client Industry: High-tech manufacturing and services

Service Line: Staff augmentation, or full time extension (FTE) of Dell team

Project Description: Dell Master Data Management (MDM) project migration. MDM is the system of record for global product data. Product attributes related to sales, marketing, and order management. Service oriented architecture (SOA) to support a variety of customer-facing and internal applications. Scalable, reliable data management environment.

Technology Platform:

- SQL Server 2000, Oracle 10G, C# / .NET

Number of staff involved in China: Double-digit FTE, growing as partnership continues

Project Size: Under US$1 million

Dell-I.T. United: Smooth Project Migration Offshoring

This case study is an example of how a successful offshoring work relationship evolved from fixed-fee projects, maturing into a long-term staff augmentation partnership that now expands into various business units of Dell.

China—Looking for a Strategic Offshore Alternative

When Dell decided to become involved in China as an offshoring destination, the global development strategy decision makers turned to I.T. UNITED as their partner. The main objective from Dell's perspective for entering China was to leverage China's talents, cost advantages, and increase supplier flexibility (scalability, ramp-up time, and so on). Dell decided to launch a pilot program to validate China as an alternative strategic offshoring destination. This decision was made a little easier because it already had set up a strong presence in China, which was focused on servicing the domestic market.

Discussions between Dell and I.T. UNITED started in July 2005, as soon as Dell had confirmed its budget. As with many of I.T. UNITED's partnerships, initial contact was established through its U.S. business network (this office was already familiar with Dell's person in charge of strategic global development at Dell. Based on I.T. UNITED's proven track record with Fortune 500 clients, it was retained by Dell for the pilot. Dell evaluated the rates for required skill-sets and the related effort estimation details that were submitted once the scope of the pilot was determined. I.T. UNITED's challenge was to provide flexible support, while upholding a quality work process in a way that did not hamper work flow. It was agreed that a Capability Maturity Model Integration (CMMI)-inspired iterative approach, which included regular reviews and rapid feedback cycles, was to be used.

The next step was taken in August 2005: I.T. UNITED sent its account manager and onshore U.S. team to Dell's headquarters to conduct the initial requirements analysis.

The Pilot: Validating the Partnership

The agreed pilot project was a four-month, fixed-fee engagement with a clearly defined project scope. The pilot was designed to help Dell assess I.T. UNITED's engineering capabilities and validate the chosen engagement model.

The pilot was part of an ongoing IT consolidation project at Dell, which was running several different applications, written with different technologies (e.g., Java, ASP, VB, and so on) by different groups at different times, all related to item data (item was defined as products and services being sold by Dell). I.T. UNITED's job was to support database migration, taking data and data model (i.e., the structure of DB) from two of those core applications (SQL server applications) and correctly convert and migrate the data to fit into Oracle.

The pilot was carried out in two phases: while phase one concerned data conversion and migration, phase two was all about data consolidation. While Dell led the data model conversion, I.T. UNITED validated and provided suggestions as to how to improve it. I.T. UNITED developed automated tools in .NET to migrate the data (such as character-set conversion) and converted stored procedures because the database procedures are different. The objective was clear: to keep the data the same and ensure that the stored procedures were behaving the same in both databases. Therefore, I.T. UNITED also wrote tools to validate the data after conversion and store procedures after migration.

During phase two, I.T. UNITED supported Dell in consolidating the data model. There was an overlap of the data model because there were several applications with a similar scope and function, and the original two applications were going to interface with the newly created model.

Tracking Progress and Fine-Tuning the Engagement Model

Project progress was evaluated on a weekly basis, more often depending on milestones. It rapidly emerged that the teams' development skills were complementary, thus validating the chosen engagement model. Dell was happy with the results as both phases of the pilot progressed smoothly and the DB migration and consolidation was completed successfully. All milestones including the automated SQL generation tool were delivered on time and Dell was able to realize 65 percent cost savings per FTE, which compared favorably when considering other locations that it leverages worldwide to support its global business.

The results of the pilot confirmed the partnership value of I.T. UNITED resources and China as a viable strategic option for Dell, paving the way for a long-term staff augmentation engagement. Dell had more DB work waiting to be done and was interested in securing I.T. UNITED in order to leverage efficiency gains that stemmed from this team's growing domain knowledge and familiarity with the technology. It rapidly emerged that the best way for Dell to achieve those goals was to enter into a long-term agreement. The offshore team was thus free to dedicate themselves fully to Dell and further enhance their Dell-specific knowledge.

For Dell, there were several advantages in this setup: rates were lowered and overhead costs reduced, and the work process became more fluid because the U.S.-based team did not need to come up with a clear scope and timeline for every milestone as is customary with fixed-term projects.

April 2006 saw another visit by I.T. UNITED team members to Dell's U.S. headquarters. This time, the purpose of the I.T. UNITED's project manager (PM) was twofold: first to meet with the U.S.-based team and review the technical direction for the existing dedicated team in China; and second to meet with another department at Dell's headquarters that had expressed interest in setting up their own China-based I.T. UNITED team.

Based on the high-level discussions regarding an additional staff augmentation team that had started in late February 2006, I.T. UNITED put together a candidate portfolio to be interviewed by Dell's technical experts (in this case I.T. UNITED successfully ramped up another solid FTE team with skilled, English-proficient resources, and completed the whole HR process, with client approval, within five weeks). The interviews took place in mid-April while the I.T. UNITED PM was in the United States, which was helpful in selecting the right candidates. Once the new hires were confirmed, Dell sent a technical architect from its U.S. headquarters to Beijing for a one-week intensive on-site training of the offshore team—clearly more cost effective than sending the China-based team to the United States.

Another outcome of the discussions with the existing client at Dell was to add another offshore team with four FTEs to develop internal tools for Dell's .NET development unit. The .NET offshore team started work in July 2006 and is ongoing.

Strong Partnership for Mutual Success

October 2006 saw the next visit of the I.T. UNITED project manager to Dell's headquarters to conduct a requirements analysis for a new project with the now fourth internal client at Dell. As before, I.T. UNITED's ability to rapidly ramp up the new FTE team was critical. This new project kicked off in November 2006 with the purpose of developing a support tool to automate and manage the server patching process on a monthly basis (MS Windows, Oracle, and so on). Once the support tool was delivered and signed off on the I.T. UNITED China team was to be reassigned and focus on user acceptance testing.

October 2006 also marked a turnaround point for the partnership, which started to branch out from traditional development activities when yet another of Dell's business units announced their interest in working with I.T. UNITED in China. One of Dell's product groups intended to develop a computer-based training (CBT) course for their order system. I.T. UNITED had previously done CBT work for other clients and the CBT sample courses provided by I.T. UNITED convinced Dell to give it a go. The CBT project got underway in October 2006, originally as a one-off project, but with a roadmap planning to localize the CBT for other markets. Initial development languages were English and Japanese.

So, how is the partnership expected to grow? The outlook for the partnership between I.T. UNITED and Dell is very positive because there is growing interest from other internal clients at Dell who have seen or heard how other business units successfully work with China and I.T. UNITED. The facts that the China-based offshore teams enabled Dell to realize cost savings of up to 65 percent and that Dell was were very satisfied with project delivery conveyed a clear message. I.T. UNITED's current forecast—based on the number of enquiries received from Dell internal clients and the fact that that the growth rate has been accelerating over the past months—estimates that the number of dedicated, China-based FTE resources for Dell will more than double throughout 2007and continue to grow going forward.

TYPICAL OFFSHORING CHALLENGES — AND HOW THEY WERE OVERCOME

When offshoring a project, there are a number of challenges that the project typically will face. The following three were relevant to this case study:

1. **Keeping Turnover Low.** Halfway through the project, the technical lead decided to leave. For obvious reasons, this caused a lot of concern with the client. Turnover is a risk that every project faces. As a rapidly growing market, China now offers skilled engineers plenty of career opportunities. A growing number of employers are competing for resources and larger, international providers moving into China will offer higher salaries, thus putting pressure on local providers. In this case, the I.T. UNITED HR department was able to find a suitable replacement for this position during the notice period. I.T. UNITED mitigates the risk of turnover by maintaining an up-to-date candidate database. The rest of the China-based offshore team has been very stable over the past two years. Key success factors for low turnover have been: I.T. UNITED's strong, English-speaking corporate culture, an incentive-based employee loyalty program, and individual career planning for all offshore team members.

2. **Avoiding Miscommunication.** Even though I.T. UNITED's corporate language is English and all PMs and technical leads speak excellent English, there were moments in very detailed (technical) discussions where misunderstandings could have easily happened. For that very reason, the I.T. UNITED account manager is a native English speaker, in this case a U.S. national who can serve as a bridge between the onshore and offshore teams. Apart from hiring resources with good English skills, I.T. UNITED native also places great emphasis on continuous English training for China-based resources (both with a business and technical focus) to help mitigating communication issues.

3. **Keeping Quality at Par.** Both parties need to be aware that aggressive deadlines and the team setup can affect quality. In this case study, the client decided to forego a dedicated testing team due to time constraints, opting instead for every developer to test his or her own code. Keeping up communication was therefore vital: apart from regular status reports and work reviews, I.T. UNITED established weekly conference calls as well as personal on-site visits

during milestone reviews or whenever necessary during the project. Even though those additional measures resulted in few added direct costs, they were essential in creating a personal bond and foster dedication as well as mutual understanding.

Rules of Engagement: Key Success Factors

Key Success Factors	I.T. UNITED Approach
Security	China-based staff working on segregated network
	File transfer via secure FTP: all work done by I.T. UNITED was transferred to Dell via SFTP access only (cheaper, better security control, no direct access to the Dell system)
	Restricted access to development/test environment
	CCTV protected work premises
	No external data-recording devices permitted in China-based ODC
Communication	English proficiency of key staff members in China
	Establish team spirit
	Meet deadlines (I.T. UNITED) and ensure that work is on track (repeated visits of I.T. UNITED account manager and PM to the United States to conduct requirements analysis)
	Timely decisions and feedback (Dell)
	Weekly conference calls and status reports
	On-site progress meetings at Dell U.S. headquarters as appropriate
Quality Assurance	Iterative two-step quality assurance process based on CMMI
	Cross-validation by team members and technical lead prior to delivery

Key Success Factors	I.T. UNITED Approach
On-Time Delivery	Cross-validation of offshore deliverables by local teams Routine technical training for offshore developers Performance-based incentives Clear requirement specifications Weekly status reports Project schedule reviews Issue/resolution tracking Work hand in hand with Dell for project implementation: faster problem solving with combined technical skills Effective time zone management—I.T. UNITED gets the work done overnight

Structuring a Successful Project Team

Like many multinational corporations (MNC), Dell only works with vendors who are part of the Dell preferred vendor list. Given that requirement, I.T. UNITED's contact at the U.S. headquarters put it in touch with a U.S.-based preferred vendor, InterSys Consulting, with whom I.T. UNITED entered into a Master Service Agreement. The only agreement directly in place between I.T. UNITED and Dell is a nondisclosure agreement. Despite this legal setup, I.T. UNITED always contacts Dell directly for all operational and daily work.

Exhibit B.5 shows the successful team structure that I.T. UNITED and Dell have employed. For project control, the I.T. UNITED and Dell PMs communicate on a regular basis. Technical discussions are lead by the technical leads from both parties. The I.T. UNITED account manager provides operational oversight and supervision for all Dell projects, and leads new project initiation.

About I.T. United

I.T. UNITED (Information Technology United Corporation) is a trusted brand name and major China-based provider of software development and outsourcing services. Established in 1998 with global headquarters in Beijing, I.T. UNITED has an international management team and is

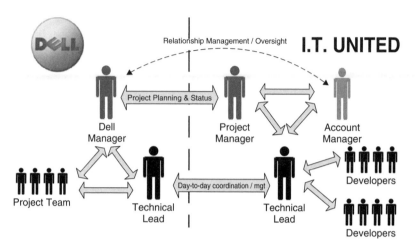

EXHIBIT B.5   Relationship and Oversight Management for Dell-I.T. UNITED Relationship

firmly committed to the highest quality standards (CMMI). The company serves as a technology supplier to global and regional IT companies, and as a solutions provider to corporate and government clients. Key services include: application development and maintenance, business process support services, systems infrastructure, and interactive marketing. I.T. UNITED consistently delivers high-performance results at the most competitive rates, globally. The company employs local talent in its development centers (Beijing, Shanghai, Xi'an), and operates a growing network of offices in North America, Japan, and Europe. I.T. UNITED is an internationally recognized Top 100 offshore player and a Class A IT company in China. Additional information can be found at www.ituc.com.

Collaboration for Synergism and Win-Win

The cooperation between Neusoft and Alpine Electronics in embedded automobile software engineering can be traced back to 1991 when Dr. Liu Jiren and two of his colleagues, founders of Neusoft, started their business at Northeastern University with three computers and RMB30.000. They earned their first bucket of gold through cooperation with Alpine. At that time, hardly anyone could see the market prospect of the software industry in China, as people had not recognized the value of software. Nevertheless, Dr. Liu was optimistic about this industry. While Mr. Kutsuzawa Kentaro, the president of Alpine Electronics, was looking for an overseas production base in China, and was touched by Dr. Liu and the Neusoft team's passion, technology, and ideas. From then on, they started their collaboration, which has lasted for 16 years to date. The cooperation in the past 16 years represents synergism, a win-win partnership, and a long-lasting friendship.

NEUSOFT GROUP LTD.

For questions concerning this case study contact:
Name: Evelyn Tang
E-mail: tangyi@neusoft.com
Phone: 86 24 83665663

Overview

Client: Alpine Electronics, Inc.

Industry: Car navigation and car mobile media solutions (car audio, driver assistant, communication)

Service Line: Embedded software development

Project Description: Car navigation: Unitive Navigation products, supporting multiple languages/mapDB/vendors, including both in-vehicle runtime and emulation on PC for debug; car audio: develop software and hardware of car audio products.

Technology/Platform:

- Car Navigation:
  - Platform: WinCE/WinCE for Automotive
  - Common Technology: COM/AUI(Automotive UI)/XML/ embedded emulation technology
  - Specified Technology: Navigation MapDB format/3D Map Display/Positioning system based on GPS and car sensor

- Car Audio:
  - OS: Uitron4.0
  - MCU: NEC V850, RENESAS M16 C/SH
  - DSP: MOTOROLA, TOSHIBA
  - TUNER: PHILIPS
  - NET: CAN, MOST

Number of staff involved in China: Car Navigation: Full-time employees: 329; Car Audio: Full-time employees: 300

Project Size: Car Navigation: $10 million (Alpine 2006 Business Contract Amount); Car Audio: $5 million/year

Alpine Electronics is a global automobile electronics company specializing in car audio and communication systems with more than 30 overseas subsidiary companies in more than 10 countries. Apart from Alpine trademark products, the company also provides original equipment manufacturer (OEM) products to well-known automobile manufacturers all over the world.

In September 1991, Alpine was listed on Tokyo Stock Exchange (First Section) as the turnover of the company reached 100 billion Yen in May of the same year. With the development of product digitalization, Alpine's software development has expanded substantially in quantity and required higher quality. In view of Japan's shortage in IT talents, utilizing China's abundant high-quality human resources to reduce research and development (R&D) costs became an obvious strategic choice for Alpine. Alpine's other strategy was to penetrate the future Chinese market, which was immature at the time but would expand dramatically in coming years. Based on these considerations, in June 1991, Mr. Kentaro and Dr. Liu set up Neu-Alpine Software Research Institute (Co. Ltd.) that marked the formal strategic partnership between Alpine and Neusoft.

In the technology space of embedded automobile software engineering, the Neusoft and Alpine team accumulated experiences from years of practice and cooperation, from using assembly language in the early days to more advanced C, C++, and Java programming languages, from no operating system to modern RTOS, such as Itron, Windows CE, and Linux, from programs of several thousand lines of code to the whole system with over a million lines of code nowadays, from code hacking with no software design to using most advanced engineering tools and sophisticated design focusing on architecture and reuse; from no development process to process maturity following CMMI Level 5 and using the life-cycle model for development. Technologies and engineering have changed in a short span of 16 years: in the past, embedded automobile software development meant simple programming on a single-chip computer; now it is a large-scale software engineering project delivered by a dedicated professional team of tens to hundreds of engineers under standard engineering process and supported by advanced software tools and methods.

Achievement in Car Navigation   In the past, Alpine software development was conducted in a hardware environment with very high costs. Soon after the initiation of cooperation, Neusoft proposed to Alpine to build an integrated development environment, which would substantially boost software development efficiency and shorten development cycle time.

The two companies began to work together on a car navigation system in 1995 by performing minor modification and maintenance on Alpine's existing system, and developing some tools to facilitate Alpine's research and

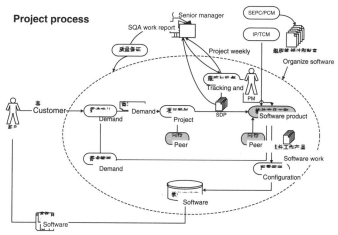

Project process

Quality is a reflection of value and respect

EXHIBIT B.6 Process Project Management

development. From 1997 to 2001, the cooperation expanded to software development and mass-production, and Neusoft and Alpine codeveloped some high-quality car navigation software products. From 2002 to 2006, Neusoft helped Alpine to establish Alpine's global navigation development platform, which helps to ensure consistent product launch in different locations with reduced costs. With the successful development of this navigation system, Neusoft also helped Alpine successfully enter the China market by winning the first very important Chinese customer. Since then, Alpine has obtained orders for product development from four other high-end customers in China.

At present, one third of Alpine's total R&D for the global navigation system is done by Neusoft. For Alpine, cooperation with Neusoft helps reduce its total cost, increase its market share, strengthens its development capability, and boosts its global competitiveness. In 2006, Seizo Ishiguro, President of Alpine Electronics, presented a special award to Neusoft to recognize its spectacular contribution in assisting Alpine in expanding into China's navigation system market.

Achievement in Car Audio Alpine and Neusoft began their cooperation in car audio software development in 1998. Initially, only two to three models were developed each year, but, by 2006, the volume had increased to several dozen models each year. The products developed also evolved from simple CD series in the beginning to all CA models and DVD models, including models of Alpine's own brand, such as IS and AMP. Neusoft and Alpine began to develop OEM products in 2003; since then, they have been developing OEM car audio products together for many well-known world-class auto brands.

In 2004, the Alpine Dalian Car Audio R&D Center was established. Today, when you enter the R&D facility, you see the entire staff wearing the same style of uniforms, even though some of them are Alpine employees while others are Neusoft employees. As most of the staff in the R&D center speaks Japanese, you can hardly tell which company an employee belongs to. In the three-story R&D center, the third floor is Alpine's hardware design center, the second floor is Neusoft's software design and R&D center doing the outsourced work from Alpine, and the first floor is Alpine's product testing center. This is the new way of off-shore outsourcing in which the original meaning of the word "shore" has disappeared; instead, tight integration and cohesion of outsourcer and outsourcee working in the same building makes the shore irrelevant The cooperation between Alpine and Neusoft truly proves that the world is flat.

Such a tight integration and cohesion of software and hardware development enables Alpine's products to win top international awards and obtain recognition by automobile manufacturers and end users, and thus helps Alpine to increase its market share globally. For example, the car audio product, CDA-9855JI, with its hardware developed by Alpine and software developed by Neusoft, won the 2005 Auto Supplies Award from Japan Automobile News Agency in recognition of its excellence in product planning and conceptual design that caught the attention of the auto parts market. Another car audio product, 06InfoVisor, with its hardware developed by Alpine and software developed by Neusoft, won Best Innovation prize in U.S. Winter Consumer Electronics Show (CES), the first time in Alpine's history it won such an award.

Today, the size of the Neusoft and Alpine team has grown to more than 700 people. At the same time, Neusoft has grown to become the largest embedded software engineering services provider in China.

Conclusion

The cooperation with Alpine enabled Neusoft to become the first software company in China accredited with CMM5 and CMMI5. The company has recently also achieved ISO27001 certification for Information Security Management. Founded only 16 years ago, Neusoft has become the largest software company in China, with more than 10,000 employees, and its offshore outsourcing revenue has been ranked number 1 in China for three consecutive years since 2004. The intimate collaboration between Neusoft and Alpine has brought significant business growth and is a win-win for both companies.

In the future, the development of the manufacturing industry in China will bring more software development business to China. Software has become a significant part of many kinds of electronic equipment, such as mobile phones, communication devices, home appliances, and so forth. Also, all the equipment manufactured in China will facilitate having corresponding software developed in China. In fact, China has already become the leading provider of product software engineering services. Following the first shift of moving manufacturing to China about a decade ago, multinational companies will now move more product R&D and software engineering to China. As the world has become flat, global sourcing and win-win partnership, exemplified by the collaboration between Neusoft and Alpine, will become a mega trend.

The Challenge: Aging Product, Drop in Sales

This case study demonstrates that smaller companies benefit just as much as big ones when outsourcing their product development to a skilled offshore team in China. It all began when Document Science, a US$20 million-plus software development company, realized that it had an aging software product on hand that no longer met the needs of its core customers, the multibillion dollar North American financial services sector.

The situation was compounded by the internal staff's lack of expertise in any of the new technologies critical to revamping the product line, which demanded easy integration with major enterprise resource planning (ERP) systems. Document Sciences made several attempts to utilize its staff's skill-sets to create a new design, but to no avail.

Document Sciences realized that it was in a dilemma: it had an in-house team with extensive industry knowledge but unable to adapt the new technology to continue servicing the market.

The Solution: A Complete Makeover

In order to maintain its position as a market leader in the document content management field, Document Sciences products required a complete makeover. Management recognized that it needed not only to re-architect its core software products but also to reimplement the whole product suite using new technologies such as J2EE, XML, and Web services. While evaluating different solutions, Document Sciences had conflicting internal factions, each proposing a different solution.

While the marketplace continued to show signs of discontent with functional point software, Document Sciences intensified its search for an affordable solution. Document Sciences decided to utilize an external consulting firm to propose a solution. This started an extensive review with

OBJECTIVA SOFTWARE SOLUTIONS

For questions concerning the case study contact:
Name: Jeanne Beyer/Daniel Xu
E-mail: jbeyer@objectivasoftware.com or dxu@objectivasoftware.com
Phone: 1-866-688-9020

Overview

Client: Document Sciences Corporation delivers real-time dynamic content publishing solutions that organizations depend on to realize productivity improvements and increase competitiveness. xPression, Document Sciences' proven award-winning technology, integrates with existing core business systems to create and deliver real-time high-volume customer communications, highly customized for each recipient. xPresso, the latest addition to the xPression product suite, uses digital assets within an organization to design, publish, and transform static marketing documents and statements into highly creative and compelling personalized customer communications with targeted marketing offerings.

Document Sciences offers worldwide sales, distribution, and support with its corporate headquarters in Carlsbad, California, and offices in Beijing, China, and London, England as well as regional offices throughout the United States and Europe.

More than 600 customers in the financial services, healthcare, government, and manufacturing industries rely on Document Sciences' software and services to automate the design, creation, production, and multichannel delivery of customer communications.

Industry: Software-content and documents management.

Service Line: Product development (design through quality assurance) for commercial software applications to replace flagship legacy product.

Project Description: Re-architect core software product technology to develop state of the art infrastructure that was scalable, reliable, and open. The application was developed with a rich set of features required for enterprise deployment.

Technology/Platform:

- Languages: J2EE,XML/XSD

- Operating Systems: NT/2000, Solaris, OS390, Linux, and AIX
- Applications Servers: WebSphere, WebLogic

Number of staff involved in China: 45
Project Size: US$6 million

a U.S.-based firm. However, the project plan delivered by the consulting company far exceeded the expected budget. In addition, the proposed technical path was extremely complex and delivery was not incremental. Additional discussion offered a possible compromise: a low-cost, high-tech team to work with their industry consultants to design and execute a software product.

Document Sciences therefore turned to an offshore option. While India was certainly the current leader in offshoring, Document Sciences looked for a local U.S. company so that both organizations could fully and easily integrate their business knowledge.

The key selection criteria were a combination of experienced senior-level technical leadership (familiar with the U.S. marketplace) and a skilled product development team in a cost-effective location.

Objectiva fit the bill because the team fulfilled all selection criteria: they had senior U.S. technical resources with solid corporate development experience and excellent academic qualifications from renowned institutions such as MIT and Columbia, as well as an experienced, cost effective, professional technical team in Beijing.

After conducting an initial requirement analysis together with the client, Objectiva proposed a codevelopment effort. This optimized resource deployment: utilization of internal Document Sciences industry consultants and implementation of a new technical delivery team. The Objectiva China team members worked on site with their Document Sciences counterparts in California during the product architecture phase. Once the integrated team agreed on the project management plan, the China offshore team leaders returned to China and deployed product requirements to their team members.

Global Deployment Methodology

The Document Sciences U.S. organization worked with U.S. technical managers from the Objectiva organization to develop an iterative design process:

1. Step One: Utilize legacy pieces of code, and enable new architected software that would migrate the application to a more robust framework.

2. Step Two: Using the knowledge gained during the first stage, the Objectiva China team designed and implemented replacement modules for the legacy code. Because the China team was integrated into the design process and started the business knowledge transfer, the team could complete the migration with limited assistance from the Document Sciences industry consultants.

The industry knowledge transferred to the China-based offshore team enabled Document Sciences to generate another revenue stream for the company: professional services. As the China team built their industry knowledge, Document Sciences had the opportunity to grow a significant professional services department.

The integrated team leadership met in both the United States and China for ongoing development reviews and planning over a two-year period. These quarterly meetings were supplemented by weekly conference calls of the subteams and daily technical progress check in.

The success of the global deployment was based on a modular approach to development, that is, work was divided so that each team had clear ownership. In this case, it meant that the China development team could send code for review and verification of design choices to the U.S. business knowledge team with a next day response. Document Sciences was able to deploy a "follow-the-sun" development and have the time zone work to its advantage.

Document Sciences chose resources that enabled an iterative product development approach, which was a critical decision and enabled Document Sciences to capitalize on market opportunities with critical product features. The remaining legacy components were incrementally built after the initial release of the product.

Document Sciences' goal was to develop a robust, reliable, scalable, and open state-of-the-art infrastructure. The platform restructuring gave the company an opportunity to leapfrog over the competition with an enterprise software application. In addition, the new product was fully internationalized to allow for the localization of the product in Chinese and other languages.

The Result: Happy Customers, Growing Sales

Documents Sciences' financial-services clients recognized the high quality of the new software, which had been developed in China based on an in-depth understanding of the industry. The excellence of the product delivered to the client was also officially confirmed when it was awarded "Best in J2EE Architecture" by the Association of Information and Image Management (AIIM).

As a direct result of its decision to tap into Chinese talent, Documents Sciences was able to fast track its professional services business unit. The China team had gained industry understanding and was able to provide value to customization projects for North American clients.

Document Sciences was one of the first small U.S. public companies to utilize an external Chinese team to deliver a commercial product for the North American market. This achievement verifies the capability of small companies to successfully deploy a China-based software development team.

About Objectiva Software Solutions

Objectiva Software Solutions, a division of Document Sciences Corp (NASDAQ: DOCX) is a leading provider of software outsourcing services to China. Objectiva's teams have been delivering projects and building dedicated offshore development centers in China since 1999. With offices in San Diego, San Francisco, Toronto, and Beijing, Objectiva helps its clients develop customized enterprise software solutions (J2EE, COM+, and MS.NET), Web-based and client-server applications, and software for the wireless Internet.

Objectiva's teams are run by U.S.-based technical leaders with several years of experience in managing global software development efforts to take the burden off the client. Objectiva reduces the cost of software development without sacrificing quality, on-time delivery, and time to market.

Introduction

Founded more than 20 years ago, the customer's mission was to automate the then highly manual portfolio accounting functions of the investment-management business. Since its founding, it has been providing reliable, trusted solutions to investment management organizations of all sizes and investment strategies. The customer, with more than 4,000 client firms and 800 employees, has established itself as a leading provider of mission-critical applications meeting the demands of investment management operations around the world.

In May 2005, the customer's CTO came to China to investigate the Chinese market as it had been considering entering it for a long time, but was not sure whether China was mature enough to recognize its software product with very advanced management principles. The CTO met with the VP of UFIDA Software Engineering in charge of the European and U.S. markets. Hearing that UFIDA is the largest management provider in China, the CTO had great interest in cooperation with UFIDA to develop the China market. During the communication process, the customer learned that UFIDA has been providing software outsourcing services for three years

UFIDA SOFTWARE ENGINEERING

For questions concerning this case study contact:
Name: Yvette Pang, Yan, Director, Strategic Marketing
E-mail: pangyan@use.com.cn
Phone: 8610-82373737 ext:8099; 8613910793615 (mobile)

Overview
Client: A leading provider of mission-critical applications.
Industry: Software industry.
Service Line: Application development.
Project Description: To develop their portfolio software product with a high speed and low cost; to establish a dedicated development team with UFIDA.
Technology/Platform:

- C++; .Net; Java; RSL (a report language developed by the Customer); SQL Server 2005; Microsoft SQL Server Reporting Services; OLAP; SilkTest; TCM (test case management); Tracker (bug tracking system).

Number of staff involved in China: 60.
Project Size: US$1 million per year.

and had performed well in the area of software product research and development. The customer asked to visit UFIDA's offshore development center and wanted to learn more about the capability of UFIDA's outsourcing business. After this visit, the customer told UFIDA that it had outsourced some testing and developing work to a small company in Shanghai, but was not satisfied with the services that company provided. That decision was based on the following:

- The resources are not assured. The small company could not recruit or train qualified engineers for the customers.
- There is no comprehensive management methodology in place to guarantee the success of each project. Customers need mature methods of development process management, project management, and offshore outsourcing management.

■ The small company did not have the finance and technology background to provide valued services, such as core technology research, to customer.

The company scale of UFIDA, professional management, and technology capability impressed the customer deeply. So it started to discuss first cooperating with UFDIA on software development outsourcing. In August, it issued a formal request for proposal to UFIDA and another big player in China. After evaluation for nearly a month, it chose UFIDA as the outsourcing partner. In mid-September, UFIDA finished building its offshore development center (ODC) with a team of ten engineers and dedicated facilities. With the purpose of establishing management process and knowledge transfer, a pilot lasting for one month began. After that, the long-term cooperation and gradual enlargement of ODC became a certainty for both sides.

Currently, five teams are working for the customer on different products on both quality assurance and development project. Knowledge transfer is the first and most important step to initiate cooperation. Regarding knowledge transfer, at the very beginning, the project manager (PM) and leads receive intensive face-to-face training from engineers from the customer's headquarters. After the on-site training, the PM and leads take responsibility of giving training to whomever joined the team later. Moreover, whenever it is necessary, online trainings by WebEx and audio conference are always available. When the relationship is taking a big step forward, more new business knowledge is demanded. To break through any bottleneck, their best engineers go to the United States and work on-site with our client to learn first-hand. These engineers will pass on their understanding to the whole team. Several configuration tools are used, such as ClearCase and SourceSafe, to share the knowledge with the team.

Weak communication skills are often the greatest challenge in an outsourcing project. UFIDA adopted that various efficient methods to ensure that work moves smoothly. For quality assurance, daily reports via e-mail provide an effective way to inform each side of the updated progress. Weekly reports are used to summarize what has been done during the week, which help the PM to adjust the assignment and fine-tune the schedule accordingly. Instant messaging tools are also employed in daily work. Whenever any problem that cannot be solved is encountered, if the client is also online, UFIDA can ask and usually receive an answer immediately.

The project has been making tremendous progress since it was first launched in late 2005. Right now, more than 50 highly educated and experienced engineers are working in the team. The five subgroups have been cultivated and expanded in the project team. Recently, six team leaders of the group have been invited to the United States to further cooperation with the client. These six people have further improved ties with the client and showed their respect and dedication, to make the development team more stable and professional. During this on-site training, they have learned valuable knowledge and strengthened mutual understanding. Moreover, they have gained confidence as well as affirmation from the client, which, in a broad sense, is conducive to the long-term success of the project.

About UFIDA

UFIDA Software Co. Ltd. (UFIDA) is one of the leading providers of management software solutions and service in Asia. Established in 1988, UFIDA has been recognized as an outstanding software company in the marketplace due to its quality products, professional service, and a vast customer base of 400,000 in China and other regions in Asia.

With persistent efforts in improvement of software development and quality, UFIDA has been a leading global provider in IT application consulting, software system development, related IT operation and support services in mainland China, Japan, Europe, and the United States. As one of the CMM Level 5 certified software services companies in the world, UFIDA adds exceptional values to our clients through professional IT services.

Headquartered in Beijing, UFIDA has established five branches in Shanghai, Xi'an, Dalian, and Chengdu in China, and one branch in Tokyo. USE global employees reached 600 in 2006. For more information, visit www.use.com.cn.

Business Background

SoftCo's B2B suite provides a standards-based business-to-business integration platform for secured transmission of business documents and messages among disparate partner systems. Some of the standards-based B2B protocols supported are EDI, RosettaNet, SOAP, ebXML, etc.

The Internet enables buyers and sellers to interact more directly than ever before—it helps the suppliers to exploit new markets and sell products more efficiently and enables buyers to find the best vendor for a particular product or service. In addition, globally accessible e-marketplaces are changing the nature of B2B commerce by bringing businesses together in dynamic trading environments.

These intermediaries are making markets look and act much like financial-trading floors with real-time, straight-through processing. To maintain a competitive edge in the Internet economy, enterprises must

WORKSOFT CREATIVE SOFTWARE TECHNOLOGY, LTD.

For questions concerning this case study contact:
E-mail: info@worksoft.com.cn
Phone: 86-10-82825266 ext 8600

Case Study Overview

Client: A Major Software Company (SoftCo).
Industry: Enterprise application integration.
Service Line: Application development and testing.
Product Description: SoftCo's B2B suite provides a standards-based business-to-business integration platform for secured transmission of business documents and messages among disparate partner systems.
Technology/Platform:
Java/J2EE, XML, Web Services, Internet Security, Internet Transports, Protocol, etc.
Number of staff involved in China: 15.
Project Size: 200 months.

be able to securely and efficiently communicate and transact with partners, customers, and vendors.

SoftCo B2B leverages SoftCo's experience with enterprise application integration (EAI) to completely integrate systems and processes across boundaries among companies.

Development Requirements

For B2B development, there are several technology requirements:

1. The need to understand leading industry standard protocols, for example, the traditional EDI standard or the new protocols based on XML, RosettaNet, ebXML, and so on.
2. XML processing and parsing. Many B2B protocols are based on XML technology, including SOAP, XML signature, and so on, so there are many processes focused on XML file parse and generation.
3. Security and authentication based on PKI (Product Key Infrastructure) platform. At the business level, customers expect strict security procedures for important transactions. The PKI infrastructure provides authentication and authorization methods based on encryption/decryption, digest algorithm, and digital signature; it is also useful for nonrepudiation and antitamper purposes.

4. Java language for platform independent. SoftCo B2B products use Java as the implementation language, so they can be deployed on a wide range of platforms.

Worksoft's Roles and Responsibilities

Worksoft started its cooperation with SoftCo through SoftCo CDC (China Development Center) in early 2006, when SoftCo decided to enter the Chinese market. To identify the best vendor from six candidates, SoftCo conducted several rounds of evaluation, including a detailed request for proposal (RFP) and on-site investigation. In the whole evaluation process, Worksoft demonstrated proven experience in CDC operation for U.S. customers and highly mature managerial capabilities over its competitors, and finally won the deal.

Based on the successful project implementation, the partnership quickly expanded into more product lines and services business. Based on the successful and fast-growing operations at the SoftCo CDC, the customer chose Worksoft to develop the B2B product.

During the kickoff phase, Worksoft engineers flew to the United States, worked together on site with managers at SoftCo's global headquarters, Silicon Valley, California, to develop the cXML protocol.

The offshore B2B team played a very important role in the whole production implementation. The CDC members were engaged in the full processes of framework design, concrete coding QA testing, and documentation.

Both the Worksoft team lead and the architect worked closely with the engineers in SoftCo headquarters.

The Worksoft offshore software engineers implemented the functions and features, and the QA team in SoftCo CDC provided the testing/QA after the coding was completed.

Last but not least, the Worksoft technical writer created development documents to ensure that all processes were properly documented and the know-how saved for future reference. Different teams jointly completed the work on the schedule drafted out by the engineers from both parties.

Development Life Cycle/Methodology/Issues/Solutions

Throughout the project, there were a number of challenges, which required special attention:

1. **Issue 1: How to master the exact business requirements?** Because the end user community of SoftCo B2B product is mainly in the United States and Europe, it was very important for Worksoft's Chinese engineers to have a clear understanding of user requirements and be aware

of issues arising from different business and cultural environments. At each stage of the development, the Worksoft team wrote specifications on product features, functions, and designs and got feedback for amendments and refinements from SoftCo headquarters. There were also question-and-answer sessions to make sure customer requirements are understood in an accurate way.

2. **Issue 2: How to ensure a good communication flow?** Because 90 % of the development was carried by the Chinese team offshore, good communication between SoftCo headquarters and SoftCo CDC were vital to the success. To this end, many tools were used within the teams, including instant messaging (IM), e-mails, regular status reporting, and teleconferencing tools.

3. **Issue 3: How to properly track, monitor, and control the implementation process?** The Worksoft team had weekly meetings and reports to track the progress of daily operations, including resource availability, employee productivity, and ultimately operations efficiency; the technical outputs, including newly developed code, QA results, and documentation readiness in both the United States and China teams, and provide timely updates to SoftCo managers in Silicon Valley.

Deliverables and Business Impact

Right on schedule, the Worksoft B2B team delivered the product to SoftCo at the end of 2006. The new product was released in January 2007, and is now already successfully in use at leading IT companies around the world.

About Worksoft Creative Software Technology

Worksoft Creative Software Technology Ltd. (Worksoft) is a pioneer and leader of the IT outsourcing industry in China. Worksoft delivers quality assurance and testing, globalization, application development and maintenance, package applications, and business-process outsourcing services to global clients. The Company works with both large global corporations and new generation technology companies to maximize their return on investment and give them The Power to Focus. It sees itself as the ideal partner to conceptualize and realize technology-driven business transformation initiatives. By targeting a dynamic environment where business needs and technology strategy converge, Worksoft delivers a high degree of performance in cost, quality, and efficiency. For more information, visit www.worksoft.com.cn.

Contact Information for Major Government Offices, Outsourcing Centers, and Online Resources

KEY CHINA CENTRAL GOVERNMENT OFFICES

General Administration of Customs

Telephone: 86 10 6519 4114
Web: www.customs.gov.cn

- The General Administration of Customs (China Customs) is a government agency that supervises and manages all arrivals in and departures from the Customs area of the People's Republic of China.
- China Customs exercises a vertical and three-tiered management structure. The top tier is the General Administration of Customs (i.e., the headquarters in Beijing).
- The middle tier is composed of the Guangdong Sub-Administration of Customs (in charge of 7 customs regions located in Guangdong Province), 2 Supervising Offices (located in Tianjin and Shanghai respectively), 41 Customs regions, and 2 Customs educational institutions.
- The third tier refers to the 562 Customs houses or offices under those 41 Customs regions. In addition, it has posted overseas offices or officials in Brussels, Moscow, Washington D.C., and Hong Kong. Its staff is numbered at over 48,000 (including Customs anti-smuggling police).

Ministry of Education[1]

Telephone: 86 10 6609 6114
Web: www.moe.edu.cn

- The Ministry of Education (MOE) is a central government agency under the State Council, responsible for China's educational undertakings and language work.
- The Ministry of Education's main mission is:
- To investigate and put forward the guiding principles and policies for China's educational undertakings, and to draft relevant rules and regulations.
- To investigate and put forward strategies of educational reform and development and master plans for China's educational development; to formulate the policy of educational structural reform as well as the focus, structure, and speed of educational development, and to direct and coordinate the implementation of this work.
- To manage educational funds, take part in formulating guidelines and policies of fund-raising, financial allocation, and capital construction for educational purpose. To monitor educational fund-raising and the expenditure for educational purposes across the country; to manage in accordance with relevant regulations educational aids and loans from abroad.
- To investigate and put forward the establishment standard, basic teaching requirements and basic teaching documents for secondary and primary schools; to organize the examination and approval of unified teaching materials for secondary and primary schools; to direct the pedagogical reform of secondary education and types of education lower than that level, and to organize the supervision and evaluation of the implementation of nine-year compulsory schooling and the eradication of illiteracy among young and middle-aged adults.
- To manage regular higher education, postgraduate education, tertiary vocational education and adult higher education, higher education offered by social forces, as well as the state-administered examinations for self-taught adult learners seeking tertiary qualifications and continuing education. To investigate and put forward the standards for establishing higher education institutions, to examine and verify the establishment, rename, abolishment, and adjustment of higher education institutions; to formulate the curriculum and basic teaching documents; to direct the pedagogical reform of higher education institutions and the evaluation of higher education; to undertake the

implementation and coordination of Project 211, a Chinese government initiative designed to raise the level of technology education.

- To plan and direct the educational work for the minority nationalities, and to coordinate the educational aid to the minority areas.
- To plan and direct the work on the construction of the Chinese Communist Party in institutions of higher learning and the work of ideology and politics education, moral, physical, health, arts, and national defense education in schools of different levels.
- To administer teachers' work, to formulate and supervise the implementation of the professional qualifications for teachers of different levels; to work out the organizational standards for schools of different levels; to make overall plans for the team construction of teachers and administrative staff for schools.
- To make plans and manage the students recruitment work for higher education institutions of different levels; to be responsible for the management of student registration for higher education institutions of different levels; to manage the reform of graduate placement for higher education institutions, to put forward relevant policies, and to organize the implementation of this work.
- To plan and direct the research work of higher education institutions in natural science, philosophy, and social science; to undertake macro-instruction on higher education institutions in the application, research, and popularization of new high-technology, in the transform of scientific and research achievements and in the efforts of combining industry, teaching and research; to coordinate and supervise higher education institutions in the implementation of state key scientific and research programs and national-defense scientific-tackling programs; to direct the development and construction of national key laboratories and research centers for national projects.
- To manage, coordinate, and direct educational foreign affairs, to formulate guidelines and policies for Chinese students studying abroad and international students studying in China; to plan, coordinate, and direct the work of teaching Chinese as a foreign language; to direct the work of Chinese educational institutions abroad. To be responsible for coordinating the educational cooperation and exchanges with Hong Kong Special Administration Region (SAR), Macao SAR, and Taiwan.
- To be responsible for collecting, analyzing, and releasing basic educational information.
- To formulate guidelines and policies of national language work; to compile medium and long-term plan for language work; to formulate the standard and criterion for Chinese and minor nationalities' languages

and to coordinate and supervise the implementation of this work; to direct the popularization and testing of Mandarin.

- To undertake overall plan on the conferral of academic degrees, and to draft relevant regulations; to be responsible for the implementation of the academic degrees conferral system; to be responsible for the work of international equity on same academic degrees, mutual recognition of academic degrees and so on; to carry out the work assigned by the Academic Degree Committee of the State Council.
- To be responsible for the coordination between the National Commission of the People's Republic of China for UNESCO (United Nations Educational, Scientific, and Cultural Organization) and UNESCO itself for cooperation and exchanges in education, science, technology, culture, and other sectors; to be responsible for keeping in touch and exchanging with the head office, Asia-Pacific office and Beijing office of UNESO; to be responsible for connecting with Chinese permanent delegation to UNESO and to supervise its work.
- To carry out the work assigned by the State Steering Committee of science and Technology and Education.
- To carry out other work assigned by the State Council.

MOE has 20 Departments
1. General Office,
2. Policy Research and Law Construction Department,
3. Personnel Department,
4. Development and Planning Department,
5. Finance Department,
6. Elementary Education Department,
7. Vocational Education and Adult Education Department,
8. Higher School Education Department,
9. Minority Education Department,
10. Teacher Education Department,
11. Education Supervision Office,
12. Social Science Research,
13. Ideological and Political Work Department,
14. University Student Department,
15. Science and Technology Department,
16. Physical, Sanitation and Art Education Department,
17. Language and Character Administration Department,
18. International Cooperation and Communication Department,
19. Degree Committee of the State Department,
20. Secretariat of the National Committee of the United Nations Scientific, Education, and Cultural Organization (UNESCO).

Ministry of Finance[2]

Telephone: 86 10 6855 1114
Web: www.mof.gov.cn

The Ministry of Finance (MOF) is a central government agency under the State Council, responsible for formulating and implementing China's financial strategy and related policies.

The MOF has the following mandates:

- Formulating and implementing strategies, policies and guidelines, medium- and-long-term development plan and reform programs of public finance and taxation; participating in macroeconomic policy making; providing policy advice on macroeconomic regulation and balanced allocation of public fund with fiscal instruments; formulating and implementing policies regarding income distribution between the central and local governments and between the state and enterprises.
- Drafting laws and regulations on public finance and financial and accounting management; laying down and implementing regulations and rules on fiscal, financial, and accounting management; organizing negotiations concerning external finance and debts and signing related agreements/accords.
- Preparing the draft annual budget of the central government and its final accounts; organizing budget implementation; presenting reports on the central and local budgets and the implementation to the National People's Congress and reports on the final accounts to the Standing Committee of the National People's Congress on behalf of the State Council; administering the public revenue, the extra-budgetary fund, and the special accounts of the central government; administering other governmental funds.
- Proposing tax legislation plans; reviewing proposals on tax legislation and tax collection regulations with the State Tax Administration before reporting to the State Council; formulating tax collection plans according to the budget; proposing adjustments on tax items, tax rates, and tax incentives, including those temporary and special tax incentives that have a major bearing on the central finance; participating in foreign-related tax negotiations and international tariff negotiations; signing foreign-related tax agreements/accords; formulating model tax agreement and convention; performing the secretariat functions for the Tariff/Tax Regulation Committee of the State Council.

- Administering the central expenditures; formulating and implementing government procurement policies; managing the budgetary non-trade-related foreign exchange of government agencies, public institutions, and social organizations as well as budgetary balance of payment; promulgating national uniform standards and policies of some expenditures; formulating and implementing "Accounting Regulation for Public Institutions" and "Accounting Regulation for Government Agencies"; formulating financial regulations on capital construction.
- Formulating and implementing the policy of distribution between the state and enterprises, managing expenditures from the central coffers to support enterprises; promulgating and implementing "General Principles of Enterprise Accounting"; supervising financial management of the enterprises directly affiliated to the central government and managing the return of state-owned capital; consolidating and analyzing the final annual financial accounts of national enterprises.
- Administering and supervising the central government expenditures for economic development, the appropriation for central government financed projects, and funds for technological innovation and new product testing; managing central government funds for comprehensive development of agriculture; formulating and supervising implementation of "General Principles on Enterprise Accounting."
- Managing the social security expenditures from the central government; formulating the accounting management rules on social security funds; monitoring the utilization of the social security funds.
- Formulating and implementing policies, rules, and regulations on managing government's domestic debts; preparing plans for treasury bond issuance; formulating policies, rules, and regulations on managing government's external debts; undertaking external negotiations/consultations on loans from foreign governments, World Bank, Asian Development Bank, and Japan Bank for International Cooperation; participating in international financial organizations on behalf of the Chinese Government.
- Formulating and implementing accounting regulations and "Enterprise Accounting Standards"; formulating and monitoring the implementation of the government's overall budget and accounting regulations governing the government agencies, public institutions, and industries; guiding and monitoring the business of certified public accountants and accounting firms; guiding and regulating the auditing business; reviewing and approving the establishment of representative offices and branches of foreign accounting firms in China.

- Monitoring the implementation of fiscal and tax policies, laws and regulations; identifying the main problems in the management of fiscal revenues and expenditures; proposing policy suggestions on strengthening fiscal management; administering resident offices of Fiscal Supervision Commissioners.
- Formulating fiscal research and education plans; organizing fiscal training; promoting fiscal information dissemination.
- Undertaking other assignments of the State Council.

Ministry of Commerce

Telephone: 86 10 66512 1919
Web: http://english.mofcom.gov.cn

The Ministry of Commerce (MOFCOM, formerly MOFTEC) is a central government agency under the leadership of the State Council, responsible for China's economic development.

MOFCOM has 25 departments
1. American and Oceanic Affairs Department
2. Asian Affairs Department
3. Electro-Machinery Products Import/Export Department. Manages imports and exports of electro-machinery products; participates in setting tariff rules and rates and in international negotiations.
4. Fair Trade for Imports and Exports Bureau
5. Foreign Aid Department
6. Foreign Affairs Department. Manages protocol and foreign affairs.
7. Foreign Economic Cooperation Department. Oversees development of overseas markets and regulates overseas operations; processes registration of contracting, labor-export, design, and consulting projects in sensitive countries or regions.
8. Foreign Investment Administration Department. Reports regularly to the State Council about foreign investment developments and proposes policies, regulations, and plans for foreign investment. Compiles and publishes the Industrial Catalog for Guiding Foreign Investment. Plans annual import/export quotas for foreign-invested enterprises; verifies contracts and articles of association of FIE projects; approves establishment of Foreign-Invested Enterprises (FIEs) exceeding prescribed investment amounts or involving quotas and licensing; verifies and approves contracts and associations of large FIEs and their changes; supervises law and contract enforcement of FIEs; supervises investment promotion work; supervises foreign-investment statistics.

9. Foreign Trade Department. One of the biggest departments in MOF-COM; established in 2001 to face the challenges of China's accession to the World Trade Organization (WTO). Studies and proposes solutions to major problems in foreign trade. Proposes policies, strategies, and reform plans for the foreign-trade sector; promotes new trade instruments; drafts and reviews qualifications for licensing foreign trade companies; and proposes rules and policies for overseas investment. Licenses domestic enterprises to open businesses abroad (except for financial businesses) and supervises their management. Oversees trade fairs and exhibitions and proposes rules for attending overseas fairs. Manages the approval of resident representative offices of foreign countries and Hong Kong. Supervises ads for exports; plans import/export quotas of various industries; manages import/export licenses; manages imports/exports of toxic chemicals; catalogs import/export commodities.

10. Policy Research Department. Manages international shipping agencies and participates in multilateral negotiations on transportation.

11. General Office. Manages day-to-day affairs, meetings, news briefings, security, and communications, among other areas.

12. Industry Damage Investigation Bureau

13. Informatization Department

14. International Economic and Trade Relations Department. Organizes multilateral trade negotiations (including with international organizations), negotiations on international service trade, and international treaties and conventions. Coordinates Chinese positions among various departments under the State Council. Manages multilateral and bilateral aid and donations.

15. Market Operation and Adjustment Department

16. Market System Construction Department

17. Personnel, Education, and Labor Department. Oversees personnel affairs, labor, wages, appointment of personnel posted overseas, and training.

18. Planning and Finance Department. Formulates medium- and long-term plans for foreign trade; proposes policies for import/export balance and structural adjustment; participates in policy making for tariffs, foreign exchange, taxation, credit, pricing, and insurance. Monitors and analyzes performance of the foreign-trade sector; supervises auditing and finance of MOFTEC and affiliated organizations, enterprises, and foreign aid.

19. Taiwan, Hong Kong, and Macao Affairs Department

20. Science and Technical Development and Technology Trade Department. Supervises technical trade; proposes a catalog for high-tech product exports and for technologies prohibited or restricted from/for

import/export; proposes and implements export-control policies by issuing export licenses for products related to prevention of nuclear proliferation.

21. Treaties and Law Department. Oversees foreign-trade law making and drafting, and review of multilateral and bilateral treaties; participates in conclusion of major agreements, contracts, and articles of association, as well as arbitration of major disputes. Harmonizes domestic regulations with international conventions; undertakes multilateral and bilateral negotiations on intellectual property rights; supervises anti-dumping and anti-subsidy lawsuits.

22. West Asian and African Affairs Department

23. Commerce Reform and Development Department

24. European Affairs Departments. These departments draft bilateral trade policies with the relevant countries (regions); organize bilateral committees and negotiations; manage overseas trade fairs; manage trade relations with countries with which China has not established diplomatic relations; coordinate with commercial sections of Chinese embassies abroad and foreign embassies in Beijing.

25. World Trade Organization Affairs Department

Ministry of Information Industry[3]

Telephone: 86 10 6601 4249
Web: www.mii.gov.cn

As an integral part of the State Council, the Ministry of Information Industry (MII) is a regulatory body in charge of the manufacture of electronic and information products, the communications and software industry, as well as the promotion of informatization of the national economy and social services in the country.

The major responsibilities of MII are:

- To study and formulate the government's development strategies, guidelines, policies, and overall plans of the information industry with a view to invigorating the manufacturing industry of electronic and IT products, the communications and the software industry, as well as promoting the informatization process of the national economy and the social service.
- To stipulate laws and regulations of the manufacturing industry of electronic and IT products, the communications industry and the software industry, issue administrative rules and be responsible for the administrative enforcement of laws and the supervision of the enforcement of laws.

- To make overall plans for the development of national public communications networks (including local and long distance telecommunications networks), radio and TV broadcasting networks and dedicated networks of other sectors and exercise sector management.

- To establish technical policies, systems, and standards for the manufacturing industry of electronic and IT products, the communications industry and the software industry; to establish technical systems and standards for radio broadcasting and TV transmission networks; to exercise control over the network access verification of telecommunications network equipment and the network access of telecommunications terminal equipment; and to provide guidance to quality supervision and control of electronic and IT products.

- To be responsible for nationwide distribution and management of such public communications resources as radio frequencies, satellite orbit positions, communications network numbers, domain names and addresses; to be responsible for the examination and approval of the establishment of radio stations as well as detection and supervision of the use of radio frequencies; and to regulate radio frequencies and help settle radio interference related matters according to laws and maintain radio wave order in the air.

- To exercise supervision and control over telecommunications and information service market, implement licensing for operation as necessary, exercise supervision over service quality, ensure fair competition and universal service and safeguard the interest of both the state and users; and to establish arrangements for network interconnection, interoperation, and accounting, and supervise their implementation.

- To formulate tariff policies for communications and information service, set tariff standards for basic postal and telecommunications services and supervise their implementation.

- To organize the planning, construction, and management of dedicated government communications networks; to manage the supervision and dispatch center of the national communications networks and international communications gateways; to deploy and coordinate dedicated government communications, emergency and disaster relief related communications and mission-critical communications; and to ensure security for communications of the government.

- To provide guidance and foster the growth of the information industry in compliance with the industrial and technological development policies, by giving directions to the adjustment of its industrial structure, product mix, and enterprise structure, as well as the reorganization of state-owned enterprises and the establishment of enterprise groups; and to rationally allocate resources and prevent duplicated construction.

- To facilitate research and development (R&D) in the manufacturing industry of electronic and IT products, the communications industry and the software industry, organize projects to tackle major technical problems and promote the digestion, absorption, and improvement of the imported technologies with a view to applying R&D results to production; and to offer support to national industries.
- To study and formulate development plans for the informatization of the national economy and help project owners and initiators in promoting the key informatization projects; to direct, coordinate, and organize the development and utilization of information resources; and to give guidance to the popularization of electronic and information technologies and education on informatization.
- To organize and give guidance to the consolidation of financial data, the submission of profits, the allocation of funds and clearing of postal and telecommunications enterprises, coordinate operational relations between postal enterprises and telecommunications enterprises, mobilize funds for subsidies for universal service and for posts, and take charge of personnel matters concerning the Ministry and units directly under the Ministry.
- To present China in relevant international organizations and when signing inter-governmental agreements, organize foreign economic and technical cooperation and exchanges, and handle matters concerned with other countries.
- To study communications and information policies concerning the Hong Kong Special Administrative Region (SAR), Macao SAR, and Taiwan and deal with related issues.
- To be responsible for the publication of sector statistic and information.
- To handle other matters entrusted by the State Council.

The MII also supervises the State Post Bureau as authorized by the State Council.

MII has 13 departments:

1. **General Office.** It handles the day-to-day work of the Ministry, coordinates the working relationship among the departments, and organizes important meetings of the Ministry. It engages in such work as information collection, news release, publicity, and public relations. It provides the ministerial leaders with secretarial service and the Ministry with administrative management over its documents, achieves matters related to confidentiality, safety and security, petition letters and calls handling, intra-ministry finance, state-owned property, and so forth.
2. **Department of Policies and Regulations.** The Department of Policies and Regulations examines and formulates general policies and major

reform plans. It drafts laws, administrative rules and regulations governing the information industry, and exercises supervision over and makes administrative review of law enforcement. It develops opening-up policies for communications. It studies communications and information policies regarding the Hong Kong SAR, Macao SAR, and Taiwan and settles related matters.

3. **Department of Planning.** The Department of Planning examines, studies, and formulates development strategies to invigorate the manufacturing industry of electronic products, the communications industry, and the software industry and mid- and long-term development programs, coordinates the construction of basic telecommunications networks, computer-based information networks, radio and TV broadcasting networks, and all types of dedicated networks in order to bring about harmonious development between public and private networks and between service and manufacturing industries. It rationally allocates resources and avoids duplicated construction projects. It exercises control over the budgeted construction funds of the state according to relevant regulations and provides guidance for the importation of technologies, foreign capital utilization, and the setting up of joint ventures and cooperative ventures with foreign partners. It is responsible for the formulation of construction standards and design specifications for communications and information networks, and exercises macro control over the construction of such networks. In addition, it maintains statistics and releases information about the industry.

4. **Department of Science and Technology.** The Department of Science and Technology keeps track of the trend of information development worldwide and formulates scientific and technological development plans and technology policies. It coordinates and establishes technical standards for public telecommunications networks and network numbering plans and defines technological systems and standards for radio broadcast and TV transmission networks. It coordinates projects for tackling major R&D subjects and promotes the application of R&D results to production. Finally, it supervises the quality of electronic and information products, regulates their standards and measurements, and organizes information collection and analysis associated with information technology.

5. **Department of Enterprise Restructuring and Operation.** The Department of Enterprise Restructuring and Operation examines and formulates reform plans and programs for enterprises, gives directions to the reform, reorganization, upgrading, and management as well as helps settle major issues in enterprise reform. It works out policies and measures for the development of large enterprises and enterprise groups

and guides the strategic reorganization of the state-owned enterprises. It maintains statistics of, monitors, and analyzes the sector's economic performance. It makes annual forecasts of major development targets and exercises macro control over the electronic and information product market and coordinates the importation of these products.

6. **Telecommunications Administration Bureau.** The Telecommunications Administration Bureau studies and formulates plans, policies, and measures for telecommunications development, exercises supervision over telecommunications and information services in accordance with the law so as to maintain fair competition, ensures universal service, and protects the interests of both the state and the customer. It is responsible for approving and licensing the operation of communications and information services, and for supervising service quality and price. It develops procedures and accounting arrangements for inter-connection between telecommunications networks and supervises the implementation. It is responsible for the allocation and management of the resources of telecommunications network numbers. It manages domain names and network sites of the Internet and undertakes their coordination with other countries. It is responsible for authenticating the equipment of network interconnection according to the standard and managing terminal access to the network. The Bureau is also responsible for the organization and coordination of the construction and management of the private networks of the government. It manages the Supervision and Dispatch Center of the national communications network, the international telecommunications gateways, and the Safety Supervisory Center for the Internet. It directs and coordinates communications for disaster relief and emergency cases and other important communications. Finally, it organizes studies on the safety and security of the telecommunications networks and information with corresponding counter-measures adopted.

7. **Department of Financial Regulation and Clearing.** The Department of Financial Regulation and Clearing establishes sector financial rules and regulations and supervises their implementation in compliance with the government's policies governing the state-owned assets and relevant financial and accounting systems and sees to their implementation. It studies and formulates rules and regulations for major postal and telecommunications enterprises to consolidate their financial data, submit profits and allocate funds and clear accounts. It also coordinates the financial relations between postal enterprises and telecommunications enterprises and mobilizes funds for subsidies in support of universal service and posts. It develops tariff policies for communications and

information services and charging levels for postal and telecommunications services and manages the funds within the state budget.

8. **Department of Electronic and IT Products.** The Department of Electronic and IT Products examines and develops both mid- and long-term development programs, policies, and measures for the manufacturing industry of electronic and IT products and the software industry. It gives guidance to the adjustment of the product mix, organizes and coordinates the development and production of major systems and basic products such as micro-electronics as well as the localization of associated equipment, components, instruments, devices, and materials required by the state-level major projects. Finally, it prepares investment instructions for the sector and gives guidance to the popularization and application of electronic and information technologies.

9. **Bureau of Special Electronic Installations.** The Bureau of Special Electronic Installations is responsible for the sector management of the special electronic installations, such as large-scale government IT projects.

10. **Department of Informatization Promotion.** The Department of Informatization Promotion studies, develops, and promotes the development programs for the national economic and social informatization while giving guidance to the various localities and sectors in their informatization work. It helps project owners and initiators in advancing key informatization projects, coordinates and promotes the development of the software industry nationwide. It studies and formulates policies and determines measures for the exploitation of information resources, and gives guidance to and coordinates the exploitation and utilization of these resources and the development of technologies for information security. Besides, it promotes the enhancement of the awareness of informatization.

11. **Bureau of Radio Regulation (The State Radio Regulatory Office).** The Bureau of Radio Regulation establishes plans of radio frequency spectrum to facilitate the rational exploitation and utilization of the frequency resources. It is responsible for the assignment and management of the frequency resources, the management of radio stations and the supervision and measurement of radio equipment and the handling of electromagnetic interference related matters so as to maintain radio wave order in the air. It regulates the use of radio frequencies in the light of laws and regulations concerned and coordinates satellite orbital positions. In addition, it handles matters involving foreign countries with regard to the use of radio frequencies. Finally, it participates in international radio conferences as authorized.

12. **Department of Foreign Affairs.** The Department of Foreign Affairs is responsible for China's membership in international organizations associated with the information industry and the signing and implementation of inter-governmental agreements as well as handling matters concerning communications and information with other governments. It studies policies for economic and technical cooperation with other countries in the field of information and has the centralized responsibility for international cooperation and exchanges. It approves and administers the procedures and matters on going abroad, including relevant projects, delegations, and personnel, within its terms of reference.

13. **Department of Personnel.** The Department of Personnel is in charge of personnel affairs within its terms of reference. In particular, it is responsible for the forecasts, planning, training, and import of intellectual resources, personnel exchange, and matters related to professional and technical titles in the information sector. It determines the organizational setup and size and matters concerning the labor and wages of the Ministry and units directly under the Ministry. It also gives guidance to matters concerning personnel, education, and labor and wages in the information sector.

Ministry of Science and Technology[4]

Telephone: 86 10 6851 5544
Web: www.most.gov.cn

Missions of the Ministry of Science and Technology (MOST) are:

- To research and set forth the macro strategies for science and technology development, as well as guidelines, policies, and regulations for science and technology to promote economic and social development; to conduct research on key issues relating to the promotion of economic and social development by science and technology, to research and determine the major deployment and priority areas for science and technology development; to promote the building of the national science and technology innovation system and improve the national science and technology innovation capacity.

- To organize the formulation of the national medium- and long-term development plan and annual progress plans for civil science and technology.

- To research and set forth guidelines, policies, and measures for the reform in the science and technology system; to promote the establishment of science and technology innovation system and science and technology innovation mechanisms conforming to the socialist market economy and the intrinsic laws of science and technology development; to guide the reform in science and technology system by various ministries and local governments.

- To research measures for increasing science and technology investment through various channels, optimize the allocation of science and technology resources, and take charge of the budgets and final accounts of science operating expenses, the "three-item expenditure" on science and technology (i.e., the expenditure on trial-producing new products, the expenditure on the middle stage tests, and the expenditure on subsidies for major scientific research projects), the funds of science and technology foreign affairs managed by MOST, and so on.
- To research and formulate the policies and measures for strengthening fundamental research and high-tech development; to take charge of the formulation, organization, and implementation of Key Fundamental Research Program, High-Tech Research and Development Program, Key Technologies Development Program, Science and Technology Innovation Program, and Science and Technology Program for Social Development.
- To strengthen the work on industrialization of high and new technologies and development and extension of applied technologies; to guide the transfer of science and technology achievements; to manage the work on national level key new products of high and new technologies; to take charge of the formulation of the guidelines as well as the implementation of the science and technology development programs such as the Torch Program, the Spark Program, the Achievement Extension Program, and so on; to administer the national level high-tech industrial development zones; to promote exportation of high technologies and formulate related policies.
- To participate in the construction and development plans of science and technology bases such as key and major national projects; to formulate and implement the plans for science and technology bases including national key laboratories.
- To conduct research on the rational allocation of human resources in science and technology and set forth relevant policies that can fully encourage the enthusiasm of science and technology talents and help create a preferable environment for their development.
- To research and formulate the guidelines and policies of China's international cooperation and exchange in science and technology; to take charge of the bilateral and multilateral governmental science and technology cooperation programs as well as those programs related to relevant international organizations; to guide the work of science and

technology agencies posted abroad; to take charge of the selection and administration of the science and technology officials posted at Chinese embassies and consulates in foreign countries; to manage the work of science and technology aid from foreign governments and international science and technology organizations toward China, as well as China's science and technology aid toward other countries, to take charge of the science and technology cooperation and exchange with Hong Kong Special Administrative Region (SAR), Macaw SAR, and Taiwan.

- To research and make proposals on the formulation of science and technology laws and regulations; to manage the work such as national science and technology results, science and technology awards, science and technology secrecy, technology market and science and technology related Intellectual Property Rights (IPR) protection; to formulate the plan for science and technology popularization, and use policy guidance to promote the development of science popularization; to promote the development of social intermediary agencies working on science and technology consulting, public bidding, evaluation and assessment, and so on, and promote the establishment of science and technology service system.
- To take charge of management of science and technology information, science and technology statistics, and science and technology journals; to approve the establishment and adjustment of scientific research institutions.
- To guide and coordinate the science and technology management work of various ministries and commissions under the State Council as well as that by provinces, autonomous regions, and municipalities.
- To manage Science and Technology Daily by authorization.
- To undertake related work trusted by the National Steering Group for Science, Technology, and Education.
- To undertake other tasks assigned by the State Council.

MOST has 11 departments:

1. **Executive Office.** It has seven divisions: Division of General Affairs (Division of Complaints and Appeal); Division of Secretariat (Division of Supervision); Division I of Research and Investigation; Division II of Research and Investigation; Division of E-Documentation and Archive; Division of Publicity (Press Office); and Division of Administration.
2. **Department of Personnel.** It has four divisions: Division of General Affairs and Personnel Training; Division of Cadres; Division of Overseas Missions; and Division of Institutions, Labor, and Salary Management.

3. **Department of Policy, Regulations and Reform.** It has four divisions: Division of General Affairs and Policy Study; Division of Regulations and IPR; Division of Institutional Reform; and Division of Science and Technology Outreach.
4. **Department of Development Planning.** It has seven divisions: Division of General Affairs and Planning (Office of Confidentiality); Division of Planning and Coordination; Division of High Technology Research and Development; Division of Key Technologies Research and Development; Division of Facilities and Infrastructure; Division of Regional Technology Development; and Division of Evaluation and Statistics.
5. **Department of Facilities and Financial Support.** It has five divisions: Division of General Affairs; Division of Facilities Support; Division of Budget Management; Division of Finance and Property; and Division of Accounting and Supervision.
6. **Department of International Cooperation.** It has seven divisions: Division of General Affairs and Planning; Division of International Organizations and Conferences; Division of American and Oceanic Affairs; Division of Asian and African Affairs; Division of European Affairs; Division of Policy Study; and Division of East European and Central Asian Affairs.
7. **Department of Basic Research.** It has three divisions: Division of General Affairs and Basic Research; Division of Bases Administration; and Division of Major Projects Administration.
8. **Department of High and New Technology Development and Industrialization.** It has six divisions: Division of General Affairs and Planning; Division of Energy and Transportation; Division of Information and Space; Division of Advanced Manufacturing and Automation; Division of Materials; and Division of Industry Development.
9. **Department of Rural Science and Technology.** It has three divisions: Division of General Affairs; Division of Agriculture; and Division of Rural Industries.
10. **Department of Social Development.** It has three divisions: Division of General Affairs and Public Service; Division of Resources and Environment; and Division of Biotechnology and Medicine.
11. **Bureau of Retired Staffs.** It has four divisions: Division of General Affairs; Office for Party Committee; Division of Logistics Service; and Division of Sports and Entertainment Activities.

National Bureau of Statistics[5]

Telephone: Tel: + 86 10 6853 3618
Web: www.stats.gov.cn/english/

As an agency directly under the State Council, the National Bureau of Statistics (NBS) is in charge of statistics and economic accounting in China. In Accordance with the Statistics Law of the People's Republic of China and relevant stipulations of the State Council, major functions of the National Bureau of Statistics include:

- To work out laws and regulations on statistical work, to formulate directive rules for statistical operation, to draw up plans for statistical modernization and nationwide statistical surveys, to organize, exercise leadership and supervision over statistical and economic accounting work in various localities and departments, and to supervise and inspect the enforcement of statistical laws and regulations.
- To set up and improve the national economic accounting system and statistical country; to work out national statistical standards; to review and approve statistical standards by other government departments; to organize the administration of national statistical survey projects, to examine, approve, and manage plans and schemes for statistical surveys by other departments.
- To organize the implementation of major censuses on the basic items relating to the state and strength of the country; to exercise unified administration over socio-economic surveys in various localities and departments, to collect, process, and tabulate basic statistical information from a statistical perspective on the national economic and scientific progress and social development; to provide statistical information and relevant proposals for the Central Committee of the Communist Party of China, the State Council and government departments concerned.
- To act as the exclusive agency in verifying, approving, administering, and publishing basic national statistical data and to regularly disseminate to the general public statistical information with regard to the national economic and social development.
- To build up and minister the national statistical information system and the national statistical database system; to formulate basic standards and operational rules for statistical database networks in various localities and departments.
- To exercise leadership over directly affiliated surveying agencies in various localities; to exercise unified management over operating expenses of statistical activities for statistical agencies in local people's governments at and above county level; to assist in the management of directors and deputy directors of local statistical offices of provinces, autonomous regions, and municipalities directly under the central government; to organize and administer qualification examinations and the evaluation of professional titles for statisticians across the country.

NBS has 16 departments:

1. **Administrative Office.** Responsible for overall coordination and management of internal administration, communication of administrative information, and secretarial work.
2. **Department of International Cooperation.** Responsible for the organization and implementation of bilateral and multilateral international statistical exchange and cooperation programs, and communication with international organizations and official statistical agencies of various countries.
3. **Department of Statistical Policies and Legislation.** Responsible for working out medium- to long-term programs and implementing methods for statistical restructuring; drafting, revision and supervisory inspection of statistical laws, regulations, and operation rules.
4. **Department of Statistical Design and Management.** Responsible for working out statistical restructuring plans and schemes: organizing and establishing the system of national accounts and national statistical surveys: working out national statistical standards and examining and finalizing statistical standards by other departments; examining, approving and managing statistical survey programs and plans formulated by various departments.
5. **Department of Comprehensive Statistics of the National Economy.** Responsible for conducting monitoring, forecast, and comprehensive analysis on the performance of the national economy and preparing macro-regulation proposals.
6. **Department of National Accounts.** Responsible for organizational work in the implementation of the system of national accounts; preparing gross domestic product accounts, input-output tables, flow of funds accounts, balance of payments, asset-liability accounts and resources and environment accounts.
7. **Department of Industrial an Transport Statistics.** Responsible for organizational work in the implementation of surveys for industrial and energy statistics, collecting, processing and providing statistical data on transportation, post and telecommunications as well as conducting statistical analysis.
8. **Department of Statistics on Investment in Fixed Assets.** Responsible for organizational work in the implementation of statistical surveys on investment in fixed assets, on construction industry and real estate, collecting, processing, and providing statistical data relating to geological prospecting, urban housing, and public utilities as well as conducting statistical analysis.

9. **Department of Statistics on Trade and External Economic Relations.** Responsible for organizational work in the implementation of statistical surveys on wholesale and retail trade, catering and on the performance of market operation, collecting, processing, and providing statistical data concerning foreign trade, foreign investment, and tourism as well as conducting statistical analysis.

10. **Department of Population, Social, and Science Statistics.** Responsible for organizational work in the implementation of statistical surveys on population and labor, collecting, processing, and providing statistical data pertaining to social development and scientific and technological advancement as well as conducting statistical analysis.

11. **Organization of Rural Socio-Economic Survey.** Responsible for collecting, processing, and providing statistical data on agricultural production, income and expenditure of rural households, rural economy, farming activities, and distribution of income as well as conducting statistical analysis.

12. **Organization of Urban Socio-Economic Survey.** Responsible for collecting, processing, and providing statistical data relating to market prices, income and expenditure of urban households and urban development as well as conducting statistical analysis.

13. **Organization of Enterprise Survey.** Responsible for collecting, processing, and providing statistical data through sample surveys of enterprises of various types of ownership and through special surveys as well as conducting statistical analysis.

14. **Census Center.** Responsible for studying and working out census plans on major items reflecting the state and strength of the country, studying special technical problems in censuses, organizing the implementation of censuses of basic statistical units and the tertiary industry, providing relevant statistical data and conducting analysis.

15. **International Statistical Information Center.** Responsible for providing Chinese statistical information to international organizations and to foreign government statistical agencies through statistical data exchange programs, collecting, processing, and utilizing statistical information from other countries as well as from Hong Kong, Macau, and Taiwan, and conducting studies on International Comparison Program (ICP).

16. **The Computing Center.** Responsible for organizational work in the development and management of the national statistical information system, application and development of information technology, processing and administration of data from national statistical surveys, and the establishment of the national statistical database system as well as the operation, maintenance, and management of statistical information networks across the country.

Apart from these departments, there are also departments in charge of personnel management and training of statisticians, budget management, statistical research, publishing, new release and press relations, economic performance survey, information service, and logistics support.

National Development and Reform Commission

Telephone: 86 10 6850 2114
Web: http://en.ndrc.gov.cn

Arising from the State Planning Commission (SPC, founded in 1952 and later renamed as the State Development Planning Commission [SDPC]), the National Development and Reform Commission (NDRC) is a central government agency in charge of macroeconomic management under the State Council. It is responsible for studying and proposing strategies and plans for national economic and social development, the overall balance of supply and demand, and structural adjustments.

The NDRC has 26 departments directly under the commission offices:

1. **Communications and Transportation Department**
2. **Department of Industries**
3. **Development Planning Department.** Proposes strategies for national economic and social development and distribution of productive forces; proposes objectives and policies for medium- to long-term national economic growth, balance of total demand and supply, and structural adjustments; formulates medium- to long-term development plans; coordinates and balances plans and policies of various industries.
4. **Economic Performance Bureau.** Analyzes trends in economic performance; coordinates emergency dispatches of strategic commodities; coordinates the foreign trade shipping industry.
5. **Economic Restructuring and Comprehensive Reform Department.** Analyzes balance of capital from all sectors; studies fiscal and monetary policies; analyzes fiscal and monetary policy implementation and proposes solutions to problems. Proposes strategies and policies for direct financing; participates in determining the total size, structure, and destination of marketable securities; consults the People's Bank of China in proposing total scale of enterprise bond issues and industrial investment fund issues; determines fund destinations; supervises fund use. Proposes objectives and policies for regulating overall price levels; monitors and forecasts fluctuations of overall price levels.
6. **Employment and Income Allocation Department**
7. **Energy Bureau.** Regulates industries, including oil, power, and coal.

8. **Environmental and Resources Comprehensive Utilization Department**
9. **Finance Department**
10. **Fixed Asset Investment Department.** Studies macro-regulatory policies for investment and proposes total amount and structure for fixed-asset investment and sources of funding. Monitors the operation of investments in fixed assets; arranges construction projects and key projects; supervises policy financing.
11. **Foreign Affairs Department.** Oversees bilateral and multilateral cooperation between the NDRC and foreign governments and departments, as well as routine foreign affairs.
12. **Foreign Capital Utilization Department.** Proposes strategies, total scale, and destinations for foreign capital utilization. Controls, optimizes, and monitors foreign loans. Studies and formulates plans for controlling the total amount of loans by international financial institutions, foreign governments, and commercial banks. Proposes total amount and destinations for foreign direct investment and overseas investment; proposes Industrial Catalog for Guiding Foreign Investment, except for industry and commerce; monitors and analyzes utilization of foreign capital. Schedules major projects financed with foreign and overseas investment.
13. **General Office.** Supervises conference organization, communications management, secretarial affairs and administrative affairs in areas such as finance, asset management, and security.
14. **High-tech Industry Department.** Proposes strategies and coordinates plans for high-tech industrial development; organizes research and development and demonstration projects of key technologies and of plant equipment needed for key industries; optimizes funding for commercialization of research results. Promotes the formation of new industries of the national economy; proposes relevant policies; schedules major high-tech projects.
15. **Industry Policymaking Department.** Formulates industrial and foreign-investment policies for industrial development; produces a catalog of investment restrictions.
16. **Law and Regulation Department**
17. **Medium- and Small-Sized Enterprises Department.** Supports medium- and small-sized enterprises.
18. **National Economy Department.** Proposes annual plan for national economic and social development, including objectives and policies for the balance of total demand and supply, growth rates, and structural adjustments. Analyzes macroeconomic situation. Proposes plans for strategic material reserves; coordinates plans for the economy, society, and national defense.

19. **Personnel Department.** Manages human resources for the NDRC and directly affiliated organizations.

20. **Policy Research Department.** Drafts major documents and releases economic information; organizes, participates in, and coordinates the drafting of economic regulations; oversees publication of relevant laws and regulations. Monitors trends in international economics and their impact on China; studies problems in China's economic development and restructuring; supervises administrative litigation.

21. **Price Supervision Department.** Supervises price checks and trials of cases involving violations of price regulations by central ministries, provincial governments, and centrally managed enterprises; hears appeals by provincial-level pricing departments against punitive decisions.

22. **Pricing Department.** Proposes policies for pricing major commodities and services; proposes the range, principles, and methods for commodities subject to government-controlled pricing; adjusts prices and fee structures of government-controlled commodities; organizes cost surveys of major farm products; supervises pricing policy on government-set prices and government-advised prices.

23. **Regional Economy Development Department.** Compiles development plans for regional economies; suggests guidelines and policies and coordinates regional economic development; introduces policy measures to gradually narrow regional gaps. Drafts and coordinates policies on land improvement, development, utilization, and protection. Participates in the drafting of plans for balanced water resources and environmental protection; narrows regional gaps and realizes sustainable development. Drafts economic development programs for border areas, less-developed areas, and minority-dominated areas; formulates projects of providing relief to these areas.

24. **Rural Economic Development Department.** Proposes strategies for rural economic development; coordinates plans and policies for agriculture, forestry, water conservation, meteorology, aquatic production, animal husbandry, and wasteland development; formulates plans for aiding poverty-stricken areas and plans for public-works-as-relief projects; formulates and implements plans for national ecological preservation; monitors and analyzes agricultural and rural economic development.

25. **Social Development Department.** Proposes strategies for social development; coordinates and balances plans for the development of population, employment, labor, culture, education, public health, sports, radio, television, filmmaking, tourism, legal affairs, civil affairs, and social security. Arranges special funds for social development.

26. **Trade Distribution Department.** Proposes strategies for developing internal and external trade; tracks, monitors, and analyzes developments in the internal and external markets; studies the supply/demand and import/export balance of strategic commodities; proposes policies for regulating strategic commodities. Consults relevant departments in formulating import/export plans for strategic commodities, bulk goods, and sensitive goods. Drafts plans for the balance of international payments. Supervises state ordering, warehousing, replacement, and supply of strategic commodities. Guides and regulates the market.

State Administration of Foreign Exchange

Telephone: 86 10 6840 2255
Web: www.safe.gov.cn

The State Administration of Foreign Exchange (SAFE) is designated with the following functions:

- Designing and implementing the balance of payments (BOP) statistical system in conformity with international standards, developing and enforcing the BOP statistical reporting system, and collecting relevant data to compile the BOP statement;
- Analyzing the BOP and foreign exchange positions, providing policy proposals with aim to achieving an equilibrium BOP position, and conducting feasibility study on the convertibility of the renminbi under capital account;
- Drafting rules and regulations governing foreign exchange market activities, overseeing the market conduct and operations, and promoting the development of foreign exchange market; analyzing and forecasting the foreign exchange supply/demand positions and providing the People's Bank of China (PBC) with propositions and references for the formulation of exchange rate policy;
- Promulgating regulatory measures governing foreign exchange transactions under current account and supervising the transactions accordingly; monitoring and regulating the foreign exchange account operations both in China and abroad;
- Supervising and monitoring foreign exchange transactions under capital account, including inward and outward remittance and payments;
- Managing foreign exchange reserves of the country in accordance with relevant rules and regulations;
- Drafting foreign exchange administration rules, examining the domestic entities' compliance with foreign exchange administration rules and regulations, and penalizing institutions engaging in illegal practices;

- Participating in relevant international financial activities; performing other duties and responsibilities assigned by the State Council and the PBC.

State Administration of Taxation

Telephone: 86 10 6341 7114
Web: www.chinatax.gov.cn

The State Administration of Taxation (SAT) is the highest tax authority in China. The SAT is the ministry-level department directly under the State Council, which is the functional department in charge of the State revenue work. Its mandates are mainly the following:

- Drafting the relevant tax laws, regulations, and the detailed rules for the implementation thereof; putting forward suggestions on tax policy and submitting it to the State Council together with the Ministry of Finance, and formulating the implementation procedures.
- Being involved in studying macro-economic policy and division of tax power between the Central and local governments; studying the overall level of tax incidence and proceeding with suggestions on how to regulate and control the macro-economy by means of taxation; formulating, and monitoring the implementation of the rules and procedures of taxation work; supervising local tax administration and collection.
- Organizing and carrying out tax administration system reform; formulating tax administration procedures; monitoring the implementation of tax laws, regulations, and tax policy.
- Organizing and executing the collection and administration of Central taxes, shared taxes, Agriculture Tax, and contributions to funds designated by the State; preparing revenue plan; providing interpretation for any administrative and general tax policy issues arising in implementation of tax laws; handling matters of tax exemptions and reductions.
- Promoting international exchange and cooperation in the field of taxation; participating in international tax conventions, initialing and executing relevant treaties and agreements.
- Dealing with collection and refund of value added tax (VAT) and/or Consumption Tax on importation and exportation.
- Managing personnel, salaries, size, and expenditure for all SAT offices across the country; being in charge of directors and deputy directors, and staff at similar level, of SAT offices at provincial level; providing comments on appointment or removal of directors of provincial local tax bureaus.

- Being in charge of education, training, and ideological education for tax staff in China.
- Organizing tax propaganda activities and tax theoretical research; administering registered tax agents; and standardizing tax agency services.

There are 14 functional departments within the headquarters of SAT, each of which consists of several divisions (offices) as follows:

1. **General Office.** Consisting of Division of Secretaries, Secretariat Division, Supervisory Division, Comprehensive Research Division, and News Division and Financial Division.
2. **Policy and Legislation Department.** Consisting of Division of Comprehensive Affairs, Tax Reform Division, Legislative Division, and Appeal Division.
3. **Turnover Tax Department.** (in charge of the administration of VAT, Consumption Tax and Business Tax). Consists of Comprehensive Division, VAT Division, Consumption Tax Division, and Business Tax Division.
4. **Income Tax Administration Department.** (in charge of administration of Enterprise Income Tax and Individual Income Tax). Consists of Comprehensive Division, Central Enterprise Income Tax Division, Local Enterprise Income Tax Division, and Individual Income Tax Division.
5. **Local Tax Department.** (in charge of administration of Resource Tax, City and Township Land Use Tax, City Maintenance and Construction Tax, Fixed Assets Investment Orientation Regulation Tax, Land Appreciation Tax, House Property Tax, Vehicle and Vessel Usage Tax, Stamp Tax, Slaughter Tax, and Banquet Tax). Consists of Comprehensive Division, Local Tax Division I, Local Tax Division II, and Local Tax Division III.
6. **Agriculture Tax Bureau.** (in charge of administration of Agriculture Tax, Animal Husbandry Tax, Deed Tax, and Farmland Occupation Tax). Consists of Comprehensive Division, Agriculture Tax Division I, and Agriculture Tax II.
7. **International Taxation Department.** (Offshore Oil Tax Bureau). Consists of Comprehensive Tax Policy Division, Tax Administration Division, Anti-Tax Avoidance Division, Offshore Oil Tax Division, International Tax Treaty Division, Foreign Affairs Division, and Foreign Cooperative Division.
8. **Import and Export Tax Department.** (responsible for VAT and Consumption Tax on importation and exportation). Consists of Comprehensive Division, Import Tax Division, and Export Tax Division.

9. **Administration and Collection Department.** Consists of Comprehensive Division, Tax Propaganda Division, Invoice Management Division, and Open Market Tax Division.
10. **Tax Investigation Department.** Consists of Comprehensive Division, Procedure Division, Investigation Division I, and Investigation Division II.
11. **Financial Management Department.** Consists of Funding Division, Infrastructure Division, and Equipment Division.
12. **Planning and Statistical Department.** Consists of Comprehensive Division, Planning Division, Statistical Division, and Macro-Analysis Division.
13. **Personnel Department.** Consists of Comprehensive Division Personnel Division for Headquarters, Personnel Division for Local Offices, Recruit Division, and Grass-root Work Division.
14. **Supervision Bureau.** (representative office of Supervision Ministry). Consists of Secretariat Division, Discipline Inspection and Supervision Division, and Division for Letters of Complaints.

Besides, some nongovernmental institutions directly under the Headquarters of SAT are Education Center, Logistical Service Center, Information Technology Center, Registered Tax Agent Management Center, Tax Science Research Institute, China Taxation Magazine, China Taxation Newspaper, China Taxation Press, Yangzhou Training Center, and Changchun Tax College.

State Intellectual Property Office[6]

Telephone: 86 10 6208 3114
Web: www.sipo.gov.cn

Formerly under the name "China Patent Office," the State Intellectual Property Office (SIPO) falls within the category of direct authorities under State Council and is responsible for patent work and comprehensive coordination of the foreign related affairs in the field of intellectual property.

Web sites of Interest

Beijing Foreign Economic and Trade Commission	www.tpbjc.gov.cn
Beijing Investment Promotion Bureau	www.investbeijing.gov.cn

Web sites of Interest

China Economic Information (Network)	www.cei.gov.cn
China Council for the Promotion of International Trade (CCPIT)	www.ccpit.org
Chinese Embassy in Washington, D.C.	www.china-embassy.org
Ministry of Construction	www.cin.gov.cn
Ministry of Culture	www.ccnt.gov.cn
Ministry of Foreign Affairs (MOFA)	www.fmprc.gov.cn
Ministry of Health	www.moh.gov.cn
Ministry of Labor and Social Security	www.molss.gov.cn
Ministry of Personnel	www.mop.gov.cn
Ministry of Public Security	www.mps.gov.cn
Ministry of Railway	www.chinamor.cn.net
People s Bank of China	www.pbc.gov.cn
State Economic and Trade Commission, PRC	www.setc.gov.cn
Shanghai Foreign Investment Commission	www.sfisc.com
Shanghai Foreign Investment Development Board	http://www.fid.org.cn/edaohang.jsp

OUTSOURCING-RELATED OFFICES AND AGENCIES

Academy of Macroeconomic Research (AMR, affiliated to NDRC)

Telephone: 86 10 6390 8063
Web: www.amr.gov.cn

The major role of AMR is research and consulting. It provides services for China's macroeconomy and social development decisions. At the same time, it also provides consulting services to industries, governments, and Chinese and foreign companies.

Administrative Center for China's Agenda 21

Telephone: 86 10 5888 4840
Web: www.acca21.org.cn

Agenda 21, based on China's specific national conditions and paying attention to population, environment, and development, sets up a strategic goal of sustainable development that can promote coordinated development of economy, society, resources, and environment.

Beijing Software International Promotion Center (BSIPC; affiliated with Beijing MOFCOM)

Telephone: 86 10 8233 1717
Web: www.bsipc.org

BSIPC is a nonprofit organization for promoting software industry development, the management office for Beijing software enterprises certification and software products registration, and the strategy research and center of Beijing software development. It is also a software testing and quality assurance (QA) center, and a software industry productivity center training school.

China Economic Trade Herald (affiliated with NDRC)

Telephone: 86 10 85229344
Web: www.chinacetm.com

The China Economic Trade Herald is the publication of the National Development and Reform Commission. Its mission is to develop a comprehensive study of economic and social development policies.

China Industry Association of Overseas Development and Programming (affiliated with NDRC)

Telephone: 86 10 6839 1521/1524/1540
Web: www.ciodpa.org.cn

China International Center for Economic and Technical Exchanges Ministry of Commerce (CICETE; affiliated with MOFCOM)

Telephone: 86 10 8400 0588
Web: www.cicete.org

CICETE's main mandate delegated by MOFCOM is to coordinate, on behalf of the Ministry, the cooperation between China and the United Nations Development Program (UNDP) and the United Nations Industrial

Development Organization (UNIDO), and to undertake the execution of the assisted programs and projects.

China National Association of Enterprises Consulting (affiliated with NDRC)

Telephone: 86 10 6836 4846/4838
Web: www.cnaec.com.cn

China National Center for Biotechnology Development

Telephone: 86 10 6211 1948
Web: www.cncbd.org.cn

Evaluation Center (affiliated with MOST)

Telephone: 86 10 8823 2449
Web: www.ncste.org

High Tech Research and Development Center (affiliated with MOST)

Telephone: 86 10 6833 9522/9089
Web: www.htrdc.com

Information Center (affiliated with MOST)

Telephone: 86 10 5888 1240
Web: www.mostic.gov.cn

Institute of Scientific and Technical Information of China (ISTIC, affiliated with MOST)

Telephone: 86 10 5888 2584
Web: www.istic.ac.cn

International Cooperation Center of the National Development and Reform Commission (affiliated with NDRC)

Telephone: 86 10 6853 5917/5909
Web: www.icc-ndrc.org.cn

Investment Association of China (affiliated with NDRC)

Telephone: 86 10 6809 6329
Web: www.iac.org.cn

Investment Promotion Agency of MOFCOM

Telephone: 86 10 8522 6561
Web: http://tzswj.mofcom.gov.cn

National Investing Project Apprising Center (affiliated with NDRC)

Telephone: 86 10 6852 9398
Web: http://pszx.ndrc.gov.cn

National Science and Technology Facilities and Infrastructure Center

Telephone: 86 10 5888 1463
Web: N/A

Software and Integrated Circuit Promotion Center (CSIP; affiliated with MII)

Telephone: 86 10 6395 1881
Web: www.csip.org.cn

CSIP is responsible for establishing the public service platform for China's software and integrated circuit, and providing public, neutral, and open services to develop China's software and integrated circuit industry and enterprises.

State Information Center (affiliated with NDRC)

Telephone: 86 10 6855 7000
Web: www.sic.gov.cn

Torch High Technology Industry Development Centre (affiliated with MOST)

Telephone: 86 10 6859 8371
Web: www.chinatorch.gov.cn

The Torch Centre is the administrative arm of China's Ministry of Science and Technology with the mission of developing high technology and achieving industrialization for China's high-technology industry. Its aims are also to promote the commercialization, industrialization, and internationalization of new technology and high-tech enterprises.

Trade Development Bureau of MOFCOM

Telephone: + 86 10 8522 6455
Web: http://wmfzj.mofcom.gov.cn

BEIJING MUNICIPAL GOVERNMENT OFFICES

Beijing Municipal Government

Mayor's Office
2 Zhengyi Lu, Beijing 100744
Telephone: 86 10 12345
Foreign Affairs Office
2 Zhengyi Lu, Beijing 100744
Telephone: 86 10 6519 2708
Beijing Municipal Bureau of Commerce
190 Chaoyangmennei Dajie, Beijing 100010
Telephone: 86 10 6523 6688
Beijing Development and Reform Commission
2 Ding, Fuxingmennan Dajie, Beijing 100031
Telephone: 86 10 6641 5588
Beijing Municipal Office of the State Administration of Taxation, Foreign Section
10 Chegongzhuang Dajie, Beijing 100044
Telephone: 86 10 8837 6074
Beijing Public Security Bureau
9 Qianmendong Dajie, Beijing 100740
Telephone: 86 10 8522 5050
Foreign Enterprise Service Corporation (FESCO)
Suite 267, 14 Chaoyangmennan Dajie, Beijing 100020
Telephone: 86 10 8561 8888
State Administration of Foreign Exchange, Beijing Branch
39 Lianhuachi Donglu, Beijing 100036
Telephone: 86 10 6398 8081

Business and Economy in China

The American Chamber of Commerce (AmCham)	www.amcham-china.org.cn
Austrian Chamber of Commerce in China (WKO)	www.wko.at
British Chamber of Commerce in China (BCCC)	www.britcham.org
Canada China Business Council (CCBC)	www.ccbc.com
China Chamber of International Commerce (CCOIC)	www.ccpitbj.com
China-Italy Chamber of Commerce (CCIC)	www.cameraitacina.com
French Chamber of Commerce and Industry in China (CCIFC)	www.ccifc.org
China-Australia Chamber of Commerce (AustCham)	www.austcham.org
Danish Chamber of Commerce in China (DCCC)	www.dccc.cn
European Union Chamber of Commerce in China (EUCCC)	www.euccc.com.cn
German Chamber of Commerce in China (GCCC)	www.ahk-china.org
Hong Kong Chamber of Commerce in China (HKCCC)	www.hkccc.com.cn
Federation of Indian Chamber of Commerce and Industry in China (FICCI)	www.ficci.com
Japanese Chamber of Commerce and Industry in China (JapanCham)	www.cjcci.biz
Korean Chamber of Commerce in China (KorCham)	www.korcham-china.net
Malaysian Chamber of Commerce and Industry in China (MayCham)	www.maycham.com
Singapore Chamber of Commerce and Industry in China (SingCham)	www.singcham.com.cn
Spanish Chamber of Commerce in China (COCECH)	www.spanishchamber-ch.com
Swedish Chamber of Commerce in China (Swedish Chamber)	www.swedishchamber.com.c
Swiss Chinese Chamber of Commerce (SwissCham)	www.swisscham.org

WORLD TRADE ORGANIZATION-RELATED OFFICES AND AGENCIES

China WTO Notification and Enquiry Center, MOFCOM
2 Dongchanganjie, Beijing, China 100731
Telephone: 86 10 6519 7313

Responsible for answering official inquiries into China's trade policies and notifying the WTO of China's policies, laws, and regulations on trade and investment.

Department of WTO Affairs, MOFCOM
2 Dongchanganjie, Beijing, China 100731
Telephone: 86 10 6519 7313

In charge of China's negotiations in future rounds of WTO trade liberalization talks.

Fair Trade Bureau for Import and Export, MOFCOM
2 Dongchanganjie, Beijing, China 100731
Telephone: 86 10 6519 8167

Deals with antidumping, antisubsidy, and related protective measures under the Department of Treaty and Law.

FIE Registration Bureau, SAIC
8 Sanlihe Donglu, Beijing, China 100820
Telephone: 86 10 6805 7995

Special bureau within the State Administration for Industry and Commerce to facilitate the registration of foreign-invested companies.

Investigation Bureau of Industry Injury, MOFCOM
2 Dongchanganjie, Beijing, China 100731
Telephone: 86 10 6519 8085

Assists in the investigation and research of cases of industry injuries stemming from dumping, subsidies, and so on.

WTO Office, State Administration of Customs
6 Jianguomennei Dajie, Beijing, China 100730
Telephone: 86 10 6519 5621

Coordinates all WTO affairs between national and local customs agencies.

CHINA OFFSHORE SOFTWARE ENGINEERING PROJECT

To support Chinese software enterprises in increasing their competitive edge in delivering outstanding services and product excellence, the Torch Center started the China Offshore Software Engineering Project (COSEP) in 2004. COSEP serves to strengthen the partnership between Chinese software enterprises on one hand and North America and Europe enterprises on the other.

COSEP's vision is to provide support for approximately 100 pilot enterprises that provide IT outsourcing (ITO) and business process outsourcing (BPO) services and software products to Fortune 500 companies and other clients in North America, Europe, and Japan.

Selected from more than 8,000 companies among 29 Software Technology Parks, they represent the leading force in China for software offshore outsourcing services.[8]

COSEP provides these pilot enterprises, as well as other enterprises, with the following:

- A training exchange platform to improve outsourcing abilities and quality control processes
- A sales and marketing platform to provide a communication channel with clients in North America, Europe, and other markets
- A common technology development and service platform to provide pilot enterprises with infrastructural needs and development environments (i.e., mainframe environments)
- A financial support platform to facilitate interaction between financial institutions and pilot enterprises, with services including loan financing, initial pubic offerings (IPOs), mergers and acquisitions, hypothecating services, and so on

COSEP represents an excellent opportunity for foreign enterprises to partner with trusted Chinese enterprises.

COSEP Software Park Index (11 National Software Bases)[9]

The China Offshore Software Engineering Project designated one software park in each of 11 major cities as a National Software Base. These bases are designed to offer resident companies the best in terms of bandwidth, technology support, and other incentives including tax breaks, to attract both foreign and Chinese companies to establish a presence there.

1. **Beijing Software Industry Base**
   City: Beijing
   E-mail: liuhx@bsw.gov.cn
   Web site: www.softdriver.org

2. **Changsha Software Park**
   City: Changsha, Hunan
   E-mail: csspo@126.com
   Web site: www.cnsia.com

3. **Dalian Software Park**
   City: Dalian, Liaoning
   E-mail: service@dlsp.com.cn
   Web site: www.dlsp.com.cn

4. **Guangzhou Tianhe Software Park**
   City: Guangzhou, Guangdong
   E-mail: ssqiu@21cn.com
   Web site: www.thstp.com

5. **Hangzhou Hi-Tech Software Park**
   City: Hangzhou, Zhejiang
   E-mail: hssib@hhhsoft.com
   Web site: www.hhhsoft.com

6. **Qilu Software Park**
   City: Jinan, Shandong
   E-mail: mengchenyan@qilusoft.org
   Web site: www.qilusoft.org

7. **Qingdao Software Park**
   City: Qingdao, Shandong
   E-mail: yuzhw@qingdaosoftware.com
   Web site: www.qingdaosoftware.com

8. **Shanghai Software Park**
   City: Shanghai
   E-mail: gyq@ssc.stn.sh.cn
   Web site: www.ssc.stn.sh.cn

9. **Shenzhen Software Park**
   City: Shenzhen, Guangdong
   E-mail: info@szsoftwarepark.com
   Web site: www.szsoftwarepark.com

10. **Suzhou Software Park**
    City: Suzhou, Jiangsu
    E-mail: customer@sipis.com.cn

Web site: www.szsp.gov.cn
11. **Xi'an Software Park**
City: Xi'an, Shaanxi
E-mail: wangyu@xasoftpark.com
Web site: www.xasoftpark.com

Overseas Missions[10]

Australia (Embassy)
Address: 15 Coronation Drive, Yarralumla, Canberra, Act 2600 Australia
Telephone: 0061-2-62734780
Fax: 0061-2-62734878
Sydney (Consulate General)
Address: 39 Dunblane Street, Camperdown NSW 2050 Sydney, Australia
Telephone: 0061-2-96985007
Fax: 0061-2-85958001
Austria (Embassy)
Address: Metternichgass 4, Wien A-1030, Austria
Telephone: 0043-1-714314920
Fax: 0043-1-7136816
Belgium (Embassy)
Address: Avenue De Tervuren 400, 1160 Bruxelles, Belgium
Telephone: 0032-2-7713309
Fax: 0032-2-7792859
Belarus (Embassy)
Address: 220071, City Minsk, Rd. Beresty Anskaya, 22, Belarus
Telephone: 00375-17-2853682
Fax: 00375-17-2853681
Brazil (Embassy)
Address: Ses-Av. Das Nacoes, Lote 51 14 Sul. Q. 813, CEP 70443-900 Brasilla-DF, Brazil
Telephone: 0055-61-3464436
Fax: 0055-61-3463299
Bulgaria (Embassy)
Address: Bl.215 ap.38 Raiko-aleksev Str. 1113, Sofia, Bulgaria
Telephone: 00359-2-9714883
Fax: 00359-2-9713345
Canada (Embassy)
Address: 515 St. Patrick Street, Ottawa, Ontario, Canada KIN 5H3
Telephone: 001-613-2342706

Fax: 001-613-7891911
Toronto (Consulate General)
Address: 240 St. George Street, Toronto, Ontario, Canada M5, R 2P4
Telephone: 001-416-9647260
Fax: 001-416-3246468
Vancouver (Consulate General)
Address: 3380 Granville Street, Vancouver, BC, Canada V6H 3K3
Telephone: 001-604-7365188
Fax: 001-604-7370154
Calgary (Consulate General)
Address: Suite 100,1011-6th Ave. S.W. Calgary, AB, Canada T2P 0 W1
Telephone: 001-403-2643404
Fax: 001-403-2646656
Chile (Embassy)
Address: Av. Pedro de Valdivia 550, Castilla 3417 Providencia, Santiago, Repubilca de Chile
Telephone: 0056-2-2345177
Fax: 0056-2-2341129
Cuba (Embassy)
Address: Calle 13, No.551, Entre CYD, Vedado, La Habana, Cuba
Telephone: 0053-7-8333005
Fax: 0053-7-333092
Czech Republic (Embassy)
Address: Pelleova 18,16000 Prague 6, Czech Republic
Telephone: 0042-02-33028862
Fax: 00420-2-24319888
Denmark (Embassy)
Address: Regards Alle 25, Dk-2900 Hellerup, Copenhagen, Denmark
Telephone: 0045-39460887
Fax: 0045-39460888
France (Embassy)
Address: 9, Avenue Victor Cresson 92130, Issy-Les-Moulineaux, France
Telephone: 0033-1-47369760
Fax: 0033-1-46750181
Economic and Social Commission for Asia and The Pacific
Address: The United Nations Building Rajadamnern Nok Avenue, Bangkok 10200, Thailand
Telephone: 0066-2-2881456
Fax: 0066-2-2883012
Egypt (Embassy)
Address: 14, Bahgat Aly Street Zamalek, Cairo Egypt

Telephone: 0020-2-3411219
Fax: 0020-2-7359459
European Union (Mission)
Address: Avenue De Tervuren, 443-445, 1150 Bruxelles, Belgium
Telephone: 0032-2-7702306
Fax: 0032-2-7704790
Finland (Embassy)
Address: Office for Science and Technology, Embassy of China
Vanha Kelkkamaki 11, Kulosaari, 00570, Helsinki, Finland
Address: Alkutie 59a, 00660 Helsinki, Finland (S&T Department)
Telephone: 00358-9-22890153
Fax: 00358-9-22890167
Germany (Embassy)
Address: Markisches Ufer 54, D-10179 Berlin, Germany
Telephone: 0049-30-275880
Fax: 0049-30-27588221
Greece (Embassy)
Address: 2a Krinon Street, Palaio Psychico,154 52 Athens, Greece
Telephone: 0030-210-6723282
Fax: 0030-210-6723819
Hungary (Embassy)
Address: Benczur Utca 17, Budapest 1068, Hungary
Telephone: 0036-1-3224872
Fax: 0036-1-3229067
India (Embassy)
Address: 50-D, Shantipath, Chanakyapuri New Delhi-110021 India
Telephone: 0091-11-26871585
Fax: 0091-11-26885486
Indonesia (Embassy)
Address: J1. Mega Kuningan No. 2 Jakarta Selatan 12950 Indonesia
Telephone: 0062-21-5761039
Fax: 0062-21-5761034
Ireland (Embassy)
Address: 40 Ailesbury Road, Dublin 4, Ireland
Telephone: 00353-1-2691707
Fax: 00353-1-2839938
Israel (Embassy)
Address: 222 Ben Yehuda Street P.O. Box 6067 Tel Aviv 61060, Israel
Telephone: 00972-3-5467277, 58392699
Fax: 00972-3-5467251
Italy (Embassy)
Address: Via Bruxelles, 56,00198 Roma, Italy

Telephone: 0039-06-8848186
Fax: 0039-06-85352891
Japan (Embassy)
Address: 3-4-33, Motoazabu, Minato-ku, Tokyo 106-0046, Japan
Telephone: 0081-3-3403-3388
Fax: 0081-3-3403-3345
Kazakhstan (Embassy)
Address: 137 Furmanov Road, Alma-Ata-Kazakhstan
Telephone: 007-3272-729332
Fax: 007-3272-638209
Korea (Embassy)
Address: 54 Hyoja-dong, Jongno-Gu, Seoul, the Republic of Korea
110-033
Telephone: 0082-2-7381038
Fax: 0082-2-7381077
Mexico (Embassy)
Address: Av. Rio Magdalena 172 Col. Tizapan, Deleg. Alvaro Obregon,
01090 Mexico, D.F.
Telephone: 0052-55-56160609
Fax: 0052-55-56160460
Netherlands (Embassy)
Address: Willem Lodewijklaan 10, 2517 Jt Den Haag, Netherlands
Telephone: 0031-70-3065061
Fax: 0031-70-3551651
New Zealand (Embassy)
Address: 2-6 Glenmore Street, Kelburn, Wellington, FS New Zealand
Telephone: 0064-4-4721382
Fax: 0064-4-4990419
Norway (Embassy)
Address: Tuengen Alle 2 B,0244 Oslo, Norway
Telephone: 0047-22-492052
Fax: 0047-22-921978
Pakistan (Embassy)
Address: Diplomatic, Enclave Ramma 4, Islamabad Pakistan
Telephone: 0092-51-2824786
Fax: 0092-51-2821116
Poland (Embassy)
Address: Ul Bonifraterska 1,00-203 Warsaw Poland
Telephone: 0048-22-313836
Fax: 0048-22-6354211
Portugal (Embassy)

Address: Rua De Sao Caetano, No 2 A Lapa, 1249-024 Lisboa, Portugal
Telephone: 00351-21-3928440
Fax: 00351-21-3975632
Romania (Embassy)
Address: Nr. 2 Soseaua Nordului, Bucuresti, Romania
Telephone: 0040-21-2328858
Fax: 0040-21-2330684
Russian Federation (Embassy)
Address: Moscow Ul. Drujbei Dom 6
Telephone: 007-095-9382006
Fax: 007-095-9382132
Khabarovsk (Consulate General)
Address: 680028 Khabarovsk, Stadium Lenin
Telephone: 007-4212-302353
Fax: 007-4212-649094
St. Petersburg (Consulate General)
Address: Kanal Griboedova, 134, St. Petersburg Russia
Telephone: 007-812-1147670
Fax: 007-812-1147958
Singapore
Address: 150 Tanglin Road, Singapore 247969
Telephone: 0065-64180224
Fax: 0065-67344737
South Africa
Address: 972 Pretorius Street, Arcadia 0002, Pretoria, South Africa
P.O. Box 95764 Waterloof 0145, Pretoria, South Africa
Telephone: 0027-12-3424194
Fax: 0027-12-3424154
Spain (Embassy)
Address: Calle De Cascanueces, 21 28043 Madrid, Spain
Telephone: 0034-91-5194242
Fax: 0034-91-5192035
Sweden (Embassy)
Address: Lidovagen 8, 11525 Stockholm, Sweden
Address: Herserudsvagen 51, Se-181 35 Lidingo, Stockholm, Sweden (S&T Department)
Telephone: 0046-8-6679704
Fax: 0046-8-6625955
Switzerland (Embassy)
Address: Kalcheggweg 10, 3006 Bern, Switzerland
Telephone: 0041-31-3527333

Fax: 0041-31-3514573
Thailand (Embassy)
Address: 57 Rachadapisake Road Bangkok 10310 Thailand
Telephone: 0066-2-2472122
Fax: 0066-2-2472123
Ukraine (Embassy)
Address: 32 Gruchevsky Road, 01901 Kyiv, Ukraine
Telephone: 00380-44-2937371
Fax: 00380-44-2302622
United Kingdom (Embassy)
Address: 49-51 Portland Place London W 1n 4jl, U.K.
Address: 42 Maida Vale, London W9 1rp, (U.K.) S&T Department.
Telephone: 0044-20-74328370
Fax: 0044-20-72866833
United Nations (Permanent Mission)
Address: 350 East 35th Street New York, NY 10016
Telephone: 001-212-655-6159
Fax: 001-212-8700333
United Nations Office in Geneva and Other International Organization
in Switzerland
Address: 11Chemin De Surville 1213 Petit-Lancy, Geneva Switzerland
Telephone: 0041-22-8795678
Fax: 0041-22-7937014
Permanent Delegation of the P.R.China to the United Nations Educa-
tional, Scientific Agency
Address: 1, Rue Miollis 75015 Paris, France
Telephone: 0033-1-45683468
Fax: 0033-1-42190199
United States (Embassy)
Address: 2300 Connecticut Avenue N.W. Washington D.C. 20008
Telephone: 001-202-3282530
Fax: 001-202-2344055
New York (Consulate General)
Address: 520 12th Avenue, New York, NY 10036
Telephone: 001-212-2449392
Fax: 001-212-3307405
San Francisco (Consulate General)
Address: 1450 Laguna Street, San Francisco, CA, 94115
Telephone: 001-415-6091789
Fax: 001-415-5630494
Houston (Consulate General)
Address: 3417 Montrose Blvd., Houston, TX 77006

Telephone: 001-713-5240780
Fax: 001-713-5247656
Chicago (Consulate General)
Address: 100 West Erie Street, Chicago, IL 60610
Telephone: 001-312-8030101
Fax: 001-312-9290489
Los Angeles (Consulate General)
Address: 443 Shatto Place, Los Angeles, CA 90020
Telephone: 001-213-8078015
Fax: 001-213-3801961
Yugoslavia
Address: Vasilija Gacese 5,11000 Belgrade, Yugoslavia
Telephone: 00381-11-2651630
Fax: 00381-11-2662747

ENDNOTES

1. Source: http://english.gov.cn
2. Source: http://english.gov.cn
3. Source: http://english.gov.cn
4. Source: www.most.gov.cn/eng
5. Source: www.most.gov.cn/eng
6. Source: www.sipo.gov.cn/sipo_English
7. Source for organizations affiliated to MOST: www.most.gov.cn/eng/organization/Affiliated/
8. Source: COSEP Directory by Torch High Technology Industry Development Center, China Ministry of Science and Technology, 2005.
9. Source: Torch Center, 2007.
10. Source: www.most.gov.cn/eng/organization/Missions/

Index

Accenture, 12, 17, 117, 120
Administration of Foreign Exchange (AFE), 167
Advanced Material Science Park, 121
Advantages of outsourcing to China, 148, 149
Alcohol consumption, 80, 81, 90
Alibaba.com, 47, 125
Alpine Electronics, 222–227
American Institute of Certified Public Accountants (AICPA), SAS 70, 152
Application Deployment Management (ADM), 96
Application service providers (ASPs), 139
Arbitration in China, 171–173
Argentina, 15, 148
Asia-Pacific corporate headquarters, 41, 42
Atari, 6, 20
Australia, 17, 18, 45, 72, 206
Aviation, 38, 39

Bai jiu (rice alcohol), 80, 90
Baidu, 47
Bangalore Software Park, 122
Baolong Industrial Park, 129
Barrett, Craig, 20
Beijing, 112–114
    administration of, 37
    as capital of China, 34
    COSEP survey results, 186, 190
    foreign residents, 73
    municipal government offices, 270
    salaries, 100
    software parks, 50, 52, 112, 114
    Tata Consultancy Services joint venture, 28
Beijing Industry University Software Park, 112
Benefits of outsourcing, 137
Beyondsoft, 48, 192–196
Biopharmaceutical Park, 121
Bo Xilai, 118

Bo Yibo, 118
Boyle, Mark Andrew, 120
Brand building, 55
    "employer brand," 104, 105
BRASSCOM (Brazil Association of Software and Service Export Companies), 23
Brazil, 21–24, 27, 49, 148
BRIC nations, 21–29, 49, 56, 57. See also Brazil; China (People's Republic of China); India; Russia
British Standards Institute, BS7799, 152
Build-operate-transfer (BOT), 60, 62, 65–71
Bulgaria, 11, 13, 14, 148
Business expansion in China market
    change, speed of, 84, 85
    cultural and business differences, 75–77, 89, 90
    due diligence, 81–83
    long-term commitment, 78, 83, 84
    outsourcing city, selection of, 85, 86
    partnerships and relationships, importance of, 79–81
    persistence, 88, 89
    and shareholder expectations, 77–79
    small and medium-sized enterprises, 78
    workforce issues, 86–88
Business incentives, 49, 85. See also Taxation
Business license, 82
Business Process Model (BPM), 153
Business process outsourcing (BPO)
    benefits of to providers of services, 8
    and BRIC nations, 21
    call centers, 5, 12
    defined, 4, 5, 146
    Egypt, 16
    Hungary, 12
    options available, 147, 148
    projected growth of in China, 178, 179
    South Africa, 17
    spending on, 7
    standards, importance of, 151
    and types of outsourcing, 138

Business process outsourcing (BPO)
(*Continued*)
vendor models, 139
Business processes
documentation of, 154, 155
selection of for outsourcing, 152–155
standards, 150, 151. *See also* Standards
Business trends
globalization. *See* Globalization
mergers and acquisitions in China, 48
outsourcing, 1, 2, 7
technology outsourcing in China, 52

Cadre capitalism, 114
Call centers, 5, 12, 13, 16, 17, 19, 28
Canada, 3, 9, 10
Capability Maturity Model for Software
(CMM for Software), 140, 144
Capability Maturity Model Integration
(CMMI), 81, 140–146, 152, 154
Capgemini, 17, 202
Captive centers
and business establishment in China, 157
expatriates, 65, 71–74, 96
Hungary, 12
India, 57
Malaysia, 18
offshore outsourcing strategies, 60–62,
65–67, 157
Career development
importance of, 100
and preventing turnover, 105
Case studies, 192–237
Central Committee of the Politburo, 37
Chamber of commerce offices in China, 271
Chanda, Nayan, 92
Chang'an Technology Park, 120
Changping Software Park, 112
Chen Baogen, 122
Chengdu, 119, 120, 186, 190
Chengdu Hi-tech Zone, 119, 120
Chengdu Software Outsourcing League, 120
China Data Group, case study, 197–202
China International Economic and Trade
Arbitration Commission (CIETAC),
171, 172
China Mobile, 46
China Netcom, 46
China Offshore Software Engineering Project
(COSEP), 273
Software Park Index, 273–275

survey results, 186–191
China (People's Republic of China)
advantages of outsourcing to, 148, 149
bordering countries, 34
call centers, 5
disadvantages of outsourcing to, 149
economic growth, 27
lessons learned, 75–90
outlook on outsourcing services, 170, 171
as outsourcing destination, 33–58, 156
tourism, 27
China Software and Integrated Service
Platform (CSIP), 179, 180
China Sourcing pavilions, 179, 180
China Telecom, 46
China Unicom, 46
Chinese language, 19, 20
Chinese New Year, 81, 107
Chongqing, 34, 37, 128, 132, 214
Cisco Systems, 26, 131
Co-operative Joint Venture (CVJ), 157, 166
Code Division Multiple Access (CDMA)
networks, 46
Communist Party of China (CCP), 36, 37
Company Law of the People's Republic of
China, 157
Confidentiality, 158, 159, 164, 165
Contract Law of the People's Republic of
China, 159–161
Contracts
BOT projects, 67, 70
Contract Law of the People's Republic of
China, 159–161
employee attitudes, 102
labor, 165. *See also* Labor law
technology development contracts, 159
Copyrights. *See* Intellectual property,
treatment of in China
Core business
focus on and need for outsourcing, 1, 2
and selecting country for outsourcing, 41
Corporate culture
and Chinese work ethic, 100, 101, 149
and loyalty, 104. *See also* Loyalty
and selection of offshore partner, 66, 81
Corruption, 149, 173, 174
COSEP. *See* China Offshore Software
Engineering Project (COSEP)
Costs of outsourcing, 137, 149, 150
"Country before company" slogan, 41, 60,
181

Courts. *See* Legal system in China
Creditors, 163, 164
Culture
    authority, 108
    cultural understanding and expatriates,
        73, 76, 77
    and disadvantages of outsourcing to
        China, 149
    etiquette, 80, 81, 90
    importance of in China, 34
    results-driven versus process-driven, 106
    and workforce issues, 87, 88
Currencies
    Argentina, 15
    Canada, 9, 10
    foreign currency management, 52
    foreign exchange, 167
    Hong Kong, 49, 184
    outlook for outsourcing in China, 171
    regulation and foreign exchange, 167, 168
    renminbi (RMB), 49, 167, 168, 184, 262
    risks and concerns, 184
    State Administration of Foreign Exchange,
        262, 263
Customs, 238
Cyberjaya (Malaysia), 18–20, 148
Czech Republic, 11, 12, 14

Dalian, 99, 117, 118, 187, 190
Dalian Hi-Tech Industrial Park, 117
Dalian Software Park, 117
DangDang.com, 98
DarwinSuzsoft case study, 202–206
Decision making
    matrix, offshore outsourcing strategies,
        61, 62
    process, 138
Definition Languages, 154
Dell, 117, 215–222
Deng Xiaoping, 33
Department of Trade in Services, 166
Deposits, 163, 164
Dice, 97
Digital Xi'an, 121, 122
Disadvantages of outsourcing to China, 149,
    170
Diversification, 135
Document Sciences, 227–231
Domestic market in China
    and advantages of outsourcing to China,
        149

early restrictions, 44
growth of, 43, 78, 149, 176, 178
and selecting country for outsourcing, 41
and talent shortage, 92
Dual-shore delivery, 71
Due diligence, 57, 63, 81–83, 142–144,
    150, 151

Economic growth
    China, 35, 36, 85, 174, 175
    India, 27
    and political stability, 37
Economic-Technological Development Zone
    (ETDV), 118
Education
    and ability to provide outsourcing, 9
    BRIC nations, 21
    Bulgaria, 11
    Canada, 9
    China, 39, 40, 51, 56, 91–95, 176, 177,
        239–241
    COSEP survey results, 190
    Czech Republic, 11
    Egypt, 16
    Indonesia, 9
    Ireland, 12
    Mexico, 10
    Ministry of Education, 239–241
    Poland, 14
    Romania, 14
    Singapore, 19
    Ukraine, 14
    United States, 97, 98
    universities in China. *See* Universities
Egypt, 15, 16, 148
Electronic Data Systems (EDS), 16, 18, 120
Electronic Industrial Park, 120
Embassies, missions, and consulate generals,
    275–281
Employees. *See* Workforce
Employment agencies, 166
Engineering
    "blue collar programmers," 63
    career development, importance of in
        China, 102, 105
    Chinese education, 51, 58, 92–94, 97
    and Chinese work ethic, 100
    demand for engineers with English
        proficiency, 63, 98, 99
    engineers, recruiting, 98–100
    experience, 98

Engineering (*Continued*)
"high-end engineering services," 49
India, 25, 26
and loyalty issues in China, 104
and outlook for China, 182
training, 109
U.S. education, 51, 91, 92
Engineering technology outsourcing, 53
English fluency
and BPO standards, 151
Brazil, 23
Canada, 9
China, 36, 40, 43, 56, 83, 94, 95, 98, 99, 170
Egypt, 16
India, 5, 24, 28, 95
Israel, 16
Mexico, 10
Philippines, 5, 19, 56
and recruiting staff, 96
and salaries, 99, 100
Singapore, 19, 56
Environmental concerns in China, 185
Equity Joint Venture (EJV), 157, 166
Etiquette, 80, 81, 90
Europe as outsourcing destination, 10
European Union (EU), 3, 11
Evening activities in China, 80, 81
Everest, Mount (Qomolongma), 34
Expatriates, 65, 71–74, 76, 77, 80, 96, 166, 169, 170

Face concept and Asian culture, 1, 40, 89–90, 108
Fixed-price short-term engagements, 60, 62
Foreign Direct Investment (FDI), 42
Foreign invested enterprise (FIE)
hiring requirements, 166. *See also* Labor law
and market entry policies, 157, 158
tax treatment, 168, 169
types of, 157
Foreign investment. *See also* Foreign invested enterprise (FIE)
and changing market conditions, 78
in China, 41, 42, 157
India, 26
promotion efforts, 54, 55
Foreign Investment Industrial Guidance Catalogs, 157
Foreign nationals. *See also* Expatriates

individual income tax, 169, 170
Foreign Trade Law of the People's Republic of China, 161
4G network, 47
Freeborders, 48
Fujian, 37, 42
Fujitsu, 121
Functional categories of business processes, 138

Game software development, 20
Gartner ITXPO Symposium, 180
Gartner Outsourcing Summits, 179, 180
General Electric (GE), 12, 117, 125
General Motors, 11, 42
Geographical regions of China, 34
Gifts, exchange of, 81
Global business locations, 41, 42
Global Standard for Mobile (GSM) communications, 46
Globalization
backlash, 4
and business in China, 181–183
business trends, 2–4, 181–183
and growth in outsourcing, 135–137
twentieth century developments, 3, 4
"Golden Weeks," 107
Golf, 80
Google, 6, 47
Government in China, 36–38, 43. *See also* Legal system in China
administration, 171
Beijing municipal government offices, 270
contact information, 238–266
intellectual property infringement enforcement, 163
and need for industry associations, 55
regulatory approvals, 171
software licensing and protection, 162
subsidies for promoting technology outsourcing, 55, 109, 166, 167
support of high-tech development, 44, 51, 63, 85, 109, 141, 149, 176
support of higher education, 93
Gross Domestic Product (GDP), 42, 63, 180, 181
Guangdong, 42, 122, 123, 125, 127, 129
Guangdong Software Science Park, 125
Guangzhou, 10, 125–127, 187, 190

Guangzhou New & Hi-Tech Industrial Development Zone, 125
Guanlan-Longhua-Banxuegang Industrial Park, 129
Guarantees, 163, 164

"Hai-Gui," 97, 98
Hangzhou, 46, 52, 115, 116, 124–125, 187, 190
Hangzhou East Software Park, 124
Hangzhou Hi-tech Industry Development Zone, 124
Health system in China, 101
Heidrick & Struggles, 97
Hewitt Associates, 13, 14, 97
Hewlett-Packard, 11, 13, 18, 106, 121, 122
Hi-tech Export Processing Base, 121
Hiring leader, 79
HiSoft, 48, 206–210
Holidays, 81, 107
Hong Kong, 37, 42, 127, 129, 130
Housing costs, 103
HP Global Delivery China Center case study, 211–214
HSBC, 18, 120, 127, 196, 202
Hu Jintao, President, 37
Hungary, 12, 13

IBM, 12, 25, 26, 46, 64, 96, 109, 115, 117, 121–122, 131
IBM Global Services, 12, 17
Income tax. *See* Taxation
Independent service providers, 158
India
   call centers, 5
   English language education, 95
   Infosys Technologies, 12, 52
   literacy rates, 24, 27
   NASSCOM, 23, 28, 43, 51, 55
   as outsourcer to China, 28, 48, 51, 52, 58
   as outsourcing destination, 24–29
   outsourcing to China compared, 148, 149
   Satyam Computer Services, 17, 28, 48, 52, 129, 202
   and shift toward China, 2, 7
   statistics, 24, 25
   talent shortage, 26, 27
   Tata Consultancy Services, 12, 28, 52, 125, 208
   tourism, 27

turnover of staff, 57
Indonesia, 9
Industrial parks. *See* Technology zones
Industry associations
   BRASSCOM (Brazil Association of Software and Service Export Companies), 23
   Chengdu Software Outsourcing League, 120
   China, 53, 55
   NASSCOM (National Association of Software and Service Companies), 23, 28, 43, 51, 55
   RUSSOFT, 24
Information security, risks and concerns, 57
Information Technology Infrastructure Library (ITIL), 81, 152
Information technology outsourcing (ITO), 138
   benefits of to providers of services, 8
   and Capability and Maturity Levels, 144, 145. *See also* Capability Maturity Model for Software (CMM for Software); Capability Maturity Model Integration (CMMI)
   China as outsourcing destination, 35, 36
   defined, 5, 139, 140
   Hungary, 12
   offshore market, 178, 179
   processes commonly outsourced, 140, 156
   standards, role of in selecting vendor, 145
Information technology services industry in China, 35, 36, 42, 43, 50, 52–54, 141, 156
Infosys Technologies, 12, 48, 52
Infrastructure in China, 38, 39, 42, 44, 85, 86, 149, 182, 183
Infrastructure management outsourcing (IMO), 140
Infrastructure outsourcing (IO), 140
Inner Mongolia Autonomous Region, 34
Insourcing, defined, 5
Integrated Computer-Aided Manufacturing (ICAM), 154
Intel, 20, 120
Intellectual property, treatment of in China
   concerns, 43, 149, 170, 171
   and contract law, 160–163
   copyrights, 159, 161
   courts, 161–163
   enforcement, 161, 162

Intellectual property, treatment of in China
(*Continued*)
international conventions and agreements,
163
occupational inventions, 161
ownership of IP and labor contract
provisions, 174
patents, 159, 161
protection of rights in China, 43, 56, 57,
159–164
and secured interests, 164
State Intellectual Property Office, 265
transfer to foreign invested enterprise,
158
International Organization for
Standardization (ISO), 81
ISO 9000, 140, 152
Internet
BRIC nations, 21
in China, 26, 47
and growth of outsourcing, 8
India, 26
mobile phone access, 46
and selection of outsourcing city, 85
Ireland, 12, 13, 21
Israel, 16
I.T. UNITED, 41, 88, 186–191, 215–222
ITIL (Information Technology Infrastructure
Library), 81, 152

Japan, 99, 117, 118, 128, 179
Jiang Qing, 123
Jiang Zemin, 37, 115
Jiangning Economic-Technological
Development Zone, 127
Jiangsu, 42, 124, 128, 129, 132
Ji'nan, 122, 123, 187, 190
Jinmen (Quemoy), 37

Knowledge management, 105
Knowledge process outsourcing (KPO), 19,
21, 138, 146–148
Korn/Ferry International, 42, 54, 97

Labor costs
call centers, 5
China, 4, 42–45, 49–50, 99, 100, 102,
137, 148, 149, 156, 177
and global labor pool, 135, 137
and impact of foreign investment, 26, 27

Labor Day, 107
Labor law, 164–166
Labor Law of the People's Republic of
China, 164
Languages. *See also* English fluency
Brazil, 21–23
BRIC nations, 21
China, 21, 36, 40, 41, 43, 47, 72, 86, 114,
127, 149
Egypt, 16
foreign language capabilities, 8
Guangzhou, 127
India, 24, 27, 28, 95
and the Internet, 47
Israel, 16
Japanese, 99
Korean, 99
Philippines, 19
Romania, 14
Russia, 23
Singapore, 19
translation and communication issues,
72
Vietnam, 20
Leadership, 107
Lean manufacturing, 152, 154, 155
Legal system in China, 43, 57
and business establishment in China, 157,
158
civil liability, 162
Company Law of the People's Republic of
China, 157
contract law, 159–163
courts, 161, 162, 173
currency and foreign exchange. *See*
Currencies
dispute resolution and litigation, 171–175
employment law, 164–166
and foreign investment, 157
intellectual property rights. *See* Intellectual
property, treatment of in China
outlook on outsourcing services, 170, 171
Secured Interests Law, 163, 164
taxation. *See* Taxation
Liens, 163, 164
Limited liability companies, 157
Litigation, 173
Liu Jiren, 222
Liuxiandong Industrial Park, 129
Loans, inter-company, 167, 168
Loss of control, 137

Loss of face and Asian culture, 1, 40, 89, 90, 108
Loyalty, 57, 58, 79, 88, 103, 104. *See also* Turnover

Ma, Jack, 125
Macau (Special Administrative Region), 37, 119, 121, 124, 126, 128, 130
"Made in China," 4, 44, 45
"Made in Hong Kong," 45
"Made in Japan," 3
"Made in Taiwan," 3, 4, 45
Malaysia, 18–20, 148
Malta, 9, 13
Management
  and disadvantages of outsourcing to China, 149
  and successful outsourcing, 138
Manufacturing
  Asian countries, 17
  China, 41, 42, 44, 45, 49, 53, 55, 177, 182
  outsourcing, 3, 6, 10
Mao Zedong, 123
Market conditions in China, 78, 84
  barriers to market entry, 157
  and globalization, 181–183
  stability of, 180, 181
Maturity levels. *See* Capability Maturity Model for Software (CMM for Software); Capability Maturity Model Integration (CMMI)
Mazu (Matsu), 37
Meals, 81
Mechanism of Regular Communication and Coordination with Foreign Invested Enterprises, 163
Mediation and conciliation, 173, 174
Mercantilism, 2, 3
Mercer Human Resources Consulting, 97, 99, 100, 102, 104
Mergers and acquisitions, 135, 136, 183
Mexico, 3, 10
Michael, Ed, 91
Microsoft, 20, 46, 48, 96, 109, 120, 122
Microsoft Excel, 66
Mid-Autumn Festival, 81
Ministry of Commerce (MOFCOM), 157, 166, 179, 180, 244–246
Ministry of Education, 239–241
Ministry of Finance, 242–244

Ministry of Foreign Trade and Economic Cooperation (MOFTEC), 157
Ministry of Information Industry, 246–252
Ministry of Science and Technology (MOST), 179, 252–255
Mobile telephones, 45–47, 84, 85
Mongolia, 34, 113, 124
Mortgages, 163, 164
Motorola, 106, 120, 132
Multimedia Super Corridor (Malaysia), 18
Multisourcing defined, 5

Nanjing, 28, 39, 52, 115, 116, 127–129, 188, 190
Nanjing New and High-Tech Industry Development Zone, 127
Nansha IT Software Park, 125
NASSCOM (National Association of Software and Service Companies), 23, 28, 43, 51, 55
National Bureau of Statistics, 255–259
National Copyright Administration, 161, 162
National Day, 107
National Development and Reform Commission, 259–262
National Outsourcing Service Cities, 166. *See also* Chengdu; Dalian; Shanghai; Xi'an
National People's Congress (NPC), 37
Nearshore outsourcing, defined, 5
Nepal, 34
Neusoft, 54, 117, 222–227
New Zealand, 18, 300
Non-competition clauses, 164–165
Non-disclosure agreements, 164
North American Free Trade Agreement (NAFTA), 3, 4
Northern Ireland, 13
Northwest Polytechnic University Science Park, 121

Objectiva Software Solutions case study, 228–231
Occupational invention, 161
Offshore
  defined, 5
  manufacturing, 3, 6
Offshore Development Center (ODC), 68, 71
Offshore Location Attractiveness Index, 156

Offshore outsourcing
 acquisition, 60, 61
 barriers to, 64
 build-operate-transfer model, 67–71
 captive centers, 12, 18, 57, 60–62, 65–67,
  71–74, 157
 defined, 5
 dual-shore delivery, 71
 due diligence. *See* Due diligence
 factors for success, 64, 65
 and globalization, 182
 options for, 60–74
 partners. *See* Offshore partners
Offshore partners
 captive center compared, 65–67
 decision matrix for offshore strategy, 61,
  62
 due diligence. *See* Due diligence
 outsourcing strategies, 60
 selection process, 66
Olympic Games 2008, 27, 40, 56, 94, 95,
  113, 114, 181
On-site visits, 82, 83
One-child policy in China, 101, 184
Onshore outsourcing, defined, 6
Oracle, 112, 122
Outsource World 2004, 15, 51
Outsourcing, defined, 6
Outsourcing cities
 information on, 112–132. *See also*
  individual cities
 National Outsourcing Service Cities, 166
 selection of, 85, 86
Outsourcing-related offices and agencies in
  China, 266–270

Partnerships
 establishing, 80
 importance of building, 79
 offshore partners. *See* Offshore partners
Patents. *See* Intellectual property, treatment
  of in China
People's Bank of China, 120
People's Republic of China (PRC). *See* China
  (People's Republic of China)
Performance incentives, 106
Performance standards. *See also* Standards
 Western standards, 75, 78, 84
Philippines, 5, 19–21, 37, 42, 56, 148
Pledges, 163, 164

PMI (Project Management Institute), 152,
  154
Poland, 12–14, 21, 148, 278
Political stability
 Brazil, 22
 China, 36–38
 Czech Republic, 14
 Philippines, 19, 37
 Poland, 14
 Romania, 14
 Russia, 13, 24
 Thailand, 37
Population of China, 34, 40, 91, 184
Poverty in China, 184
Project management, 58
 education, 94
 experience in and salaries, 99, 100
Project Management Institute (PMI), 152,
  154
Provinces and regions of China, 34, 37
Pudong Software Park, 52, 114, 115
Pukou High and New Technology
  Development Zone, 127
Put and call options, BOT agreements, 70

Qianhai Industrial Park, 129
Qilu Software Park, 122

Re-engineering standards, 152
Reasons for outsourcing, 137, 138, 156
Recruiting staff, 96–99
References, 82, 83
Regulation on Administration of Technology
  Import and Export, 158
Regulations on Protection of Computer
  Software, 159
Relationship building, 78–81
Renminbi (RMB), 49, 167, 168, 184, 262
Representative office in China, 158, 166. *See
  also* Labor law
Requests for information (RFI), 66
Research
 Chinese universities, 93
 scientific research, India versus China, 27
Research and development
 China, 46, 92, 102, 105, 121, 159, 182
 India, 27
Respect, 104
Risks and concerns
 aging of population in China, 184

currency trading and fluctuation, 184
English language capability, 56, 183, 184.
    See also English fluency
environmental issues, 185
intellectual property rights, 56, 57, 170,
    171
international protectionism, 185
loss of control, 137
negative repercussions of outsourcing, 138
and outlook on China outsourcing
    services, 170, 171, 182
project management, 58
regulatory changes, 183
and selection of vendor, 145, 149, 150
social unrest, 184
staff loyalty and turnover, 57, 58
Romania, 10, 14, 148, 279
Royalties, 169
Russia, 13, 14, 21–24, 148, 279
RUSSOFT, 24

Salaries, 99, 100
    and advantages of outsourcing to China,
        148
    and employee turnover, 103
    and selection of outsourcing city, 86
    wages and benefits, Labor Law of People's
        Republic of China, 165
SAP, 11, 117
SAS 70, 152
Satyam Computer Services, 17, 28, 48, 52,
    129, 202
Scope of outsourcing, 138–147
"Sea Turtles," 97, 98
Secured Interests Law of the People's
    Republic of China, 163, 164
Selective outsourcing, 139
Service level agreements, 150
Service sector in China, growth of, 177, 178
Shandong, 42, 86, 122, 123
Shanghai
    administration of, 37
    as Asia-Pacific corporate headquarters, 42
    as business center, 114
    COSEP survey results, 188, 190
    foreign investment in, 42
    foreign residents, 73
    history and description, 116, 117
    National Outsourcing Service Cities, 166
    population, 114
    salaries, 100

software parks, 52, 114, 115, 274
transportation and travel, 38, 39, 113,
    115, 116
universities, 86, 93, 115
World Expo 2010, 181
Shanghai Banking Corp. (HSBC), 18, 120,
    127, 196, 202
Shanghai Software Park, 114
Shenzhen, 129–132
    as business center, 114
    COSEP survey results, 189, 190
    history and description, 130–132
    population, 129
    Special Economic Zone, 44
    technology zones, 129
    transportation and travel, 39, 115, 116,
        126, 129, 130
    universities, 129, 131
Shenzhen Grand Industrial Zone, 129
Shenzhen Hi-tech Industrial Park, 129
Shiyan Industrial Park, 129
SIM cards, 46, 84
Singapore, 9, 19, 20, 41, 56, 271, 279
Six Sigma, 152
Small and medium-sized enterprises (SMEs),
    78, 105
Social activities in China, 80
Software
    Brazil, 22, 23
    development of and benefits of providing
        outsourcing, 8
    exports from China, 51
    game software development, 20
    India, 41
    Israel, 16
    parks. *See* Software parks
    Russia, 24
Software Engineering Institute (SEI), 141,
    143, 144
Software parks, 54
    Bangalore Software Park, 122
    Beijing, 112
    Beijing Industry University Software Park,
        112
    Beijing Software Industry Base, 274
    Changping Software Park, 112
    Changsha Software Park, 274
    China Offshore Software Engineering
        Project (COSEP) index, 273–275
    Dalian Software Park, 117, 274
    Guangdong Software Science Park, 125

Software parks, (*Continued*)
  Hangzhou East Software Park, 124
  Hangzhou Hi-Tech Software Park, 274
  and job-hopping, 86
  Nanjing Software Park, 129
  Nansha IT Software Park, 125
  national software parks, 49, 50
  Qilu Software Park, 122, 274
  Qingdao Software Park, 274
  and selection of outsourcing city, 85
  Shanghai Pudong Software Park, 52,
    114–115
  Shanghai Software Park, 114, 274
  Shenzhen Software Park, 274
  Suzhou Software Park, 274–275
  taxation, 85
  Tianhe Software Park, 125, 274
  Waigaoqiao Software Park, 114–115
  Xi'an Software Park, 120–121, 275
  Zhongguancun Software Park (zPark), 50,
    52, 112, 114
Sohu.com, 98
Sough Guangming Industrial Park, 129
South Africa, 16, 17
Special Administrative Regions (SARs), 37,
  119, 128, 248, 254
Special Economic Zones (SEZs), 4, 44, 130,
  131, 168
Sports activities, 80
Spring Festival, 107
Staff augmentation, 60–62
Staff turnover. *See* Turnover
Standard Chartered Bank, 18, 120
Standard CMMI Appraisal Method for
  Process Improvement (SCAMPI),
  142–144
Standards. *See also* Capability Maturity
  Model for Software (CMM for
  Software); Capability Maturity Model
  Integration (CMMI)
  business process, 150, 151
  importance of, 150, 151
  ISO. *See* International Organization for
    Standardization (ISO)
  role of in selecting IT outsourcing vendor,
    145
  trends in China, 170, 171, 182, 183
  types of, 152
  and vendor due diligence, 150
  and vendor selection, 154

State Administration of Foreign Exchange,
  262, 263
State Administration of Taxation, 170,
  263–265
State Intellectual Property Office (SIPO),
  159, 265
Sun Microsystems, 46, 48, 122
Sun Yat-sen, 126, 128
Supply Chain Operations Reference Model
  (SCOR), 153
Swim lane process maps, 154

Taiwan, 3, 4, 37, 38, 45, 118
Tata Consultancy Services, 12, 28, 52, 125,
  208
Taxation
  business incentives, 49
  business tax, 169
  consumption tax, 169
  foreign invested enterprises, 158, 168, 169
  foreign nationals, 169, 170
  and government support of technology
    development, 167
  high-tech and software parks, 85
  non-resident enterprises, 169
  outlook for outsourcing in China, 171
  State Administration of Taxation, 170,
    263–265
  turnover tax system, 169
  value added tax, 169
Team-building, 88, 107
Technology
  Chinese focus on, 176, 177
  contributed as capital, 158
  high-tech parks, 49. *See also* Technology
    zones
  investment and development, promotion
    of, 49
  rapid changes in, 6, 7
  spending, 7
Technology development contracts, 159
Technology talent
  and BRIC nations, 21
  China, 2, 7, 63, 91, 92, 178
  Czech Republic, 11
  Hungary, 12
  India, 7, 28
  and reasons for outsourcing, 1
  research and development in China, 46
  supply of, 51, 54, 58
  Ukraine, 14

Technology zones
  Advanced Material Science Park, 121
  Baolong Industrial Park, 122, 129
  Biopharmaceutical Park, 121
  Chang'an Technology Park, 120
  Chengdu Hi-tech Zone, 119, 120
  Dalian Hi-Tech Industrial Park, 117
  Economic-Technological Development
    Zone (ETDV), 118
  Electronic Industrial Park, 120
  Guangzhou New & Hi-Tech Industrial
    Development Zone, 125
  Guanlan-Longhua-Banxuegang Industrial
    Park, 129
  Hangzhou Hi-tech Industry Development
    Zone, 124
  Hi-tech Export Processing Base, 121
  Jiangning Economic-Technological
    Development Zone, 127
  Liuxiandong Industrial Park, 129
  Nanjing New and High-Tech Industry
    Development Zone, 127
  Northwest Polytechnic University Science
    Park, 121
  Pukou High and New Technology
    Development Zone, 127
  Qianhai Industrial Park, 129
  and selection of outsourcing city, 85
  Shenzhen Grand Industrial Zone, 129
  Shenzhen Hi-tech Industrial Park, 129
  Shiyan Industrial Park, 129
  Sough Guangming Industrial Park, 129
  Tianjin Economic and Technological
    Development Area, 131, 132
  Xi'an High-Tech Park (XAHTP), 120, 121
  Xi'an Jiaotong University Science Park,
    121
Teksen, 48
Telecommunications
  China, 26, 45–47, 149
  India, 26
Terminology, 4–6
Thailand, 37
Thousand-Hundred-Ten Project, 166, 167
3G network, 47
Tianhe Software Park, 125, 274
Tianjin, 37, 39, 99, 116–118, 131, 132,
  189, 190
Tianjin Economic and Technological
  Development Area (TEDA), 131, 132

Tibet (Xizang Autonomous Region), 34, 39,
  113, 116, 119
Time zones
  Beijing Time, 34
  and BOT considerations, 69
  and disadvantages of outsourcing to
    China, 149
Toasts, 81, 90
Topjobway, 97
Torch Center, 49, 179, 180, 253, 269, 270,
  273
Total outsourcing, 139
Tourism in China, 27
  Dalian, 118
  Hangzhou, 124, 125
  Jinan, 123
  Xi'an, 121
Trade-Related aspects of Intellectual
    Property Rights (TRIPS), 162
Trade secrets. *See* Intellectual property,
    treatment of in China
Trade shows
  Chinese participation in, 51, 53, 179–180
  Gartner Outsourcing Summits, 179, 180
  Outsource World London 2004, 51, 179
  participation in, 13, 14, 18, 53
Trademarks. *See* Intellectual property,
    treatment of in China
Training, 87, 94, 106, 108, 109
Transportation in China, 38, 39, 85
  Beijing, 113
  Chengdu, 119
  Dalian, 117
  Guangzhou, 126
  Hangzhou, 124
  Jinan, 122, 123
  Nanjing, 127, 128
  and selection of outsourcing city, 85
  Shanghai, 115, 116
  Shenzhen, 129, 130
  Xi'an, 121
Treaties
  intellectual property, 163
  tax, 169
Trust, 80, 102, 104
  and meeting standards, 151
  offshore partner, 66, 67
Turnover
  Brazil, 22
  China, 57, 58, 102, 103, 148, 149
  India, 2, 26, 53, 57, 148

Turnover (*Continued*)
  minimizing effects of, 103
  person-culture fit and person-job fit, 103
  preventing, 98, 101–109
  reasons for, 99, 102, 107

UFIDA Software Engineering case study,
  231–234
Ukraine, 14
Unfair competition, 159
United Kingdom, 10, 12–14, 18, 162, 280
United Nations Convention on Contracts for
  the International Sale of Goods, 159
United Nations Development Program
  (UNDP), 184
United States
  engineering competitiveness, 51, 91, 92
  and NAFTA, 3
Universities
  and advantages of outsourcing to China,
    148
  Beijing, 112
  Chengdu, 119
  China, 40, 51, 56, 86, 91–94, 97, 98, 176,
    177
  college entrance exams, 95
  COSEP survey results, degrees awarded,
    190
  Dalian, 117
  English skills, 98
  expansion of in China, 92
  Guangzhou, 126, 127
  Hangzhou, 124, 125
  India, 28
  Jinan, 122
  private, 93, 94
  and recruiting talent, 96, 97
  Russia, 24
  and selection of outsourcing city, 86
  Shanghai, 115
  Shenzhen, 129, 131
  types of higher education, 93
  United States, 51, 91, 92, 98
  Xi'an, 121

Value-added outsourcing, defined, 6
Value-added services
  and BOT model, 68
  offshoring, 6
  Philippines, 19

trends in China, 4, 96, 177, 182
Value added tax (VAT), 169, 171
Value chain, Business Process Model, 153
Value Stream Mapping, 154, 155
Vendors
  comparing, 139
  due diligence. *See* Due diligence
  ranking system for, 153, 154
  relationship building, 80
  selection of, 149, 150, 153–154
  service models, 139
Vietnam, 20, 21, 34

Wadha, Vivek, 91
Waigaoqiao Free Trade Zone, 115
Waigaoqiao Software Park, 114, 115
Wal-Mart, trade relationship with China, 45
Web sites
  business and economy in China, 271
  government, financial, and business sites,
    265, 266
Western business practices, 57, 72, 77, 78,
  84, 89, 97, 104, 149
Wholly Owned Foreign Enterprises (WOFE),
  157, 166
Wi-Fi hotspots, 46
Wilson, Brenda, 100
Wipro, 17, 112
Work environment, 87, 106
Work ethic, 100, 101, 149
Workforce. *See also* Technology talent
  and advantages of outsourcing to China,
    148, 149
  authority issues, 108
  Chinese work ethic, 100, 101, 149
  communication, 107
  cultural issues and expansion in China
    market, 86–88
  demand for talent, 91
  global, 137
  growth of, 97
  health issues, 101
  interpersonal skills, 99, 101
  labor law in China. *See* Labor law
  new generation, potential issues with, 101
  recruiting staff, 96–99
  salaries, 99, 100
  size of, 91
  staff management, 106, 107
  team building, 107
  training, 108, 109

turnover. *See* Turnover
U.S. educated, 97, 98
Worksoft Creative Software Technology,
  Ltd. case study, 235–237
World Expo 2010 (Shanghai), 181
World Intellectual Property Organization
  (WIPO), 163
World Trade Organization (WTO), 4, 49,
  73, 114, 173, 174, 181, 245, 246
  and market entry barriers in China, 157,
  158
  offices and agencies, 272, 273
Wu Yi, 92

Xi'an, 120–122, 189, 190
Xi'an High-Tech Park (XAHTP), 120, 121

Xi'an Jiaotong University Science Park, 121
Xi'an Software Park, 120, 121
Xinjiang Autonomous Region, 34, 39
Xizang Autonomous Region (Tibet), 34, 39,
  113, 116, 119

Yahoo, 47, 98, 125
Yangzi River (Chang Jiang), 34
"Your Essential Shore" slogan, 41
Yu, Peggy, 98

Zhang, Charles, 98
Zhongguancun Software Park (zPark), 50,
  52, 112, 114
Zhu Ziqi, 50